The Golden Path

Jean Christian

Introduction

Several days a week there are special gatherings in the meditation room at my home. The Guidance Talk Circle provided a place to bring questions and to discuss spiritual and life issues. I am full of love for the diligent people who climb those steps every week to learn, share and ask.

I am full of gratitude for the immeasurable Grace that meets every question with willingness, precision and care.

I feel that I am a meeting point, an observer, a vehicle, a student, a friend and a translator of universal wisdom into human image and language. This book is a collection of questions and answers meant for more than just the few of us.

Jean Christian

This work is the result of many good hearts.
To arrive in book form, from spoken teaching, is a long journey.

My thanks to Linda Poole, for her belief in me as a channel of Grace and her many hours of transcribing and editing.

Regarding the cover

The unconscious human has only one path
The path of shadows

The becoming conscious human has two paths
The shadow path and the golden path

The fully conscjous human has only one path
The golden path

About the Author

Jean has been offering channeled Guidance ,Consciousness mentoring ,Meditation circles and Retreats ,as well as Life Guidance counselling for individuals , for 25 years. She is a Classical Homeopath as well as a mother of four daughters.

Jean has three previous books: **Cycles of Wisdom** (edited and republished as **Compositions of Grace), Tapestry of a Soul** and **Becoming Truth.**

Website: www.becomingtruth.com

Table of Contents

Section 1: Spiritual Development Teachings 1
    Grace 2
    Beauty 6
    Peace 10
    Love 13
    Higher Presence Beings 17
    Islam..32
    Current Teachers 37
    Karma..42
    Kundalini 51
    Meditative Practices 55
    Intuition 69
    Worship 74
    Dreams 79
    Life Purpose 81
    Living Our Spiritual Identity 84
    Born Complete 88
    Old Patterns of Human Nature 90
    Authenticity 98
    Levels of Consciousness 100
    Relationships..102
    After Death 108

Section 2: Consciousness in Healing... 117
    Words on Healing Practice 118
    Immunity..134
    Self-acceptance 136
    Consciousness Towards Others in Illness 141
    The Holocaust..154
    Challenges in Healing 157
    End of Life 165

Section 3: The Physics of Consciousness...................................... 173
    The State of Meditation 174
    The Mind, Brain and Soul 184
    Genetics 195
    Teleporting 198
    The Spinal Column 202

                                                    Continued over

Table of Contents Continued

    Conception 205
    Abortion 208
    Vaccination 210
    Viruses...213
    DNA 215
    Teachings on Diet 222
Section 4: World in Evolution 229
    The Future Unfolding 230
    Change of Frequency 233
    Animal Souls, Tree Souls...235
    Oceans, Water, Radiation 243
    Earth's Twelve Chakras..256
    Photon Energy 258
    Humanity in Evolution 261
    The New Fruit 275
    Postlude...292

Spiritual Development Teachings

Grace

This is a question from the heart: How can we feel some hope, and understand all that is happening with humanity in the world right now?

The Guidance shows me two aspects of the experience of humanness: One is the very linear physical framework of identifying with the world, time, the needs of the body, emotions, and mind. It is a very human and temporary frame of reality and identity. The second is the framework of the eternal essence, the undying, the non-physical, the non-linear, the essential being-ness. Every human being has this duality. The way forward is to firmly know the duality and know how to be identified within both. To have the freedom, skill and capacity to be in both frames of identity, knowing that the identity of the eternal being-ness (or on-going soul) is the source without end. It is the source for all hope, for life energy, for life force, and for nutrition in every aspect of both the subtle and the physical.

To be able to hold both frames of identity within 'who you are', and become versatile, knowing that the purpose of holding two frames of identity is to merge them, so that they flow together. The purpose is to draw the Endless Source into the human framework, into human existence. It is to learn to repeatedly express eternal values, eternal abundance and bring the endless and undying positivity of love into human nature. The purpose is to address this physical world from the framework of the eternal identity.

To lose hope is to become fixed, ensconced and overly identified in the temporary passing identity within the human form. It is to become impacted by that which will not remain, that which is changing or dying. It always was this way. The human context, the embodied context of identity is ever changing, ever dying, and ever grasping against loss and shaping its whole consciousness around avoiding loss and around survival.

The phase of evolution of human being-ness sitting before us now is to have an equal placement in both frames of identity. To have rejoicing, commitment, compassion and effort placed into the human temporary embodiment, while continually drawing from Source, for reason and purpose and direction, for the divine framework, for the eternal essence of who you are.

You ask about this time in the history of humanity. We show the transitional peaking, the end of an age, transitioning from the Age of Unconsciousness into the Age of Consciousness. There is an emptying out of the debris that remains from unconscious action. You are watching the emptying out, the stringency, the cleansing. You are watching the dying and the ending, voices rising, choices being made. You exist in a blend of perhaps the brightest and the darkest of times, a most difficult time to be embodied. *Your only recourse is to continually resource your being into the identity that never dies, that never fears for survival, is never lacking, is never vulnerable, never needs to question and has hope as part of its nature.*

The pressure of this transitional time is to be used as a push to the place where hope is never, ever questioned. To push, like all strife and destructive events push, towards the eternal identity. Pushing towards Immeasurable Grace, which is the vision held in all beings before embodying, before worlds embodied, the immeasurable vision of grace.

Understand that Immeasurable Grace is the premise, the source, and the starting point of all creation. That which is held in the starting point is the constant dictate of the ending, of the outcome and the unfolding. Unconsciousness is unstable and false. It crumbles and cannot sustain. You are witnessing this instability intensifying, because consciousness is bulging and ready to be born, ready to take dominance within beings. Consciousness is creating the instability as it pushes for more room within creation. When you feel hopeless and sad and doubtful, this is your push to reside more firmly and more fully in the stillness, the unchanging Grace that is your being and that is All-Being.

Walk into the halls of Light, increasing the numbers that stand in those halls by one, by you. As more and more walk and stand in the halls of Light, the halls of darkness empty. This creates a reality in the world, which ensues from the halls of Light. Know that to entertain thoughts of darkness, even subtly, thoughts of fear, or of doubt, is to stand in the halls of shadow, adding to the shadows of unconsciousness. To choose to breathe and move ones being into the halls of Light is to lessen the shadows for all. News casts, little threads of moments, indicators: even the newscasts change as more and more leave the shadows and stand where the light is strong.

Every subtle action in your being counts more and more in the times to come. The conscious being begins to realize there can be no clumsiness, no leeway. To host a dark thought is to stand and hold darkness within the whole being. A conscious being swiftly, quickly, moves into praise, into gratitude, into love and trust, knowing they are doing this not to meet their own despair, but to dispel despair itself. Even when hearing of an individual in despair, the first step is to attend to how you are upon hearing that. Were you pulled into the dark hall of despair? For then your first task is to remove yourself, is to stand where the truth is, more strongly with a wider stance. Truth is the premise of all beings and all creation, and it is Immeasurable Grace.

What is the definition of Grace according to this source?

There is wordlessness, an inability to place into words the true definition of Grace. Grace within the field of consciousness of the human mind, lifts the senses, lifts the understanding to its most subtle, sublime reaching and region of grasping. It lifts the human consciousness to reach for what is most beautiful, most harmonious, most perfect, most infused with meaning and purpose. Grace lifts the human consciousness to reach for that which gives it the most lift, the most hope, the most expansive vision of itself.

Grace is:

The inherent understanding of one's place in all creation.

The force of all creation.

The Presence behind the force behind all creation.

Grace as the intention of such force, such presence behind all creation and beyond creation. Grace as the meaning of creation, the intention of creation and the outcome, ever unfolding, of creation. Grace as the character trait of Supreme Being-ness, the essence of meaning and purpose of Supreme Being-ness within creation and before, and beyond.

When the un-manifest, invisible intention of Grace, named Grace, named nothing, creates a gesture into creation, the gesture is Grace. The gesture of the beauty of a flower is Grace. A flower is a gesture of Supreme Being. The human being, an intricate gesture, an intricate reflection of the gesture named Grace. All creation is a gesture of Grace. All creation is an expression of the meaning, the intention, of the unnamed, unnamable. For lack of name and for lack of words, Grace then, the word Grace.

Grace then, encompassing all creation, has the root meaning and understanding of perfect-ness, of harmonious whole, of beauteous becoming, of rightness unfolding. To all name holders, to all word seekers, all poets, and all descriptors: Be willing to let it all go into the absolute silence of the un-named, the un-worded, the direct experience.

All creation a gesture of Grace

Beauty

What are the effects of beauty on consciousness? How is beauty defined? What is beauty as an expression, its meaning? How can we define ugliness, what is it that ugliness really is?

I am given a very detailed image of our brain and our consciousness and our perceiving apparatus: how we receive and perceive reality and how we organize within the brain the forms and the experience around us.

The question of beauty is a very integral question. There is an inbuilt, inherent ability within conscious beings to see synchronicity, to see 'God', to see divine attribute, to see harmonious meaning, *the alignment that is divine being-ness in form.*

One description of beauty could then be: the absolute alignment of divine being-ness creating form. Divine being-ness utterly allowed to take shape, not interfered with while descending into form. The pure thought manifesting unbroken into form, a perfection of manifestation into molecular shape. Therefore beauty is a message, beauty is a key to understanding the synchronicity, divine alignment, the meaning, the purpose and the intention of the creative principle of God nature.

In metaphor, if you allow any molecular substance to take shape in its most un-interfered progression, it will arrive into a perfectness of itself. In actuality, non-metaphor, the quartz crystal is the molecular alignment of silica when it is absolutely allowed, in peace, to take shape or crystallize. Seeing the perfect lines, the absolute clarity. This is beauty. The human being, the conscious being recognizes it as beauty, as divine alignment of silica. If you take any atomic substance, any mineral or any seed and allow it to take perfect shape in its own name and its own identity, it will produce forms of perfection. Take the seed of a tree and give it the conditions of peace, fertility and steadiness and watch it develop into the perfect expression of itself, the divine alignment within itself.

The conscious being sees divine alignments of form as beauty. And so, this is one ultimate manifestation, the uninterrupted perfect descent from the idea of form into the substance and full manifestation of form. In this worldly matter, in the material world of substance, diamond carbon sits in many interrupted forms and you can look at these interruptions of carbon development and see them as beauty (colored diamonds hold inclusions of other minerals). But what is held in the conscious human being as the ultimate beauty is carbon in its uninterrupted form as diamond. Carbon in its most uninterrupted crystal manifestation is the diamond.

Understanding that aspect of beauty defined, understanding also that the conscious being has an inherent readiness, a place within their consciousness that notices divine alignment and upon noticing divine alignment, begins to divinely align within itself. Noticing perfect silica, quartz crystal, begins to create divine alignment within one's being on all levels. Noticing the perfected shape of a mountain, a tree, a flower unblemished in opening, creates divine alignment within the conscious form. Even more powerfully, the divine alignment of a human being such as the Christ, the perfect flower, such as the beings that have fully entered into the flowering of consciousness within form. These beings create divine alignment in all those that love, all those that attend and listen and revere. This is divine alignment occurring in the complexity of the human form.

One can look for this perfected form of being on all levels: the mineral, the plant, the animal, the human and in the infusion of the spiritual identity, the divine mind. It goes on from there, into the realms of the non-physical. Into the perfected placements and the perfected nexus of development at each level.

We move from here into the variations, what we call the disruptions. Even the beautiful rose quartz is disrupted silica infused with mineral. And all the beautiful stones and gems that have color are interrupted and infused with other elements of becoming. Or the tree that has had to withstand the strongest wind on the hilltop and doesn't grow straight is a disrupted tree form, and yet beautiful. Or the human being who has been jailed as a murderer and then comes forward into the world to be a divine servant, this is a disrupted process and yet ever the more beautiful. What makes it beautiful? What makes the rutilated quartz, with its strands of asbestos glinting in it, any different than the pure quartz? Or the human being who has been in the darkness of mind, and then in the dawning of mind…what is that then?

Beauty is the essence of all beings; beauty is the source, the journey and the end of all forms of manifestation. Beauty is another name for God, and God is an ever moving, ever dynamic process of becoming. God is the molten silica sometimes finding itself in a protected place to develop into perfection, sometimes not. It is all beauty. It is all the substance of God. It is all the substance of the indefinable name of creation.

Beauty is then the conscious being recognizing that the divine manifestation, the divine expression of God, is beautiful every step of the way and is moving every step of the way. It is the essence of hope, the essence of faith and the essence of consciousness that sees that the twisted tree is as beautiful as the straight tree because the tree stayed living, became stronger, became more conscious because of the wind. And the crystalline substance of quartz with its inclusions is beautiful because it continued into crystallization around its inclusions. In essence there is nothing but beauty, and to the conscious being, everything is beauty, even the dump. Even the dump is just the process of trying to crystallize around inclusions. Before there ever is a completed product showing the result, there is the confusion. What will occur on the Earth's body itself, when the dump has been incorporated, crystallized or shaped around? What magnificence will arrive from that, which you may see in a life a thousand years from now?

We could say that *ugliness is focusing in on one moment and seeing the confusion of disruption.* Seeing the unknown result, seeing only that moment. Seeing only the broken crushed crystal, and not understanding the indestructibility of atomic matter itself. It will always reshape and there is a calling within all substance towards shaping into alignment. We see the resultant forms, we see the old tree in its beautiful shape and we celebrate. But we must learn to celebrate when it's a young sapling whipping around in the wind looking tattered with branches torn off it. We must look to see what it can become by sitting there in that tempest, knowing that we are watching *beauty in formation.* We could then define ugliness as beauty in formation.

We must learn not to look at ugliness and let it create a lack of alignment in our being. Learn not to let it create despair and confusion. We must look at the apparent momentary disruption and ugliness with patience and with wisdom, **knowing that it will become the best it can be in most remarkable ways.**

There is only beauty, there is only God, and there is only divine purpose in every aspect of manifest creation. And yet when we are in an undefined struggle of consciousness, when we are in need, we must resource ourselves around the perfected aspects of beauty: the unbroken forests, the flower gardens in full health. We must immerse ourselves in the shape of manifesting divinity. Allow it in, allow it to reach deep and create that flowering and alignment in the heart and the soul. Furthermore, turn to the masters of perfected consciousness, and allow them in. Allow them to create the streaming alignment to the highest extent.

Peace

We ask to be taught about Peace, what is meant by 'a state of inner peace'?

The experience of peace results from alignment. It is experienced through the alignment of all aspects of being: the soul, the conscious mind, the sensory heart, the intentional will and the embodiment. As the alignment is exact and harmonious, the experience is entire. Peace is not a state of the emotional being alone, nor a state of the body in a completeness, satisfaction or contentment. It is not a description of the mind being undisturbed, nor is it an experience of the wonder in the soul. It is all of this at once. It is the alignment of a being that sees existence with wonder and awe and joy, sees their life as a thing of beauty and of wonder. It is the mind that is intelligently curious and delighted in what it knows and what it wants to know, in what it perceives as purposeful existence, the evolving and unfolding of world and humanity and systems. It is an emotional or sentient state of heart that feels deeply, love, goodness and engagement with all beings, easily. It is the body that hosts a silent wellness, a silence of symptom, a silence of wholeness.

There is no disturbance in absolute peace. There is no disturbance in any of the realms of being-ness. A being that is hosting peace as an inner state can surround disturbance of the heart or body as part of itself. The body, in its imperfections and symptoms, is enfolded in the grace and the love of the sense of intactness: "This too, is part of my being. This too, is part of the whole." The sadness or grief experienced in the heart is part of the entirety. Therefore, it isn't a disturbance but part of the beauty and part of the evolving expression of the being.

Do not understand peace as the emptiness of sensation, the emptiness of thought or feeling, or the space between crises. Do not see peace so intermittently as when one is left alone by disturbance or pain or thought. ***The inner continuum of peace exists in a being that sees the entirety in alignment and chooses and creates an alignment.*** This alignment includes all processes of physical formation, physical unfolding and emotional unfolding. It includes grief and loss, it includes pain, and it includes queries and confusions. Confusion does not go so deep as to disturb the continuum of peaceful being.

Peaceful being is the foundation, with the process of evolution surrounding it. Therefore, all life experience is met from the foundation of peace and the presumption of alignment. This is all part of what must be. It is all part of the rightness of existence and being. This death and this injury, this unknown and this confusion, this world condition or that, is all part of the greater whole of becoming. And this greater knowing of the whole, the resting into the all-encompassing purpose of evolving all systems, creates an alignment in a conscious soul, an alignment of a continuum of peace.

Why is it difficult for us to be at peace, to be grateful and realize that we are fortunate when we compare ourselves to the ones whose lives are full of great destruction and unrest?

This is a question of, *"How am I different from those who suffer?"* It is a question of standing on one side of the door, moving through, and looking at it from the other side. I am here and they are there. *"How should I view my own being, my own life, in the light of how it is for others? How am I separate and how am I not separate?"*

The mark of spiritual evolution is knowing that your being is on both sides of the door. In this separate sense of your physical embodiment, in your linear place in the world and also in all beings undergoing everything they are going through, it is all literally occurring in your being whether you hear of it or not. This is not meant to bring the mind into a scattered place of, "What do I tend to first then?" The mind can't possibly hold all this. The mind cannot hold the concept that you are here and they are there, and there is this issue and that issue, and this and that...the mind cannot identify at such a scale, nor can the mind stimulate the will to an action on such a scale.

This time (in history) requires a letting go of who you think you are.

Though you may have ease every morning and every night, the war is occurring in your being as well. The victories are occurring in your being and you are a part of everything going on in this bubble of human evolution. Open the eyes of your mind, of your will, and look before you. What is there to do within the literal, linear nature of your life? If there is no one who needs to be bandaged, what do I do? If there isn't a starving family next door, what do I do?

The general answer is that in your relative peace and ease, where there isn't an immediate need to bandage the wounded. You have a greater responsibility than the ones that are running away down the street to hide. Yours is greater than the ones that must bandage the knees and the heads of the wounded. Your action, your responsibility is greater.

You must become the Metta, you must become the song of love that lifts the outcome, that lifts the possibility for choices being made right now, and for what befalls a being that has just died in the tsunami, a being who has been cut loose from their path and is like a leaf falling. When the song of love is loud within the whole scope, that leaf is directed to its most fortuitous place of grace unfolding. Your responsibility is to infuse the entire atmosphere of human evolution with the principle of love. When you are far away in a place of peace and ease you have the most to do. You have the most to become. You become the beacon that calls the whole next step, the next footfall of human evolution. Beckoning that footfall onto solid ground, onto a higher place to stand. This is the inversion of a thought that says: "If I was close I would have the most to do, and if I am far away I have the least to do." "If I happen to be there, there is so much to do I would not know what to do first, but when I am so far away there is nothing I can do."

In the era to come there is no separation between beings. The definitions of religion become useless and they fade. The differences between races become transparently empty. The differences between cultures of ease and poverty become all part of one story. One being-ness. As all these membranes of separation, identity and consciousness dissolve, there is a swift, tremendous becoming within the human being and within the spirit. It is the dawning of great light, of great realization that each embodiment is truly a principle of love, that each embodiment is a unique being of love.

#

We ask for a teaching on love, a greater understanding of what is meant by love, to act it and feel it, to apply it to oneself and to others.

The Guidance starts by saying that there must be a balance and a health in the soul, in the mind, in the whole configuration of a being to understand love. Realize that a being is comprised of soul moving forward into embodiment with mind, with the sensory of heart, and with the creative will principle of the ego nature. There needs to be a balance within the being to understand love from the soul, the mind, and the senses, and to be informed by love in creative action, in will, and to be led by love in the identity of a human self. Love is the outcome of this balance; it is the flowering of such balance. If a being is damaged and hurt, condensed and cramped in their emotional or mental nature, if they hold deep injury in their soul, and unresolved injury resulting in unconsciousness, then their experience and understanding of love is limited. We say here that love is understood only as it comes to such a being not as it goes forth. Such a being needs love to be given. They need to be taught love by being given love. It is love and love alone that will reach through the injury, through the condensation and the unconsciousness. It is love alone that will dissolve and beckon forth this being into consciousness, into release.

To understand what love is then, we ask: What is this love being given? **Love is the absolute and total validation of another being's existence.** It is the absolute acceptance and embrace of another being in exactly how and who they are. It is a message given to that being that they have the full celebration, the full invitation to exist, to be whom they are right then. They are fully accepted and fully acknowledged. There are no conditions to the acceptance and there is no judgment of the being's point in their evolution. Love is what is meant in the action of Namaste, the pure unobstructed acknowledgement of another being's totality.

Love then, is a highly conscious act. It is not an emotional gesture. It is not in service to itself, it is an outward movement of highly conscious acknowledgement. It is to realize another being in their beauty, in their entirety. It is to realize another being in their darkness, in their struggle, but not to focus or single out that darkness, nor struggle, but include it in the beauty, include it in the validity. It is to communicate, to message to another being that all they are is beautiful and valid, and they have a right to fully exist exactly as they are. This is a highly conscious act that must come from a being of balance, able also to attend to self in the same way. Not rejecting the self, nor judging it, nor hating it, not to go against one's own being, but to hold the same full acceptance, full acknowledgement.

Holding the in-built assumption of the right to exist and the equality of being-ness to all other beings in creation. Also accepting the factor of evolution, in that *all beings throughout creation are in evolution,* all beings are perfection in movement, perfection moving into perfection. *Creation is a dynamic description of perfection unfolding itself.* The Source, the Godhead, the Supreme Being-ness, sitting in the centre of all creation holds no judgment, exists as love itself. Simply said then, understand love as giving the gift of full celebration, full acknowledgement to oneself and to all other beings, holding the full message of the right to exist as an equal, valid, beautiful being. There is no hierarchy to love.

We want to understand Metta meditation and Metta action. We wish to gain an understanding of the principles in Metta. (Metta meaning loving-kindness as a path.)

The Guidance shows the human being in its levels of expression, showing the different thrones of consciousness in the human being, the places to sit and consciously open to, connect to, and identify with: the throne of the mind, which can perceive and hold all perception; the throne of the heart, which can have sentience for all beings, can understand, interact, and be love within all beings; the throne of action and the will, which can manifest truth. Realize the levels of being, the enthronements, and **understand Metta as the enthronement at the heart.**

In Metta there is the out-pouring of one's love into all beings; **the experience of one's being as all beings.** In one's own being, becoming an embodiment of 'love itself', that all beings can be part of, thereby hosting in one's being the principle of love. When one is living this principle of love, it then creates attunement, cleansing and realignment for all.

We give the image: if all beings were just a song, a vibration in a great bubble, and one of those beings corrected their song into the highest and purest song of alignment of love's meaning, the song penetrates within the whole bubble. The song enters into all others. Metta is that. It is becoming the high vibration of love itself and becoming the principle of love. Putting aside human nature, the 'I am-ness' of separation to become the 'I am-ness' of love itself.

Hear the subtlety and process there. Putting aside the egotistical, human, separate self, even if only for that moment, is learning to become love itself, the song of love, itself. As you do this, you are the vibration, the note and the movement of love vibrating in all beings in this bubble called creation.

It is vast and yet it is not. There are five billion people, and yet it is not vast. Let go of the size and thoughts of being small amongst it all and being one amongst billions. In truth it isn't like that. There is no linear nature in truth. There is no size or measurement to love. When one individual becomes a principle of love, they sing that song of love into the entire collective being-ness. This is Metta.

The most internal description of Metta is that a being has learned to step aside, to host all beings within themselves. To identify with all as 'I am.' "I am love itself, I am all beings." The mind can't follow this, the mind is geared to host and sustain separation and individuality. The mind hosts the identity of separation; therefore, the process is for the mind to become the observer. The mind stands witness as the heart takes leadership, (the enthronement of the heart) for the identity of the heart has no separation. The heart is designed to host the identity of all being-ness.

A question about spiritual practice and path: is there a form of practice that is most direct, pleasing or most received by Supreme Nature?

Your question *"Is there a path that pleases Supreme Being-ness?"*

brings a smile and an acknowledgment of dearness. *You* are Supreme Being. It is all Supreme Being. Love itself is Supreme Being and as you become the principle of love, you manifest Supreme Nature. ***The most direct path is to become the principle of love. It is to become love itself, it is to have no dogma other than love.*** It is to have only the practices that implement and dissolve separation and that lead to the immersion into love itself. It is to involve yourself in a practice where your identity begins to shape itself as a being, an embodiment, of love.

As the human being progresses in consciousness and evolution there becomes less and less dogma, less and less format and less and less ceremony. There becomes simply the dawning of remembrance, of realizing the true identity. Looking into the eyes of others and not seeing a separate being over there, but seeing the greater being. Seeing one's own being in every pair of eyes. In seeing one's own being in every pair of eyes, there is instant compassion. To care for your body is the same as caring for my body, caring for your welfare is no different than caring for my welfare.

In the evolution of the human being, there is less and less need to maintain individuality. Individuality is maintained to mark separation, to ensure survival and as the human being evolves there is no question of survival. There is no question of dying because there is no dying. There is nothing to survive; the identity is based in the eternal nature. As the human being evolves along the principle of love, and as their identity of separation dissolves, they begin to remember the many faces they have worn, the many journeys they have taken, and none of it matters. The cloaks don't matter, only the principle of love matters. The human begins to operate as a singular being, as a Being of unity.

There is no question of what path is best, there is only the answer: to pare it down to the principle, actions and teachings of love, the meanings of love in action, the principles of love in life, and to know that this is the path taken. It is to feel the dissolving of ceremony, of ritual, of position, of uniqueness, of maintaining separation between churches and religions, between people and minds.

The generation being born knows this, and they care not for all the trappings and the dogmas of the faiths and ways, *for they are born to see the likeness of their own being in the other.* They are born ready to see the ONE set of eyes, the eyes of luminous presence and love in all beings.

Higher Presence Beings

*What is **God**? The Vedic tradition has one description of God, the Christian tradition has another, and we ask this source: What is God? How did the original concept of God change from internal to external?*

The words *"What is God?"* bring a wordless experience. They bring the consciousness to **the non-manifest original being-ness, that which sits beneath, before and precedent to all creation.** The question *"What is God"* is a very direct question and the most direct answer erases all forms, dissolves all forms into the original non-manifest being-ness. Showing God then, is showing nothing.

Showing the imprint and impression of the absolute, which can be shown to her eyes as endless and vast presence. In her eyes (Jean's inner effort at seeing the information) she would try to see it as endless and vast light, and yet light is manifest.

We could say that 'Presence' is not manifest. **Presence is the irreducible origin of God.** Presence, or consciousness, is Source. God is Source. God is Source and all that springs from Source. God is the non-manifest and all that springs into manifestation. God is Source and there is no word for Source. Source brings to the image mind 'the beginning': the beginning of a water-flow, the beginning of a seeds growth. Yet beginning is not what is meant because beginning suggests the form of time. Time is a form. Time is a form put into manifestation; the non-manifest coming into the manifest is time. Source and all its language is related to the manifest, and so the language that you use struggles to encapsulate a description and an answer to "What is God?"

The descriptions of God are purely just that, descriptions describing it as a consciousness, as a beauty, as a value system, and as a truth. They are all descriptions of the indescribable. For you to experience an understanding of God, you must experience it through form. You are a form of God. Experiencing your being, in fuller and fuller measure is to experience God Nature. You are a refined and refining manifestation of God in form and held within you is the indescribable, non-manifest source or presence. *You will find the understanding of "What is God" through your own being-ness.* If you examine a flower, if you examine God nature in the flower, you will see a simple manifestation of the absolute. If you contemplate your own being, your own capacity for consciousness, if you strive to come into the full capacity of consciousness, there you will find the answer in its most intricate and most comprehensive form. You are the answer and you hold the answer. Everything you see is but a part of, an aspect, of, an attribute of, a description of, and an expression of the indescribable and inexpressible. Yet you hold the capacity to have an absolute understanding of the indescribable. For this you are shaped, for this you have the nervous system, the brain system, for this you have the embodiment to answer that question. The embodiment that can ask "What is God" is celebrated because it can ask that in the first place. *If you can ask it then you can know it. If you can ask it then you also hold the answer.*

There are descriptive terms of God Nature: supreme source, supreme origin, timeless indescribable light, the absolute, the absolute that encompasses all that is, the absolute truth, the absolute grace, the supreme perfection of truth, the supreme perfection of being-ness, the omniscient and the endless presence of grace. And yet beyond these descriptions of vastness, beyond all that, the supreme presence of grace streams into being-ness through many forms. The source of love streams into being-ness and streams into manifestations of love. God is a being-ness of love. God is not just the boundary-less expanse of presence that is distant. God is an embodiment of love. God is father, God is all about you as well as within you. God is your elder and your guru. *God is the being-ness of love that is perfected beyond you while you evolve into the perfection within you.* God is within you and God is without you. As you awaken more and more into the God nature within your being and expand into the boundary-less presence of love, so then do you answer what is God by becoming God. And yet from the position of contraction, unconsciousness, and un-evolved awareness of being, God sits as an outside experience as well as a glimmering inside experience.

This brings the second question into answer (internal vs external God). For the human being who does not have the inner glimmering of God Nature within, the human being who is not self-recognizing, for the human being who is not inwardly becoming conscious of the great presence within, then God as an embodiment of love is on the outside, and it is grace that it should be so. These children of God have found God that way, and in the evolving, the deepening, the advancing of consciousness, there is the transitional knowing, the true knowing that each being is an embodiment of God.

A conscious being is simply one who holds full awareness of that, and who has answered the question by becoming it. A conscious being is one who has let go of any separation, of any sense of identity that creates separation from the Absolute Supreme Being-ness. They are an embodiment of grace; they exist within and for all, which is the meaning of omniscience. They are avatars embodying omniscience in form. They exist within for all, and all exist within them. There is no separation and there is no consciousness of an egotistical nature. There is the absolute identity of God Nature. Therefore they are examples of God Nature in manifestation and they are your teachers. They are outside of you and yet they are within you and as your awakening being evolves, they are only within you. Your stature rises and you become one who is as that.

The Christian words, 'you are each sons and daughters of God' mean that you hold the capacity for the full answer "What is God?"

You are created to have full consciousness, and you are created to be guardians of all creation that doesn't have full consciousness. Your patience is required to witness the humanity that must revere God as an embodiment far above and beyond them, and to know that you are simply looking at the progression of a being sitting in unconsciousness of their internal nature. It isn't a steady movement or a steady crescendo, there are those that hold full consciousness that embody and walk the Earth, and then there are those that hold very little consciousness and walk the Earth.

So yes, in the Vedic concept there was the full knowing. In the past there was the full nameless knowing of God as source, source nature to all creation, source nature, as the kernel of existence within the human being and all physical beings. And there was then reverence to all physical beings, the sleeping ones and the waking ones.

Realize that there are many streams of humanity and many streams of evolution. ***The hallmark of understanding of consciousness within that stream of humanity, is how internalized has the concept of God become.*** There needs to be patience, allowing all streams of humanity to weave, to impart to each other, to exist side by side with no judgment, for it is blessed to have God as a concept of a heavenly father. It is blessed and it is not to be judged. It is the flame that calls that being forward closer and closer, drawing the heaven to the Earth, drawing the truth within. It isn't stupid, it is the way and it is a way that is blessed.

Consider the creature that has no vision of such. Understand that the creature, many creatures turn to the human being as though they were such a divine character. Realize that you are as God to these little animals. They are looking up and you are on the outside of them. You hopefully nurture them, feed them and are an endless source of safety, plenty and purpose to their lives. You are evolving that little creature until such time as they can host that awakening, that endless source of grace, safety and goodness within themselves. It is blessed.

*Who is the **Higher Presence**? When reaching out to higher presence, to non-physical information or entity, is the being we are reaching out to our being in a larger description or a separate being?*

As you become more conscious of your greater nature, more identified with your being in its greater 'I am-ness,' there becomes less separation, less sense of division, fewer compartments of self versus other, self versus God or Guidance. This is a question that does not have a concrete answer.

Is Higher Presence a separate egoic form, that is outside of and separate from us? It is indeed Greater Being, it is a separate entity, angelic form, elder, it is God surrounding. Yet as the identity of your being and all beings widens and expands, takes in greater vistas of consciousness, there is the gradation and the slow realizing of the greater magnitude of the presence within and of the divine entity within. There can then be the sense that the sphere has become large and that the answer has come from within the sphere of 'I am.' Still, there is a vastness of Supreme Being-ness surrounding. Even the Christ, who sat in divine identity, felt the separation. He felt the vastness of Supreme Source as outside.

Don't be fixed with your understanding or your questions. Realize the ever-expanding evolution of consciousness. Sometimes the answers will arise from within the sphere of your being, sometimes from outside depending on your development. It depends on the consciousness that has developed within your being, and even that fluctuates. There may be a moment where the expansion is so great that you know the great 'I am' that breathes, watches, that is, and then again feeling the smallness, the containment of the unconscious development and feeling the gracious answer, the gracious presence as outside of you.

Ultimately, address the creation, the wordless supreme creation as a wonder that you are a part of and that you are growing into. It is your source, your origin and your infinite becoming. Address Supreme Being with devotion, realizing that there is that beyond you, and that it is the indescribable love and grace that you are called to. It is like a sun of the greatest magnitude, that you will keep coming to until you are dissolved in the greatest love and brilliance. Ultimately you are all that. You are the one coming home, and home is within you and beyond you.

You needn't grapple with this; just open your heart, soul and devotion. Be not concerned with names or structures, mental constructs of understanding; be only concerned with the love in your heart that will lead you into greater and greater love. Be in devotion to the source, the substance of creation and be in wonder that you are part of that. You are surrounded and in-filled.

What are the Angels ?

"We are your elders, we are as you, we are those who can see the entire scope. We know you, we know your origin, we know why you exist, we know where you're going, and we know you intimately. We are your elders, your guardians; we are your brothers and sisters, more intimate than guardians. We are yours. We are part of you, and yet beyond you. We are committed to you, we are your attendants and your midwives."

But what are you made of, what are you?

(Jean: There was a struggle for this to meet my consciousness. I am seeing the substance of light, the cosmic light substance of their embodiments. They are light and that frequency of energy is exquisite consciousness. Cellular substance, such as dust, stone or flesh, is a less con-

scious frequency, a less conscious substance. There are gradations of consciousness. At a certain level of unconsciousness matter starts to take shape, as we know it.

Now there is a tap on my head, the entering into my being and tremendous surges of energy through my being, direct contact, direct experiencing and knowing the peace, a sense of the reality of being so accompanied. It feels like this is the angel that I am, in this confined body and limited apparatus of mind. This is true as well. This is what each of us is: an angel in a less conscious phase.)

"We are angels in embryo and by our love wings shall grow."

The Guidance tells me of a ball of blue light speeding to the Earth. This is an image of consciousness descending, the moving of the high frequency consciousness of the angelic nature into the less conscious state of the human nature. The angelic state or strata of consciousness is a very subtle fine high speed of energy.

One can seek this understanding through just allowing the higher frequency presence into your field and being. It is yours, this eternal relationship. There are many different names for this higher stratum of consciousness, the angelic realm. The angelic realm is absolutely fluid and free. It can enter into any creature, any earth form, and any living form, as though a wave of light is passing through.

Who are Angels? What is their purpose?

The term 'angel' describes a stratum of consciousness. It is a grouping of beings that hold a fully developed divine identity and are committed to serving all life forms below. They are workers. They are beings in full attendance and in service to all beings (not just humans) that host and hold unconsciousness.

All angels are guardian angels. All beings in the angelic realm are in attendance to humanity and to all life forms trying to come into consciousness in this sphere. It is a commitment and part of their own development to be in this realm of service and being-ness. They are playing their part in the universal unfolding, and it is far more complex and intricate than books would say. There are many realms to serve, and there are so many areas of service within each realm. It is a highly organized, light filled realm of beings developing and evolving their own beings in this way.

If you could see them you would see a radiance of shaped light expressing love, thought and intention. Therefore, the shape of the light is in accordance to the need of the one being served. These beings are everywhere at all times. They are the ushers at death, present at birth, and they are the ever-present mediating force in illness. They are present in the un-embodied period of development between lives. They are the comforters, and they are the messengers of divine grace through their presence, through action, through communicating, or extruding love into unconsciousness. Embodying love close to unconsciousness so that love can be experienced. They are anchors of love, batteries of love.

Anytime you hear of someone dying, of a country dying, know that they are present. By the droves they are there. When anyone is suffering, know that they are there. They are there bringing love into a resonant closeness energetically so that it can be seen and experienced. They are the yeast in the great dough of Universal Becoming, yeasting with love. They are the embodiments of love, holding that embodiment as close as possible to lower conscious states.

*We ask about the **Energy Field of a Master**. What are the dynamics, the actual description or understanding of how we can feel the energy field of a Master through a computer or over a distance? (i.e. Nithyananda is a master in India who makes himself available to devotees through the internet)*

As soon as you step back from the fixed linear consciousness, which is streaming from a certain part of your brain, which registers the physical plane in linear terms and fills your consciousness with dictates and terms. When you step back from this, there is no distance or separation. There is no division or individuality in the same sense as you think. As soon as you link your mind, your heart, and your commitment to a being who has dissolved the linear identity and has become omnisciently conscious, your linkage has nothing to do with distance nor communication modes. Your linking is continual and always, and though you may in your human emotional and mental expression feel this, when you see or hear him on the computer you have just opened your sense to experiencing what is always there.

One who has dissolved their linear consciousness, who has dissolved their egotistical identity and come into the Greater Being-ness, has no edge to their energy field, no confinement or container. They are part of all humanity, all being and all existence. They assist those such as you by heightening your awareness. As you say "I am in the energy field of this being," you could say "I am in the universal energy field with the assistance of this being." You could name your experience by that being's name, yet realize that that being is just an elder taking your hand or an usher for you to experience who you are, for you to dissolve your boundaries and your concepts of separation. You, too, are part of all beings, all creation and all omniscience. A master takes your hand, surrounds and assists you to know 'who you are'.

In love and in gratitude, accept the assistance; deepen the awareness of what the assistance is. Be devoted to the elder, be devoted to the one who leads you and yet realize what you are to devote your being to, is the truth of who *all* are. "I am as that, I am this as well."

If you are experiencing communion through this communication mode then turn off the communication mode following and sit in the pure presence letting your mind go beyond the distance, the communication mode, the thoughts of distance, the thoughts of separateness and the thoughts of the names. In other words, take the invitation and walk all the way in. **Don't just stand in wonder and exclaim at the door, walk right in.** Realize that it was always there. It was always surrounding and within you all the time. Realize that there is no definition in terms of distance, time, place or mode in universal truth.

*This question is about the Masters, **the Avatars,** the divine embodiments throughout time and all that has taken shape around them: the religions, the faith paths, the teachings, the traditions. Are all of these very many divine embodiments the same re-embodying presence, or are they all different beings? We wish to understand more.*

The guidance is bringing us far above the question, looking far back into an arrangement or a setting up of 'the beautiful human being'. This beautiful embodiment of the human being is a formation of this substance earth, an animal form, the earthly embodiment. We look at the preparation of this earthly embodiment to host divine consciousness. With the oft-used term, the 'sons and daughters of God', we are given the image of God in physicality, in substance form. We need to know the purposes and understand the long, long road of evolution to understand the question.

There are guardians assigned to mentor this process (evolution), which is held very intimately in the hands and in the mind of Greater Being-ness It is continually being shaped, foreseen, and yet not foreseen. There is a great risk of the unknown held within this: How shall all of this converge? *The lowest wavelength form of material substance hosting the highest wavelength form of Ultimate Divine Consciousness.* How shall that evolve? How long shall it take? What are the dynamics of such an evolution? The bringing together of 'All that is' into the most expressed consciousness in all levels of description, the inert substance of physicality in its most exquisite conscious development, hosting the supreme, sublime consciousness of 'God Nature' in individuality, in community.

So then, there are assigned these positions of mentoring, the guardians (Avatars), and it is the guardians to which we refer. It is a Council, it is a realm of guardianship beings that are evolving in their explicit purpose by assisting in this implanting, this incoming of divine consciousness into embodiment through the human being.

In simple answer, yes, there is the re-embodying of the guardians in very designed cyclic ways. There are themes, the assignment to theme that each guardian holds, and there is the cyclic timing for each guardian stream and the aspect or community of souls that each guardian holds in their mission, in their riding, in their purpose. So yes, there is the re-embodying of a continual guardian, throughout time, throughout the cycles of humanity and in relationship with the souls of humanity. Therefore, there are continuing relationships between this avatar, divine en-fleshing, and the human souls that collect and are drawn in resonance to be born, to be in relationship to the teachings, to the embodiment. There are the repeating lifetimes of both. Not just the repeating embodiment of the master, but the repeated embodiment of the disciples, the students, and of the beings ever drawing closer to understanding. There are many levels of this. There are those who repeatedly embody close to the guardian, and there are those that embody in more distant ways.

The Guardian is like a great bell ringing a tone, a tone of remembrance of 'the all inclusive truths of Divine Consciousness', and the bell being rung through their incarnations. The bell is then heard in those who have woven their beings to that guardian. So, we show her the great gong ringing even before the embodiment of the guardian, calling all those who hear the bell to die and be reborn, to come closer to birth, to arrange themselves to embody, to incarnate. There is a great incarnation process around each guardian and the timing of their lifetime. And there are themes that each guardian holds. Realize that coming into incarnation is like carving into stone, the knowledge and development, implementing and manifesting more deeply the divine conscious development within each soul. It is as though each soul is saying: "I am ready, I am ready to walk it again, I am ready to walk it a little further, I am ready to print it, to hear the bell even more deeply, I am ready to start breathing with the bell, to start hearing as though the guardian speaks within." And each lifetime is a practice of embodying truth more and more.

Let us look at the span of time, and look at the bright points of the saints or the masters and their gatherings. Now look lightly upon their names and the temporary nature of their lifetime, their country and of all those who have gathered around, and know that they have held many names, as have all those who have gathered around. All are a continuation, all beings are a continuing being, and all masters are a continuing being originating from this Council. This Council with a highly directed purpose, that is an interface of the most sublime un-embodied truth nature, "God", focusing in upon the guardian beings and then focusing downwards onto the human beings. Once a human soul has attached itself to a guardian, to an avatar, to a point of light, such as a master, their entire evolution is caught in that tapestry, that weaving forward, that shaping of awakening called into embodiment. Even between incarnations there is the infusion and the development of awareness. Hold lightly to the names, to your own name, and to the name of your master and your teachers, hold lightly. Know that they are the true en-fleshing of the timeless eternal divine light, holding many names, just as you.

*What is the **Guidance** and how do we acknowledge it? (Guidance is the name given by Jean to the source of the teachings)*

The Guidance is universal knowing. Universal wisdom. It is undefined to being; it is All Being. It is that which each of you is a part of in that every one of you have created and evolved consciousness. The entire embodiment of Supreme Being-ness has evolved this wisdom and you are each part of it. This universal knowledge is available to each being for each being is part of it. Each being essentially springs from it and is part of evolving it into more and more distinct absolute clarity and becoming. It can be embodied here, before you, like this (Jean channeling), or like that, or over there...it can be embodied to you in the glory of the masters, and it is. It can be embodied to you in the silence of an elder, and it is. Yet you are to know that it is embodied in you because you are part of it.

Acknowledge it by acknowledging your own being. Acknowledging that you are the AUM, 'I am all that is.' That is the true acknowledgement. **Don't bow down to it outside of you without bowing down to it within you.** Don't identify universal knowing, universal wisdom as that which is outside of you. Don't create that separation. First and foremost, thank that which is within you. All that is being reminded and nudged and told to you within. 'I am that.' First thank that which you are before you thank it as being outside of you.

We wish to understand the difference between the teachings of **Buddha and Christ.**

The Guidance shows me the pure light form of the Christ being in his teaching state and the pure light form of the Buddha in his teaching state. Showing the absolute sameness of this light, of this very pure gathering of light, the transmission of Truth, the avenue of Truth that each is and was. Much of the difference is in how the light was received as defined by the time and the peoples and the amount of purity that was or was not absorbed or understood.

Buddha was teaching to a humanity far more prepared for sublime knowledge, inner knowledge. It was a humanity that was prepared many times over to understand divine nature within, and to expect to find liberation and divine nature within. In the sublime understanding that the Buddha came to, and then spoke of, was the unfolding of the truest identity, the God-nature within his being. It was a culmination of lives of preparation, of readying, of seeking and finally arriving in the fullness of God-nature within the human embodiment.

The moment that his life was and the purpose that his life held was to peak, to come to the mountaintop of the unfolding of divine nature within embodiment before the humanity around him. A demonstrator of divine nature for those who witnessed, the articulation of the experience and the laying down of the methods found. These culminating realizations composed his teachings. The potency of these teachings coming from a being that had just stepped free and had just, finally, in absoluteness, come to supreme mind.

The humanity in readiness around him understood not only the words given, but understood the path toward the words, understood the journey that led to the moment of supreme unfolding. The foundation of understanding was laid in humanity at that time, in that place. Therefore the witnessing was as timely and important as the unfolding. The witnesses were as ready as the one who unfolded. ***Therefore they received the teaching that Buddha is not an individual, Buddha is a state of being, a state of supreme mind that is the outcome of diligence and the movement into true identity.*** The witnesses, meaning the humanity and the students, understood that what was before them was not an individual to be worshipped, but an individual to be witnessed, as though witnessing themselves, witnessing the very process that all are in. Therefore it is held in Buddhist teaching not to worship the individual, nor to worship God as an outside entity, but to hold diligence to the process of supreme unfolding within.

The humanity surrounding the ***Jesus*** was different. It was a humanity suffering in strife, in judgment, in the lack of understanding of love. It was a humanity that was desolate, that held poverty in mind and heart. Therefore the pure light transmission of the Jesus takes a different form. ***These were a people to be embraced, to be loved, to be saved, to be given hope, to be retrieved, to be parented, to be healed.*** The mission of the Jesus was in accordance to the humanity. The absolute light of truth as defined by the receiver and the time of the receiving. The humanity surrounding Jesus had no capacity to understand divine nature within and they were not witnessing a being coming into supreme unfolding before them. They were witnessing the minister, the one who came to give succor, sweetness and healing. They were to be given hope and they were to be given a revision of understanding.

Understand the tremendous difference in the two humanities and the two times, and understand the value of both teachings for there is much humanity still lost in despair, lost in illness of mind and spirit and body, and there is much humanity ready to witness Supreme Being-ness within.

*We ask Guidance to teach us of the divine descent of **Shiva**, **Rama** and **Krishna**, these embodiments and spiritual founders in our distant past.*

Guidance brings us to the undifferentiated light of God, the light of

Supreme Being-ness, the light of Eternal Presence before manifestation, that differentiates as it embodies and as it meets the developing humanity and its needs. Understanding therefore, that ***each avatar or divine descent is a description of humanity at that time and its needs, the state of consciousness in humanity and where that state of consciousness needs assistance.***

We recall for you that the state of humanity at the time of the Shiva descent, was very childlike, very innocent, very vulnerable, very open in heart, open as a child is open, very reachable, and believing what was before them. They believed without discernment or questioning and believed what most others around them believed. The humanity at that time was highly impressionable, within the surrounding belief systems, by the one who spoke the loudest, the one with the most charismatic voice. Therefore this time in humanity was like a window, an opportunity to impress upon the soul of humanity, the divine principles, of the need to choose truth and purity and to choose, with strength, that which is right.

Humanity at this time was wildly erratic and could choose this and then that and by changing choices destroy what it had chosen first. Humanity was highly reactive and highly impressionable, and was creating great distraction to itself and each other. The light of God descended into teaching force at this time and spoke with stern discipline. The stern words: "Only this, stand strong to what is true, discard what is not and hold strong to what we give. Hold strong to these laws of righteousness, the laws of right-being, and apply the fire of dissolution to all else." The word of God as spoken to humanity at that time was like thunder, was like a tremendous reprimanding force: "Listen! Only this one path, and one truth. To vary or to wander over there is to it become destroyed." The voice of God at that time needed to instill the fear, that to wander over there is to die; to stay on the straight path is to exist in glory. There was a need to speak to this humanity in dramatic terms, for the drama created was the only way they could hear it. Shiva, the principle of fire, the father principle, the thunderous voice of truth that spoke in a blaze of brilliance that humanity heard. Supreme Presence knows exactly what it is doing.

Every decent of divine being-ness is a continuous descent, therefore all that was given through the weaving of the Shiva principal into the human soul is still there, though layered upon through time by teachers to come. Every divine descent is an active principle in continuum.

We move to the teacher **Rama.** This time we see the humanity in a much more mature place, with much more discernment, and more questioning within most beings of: "What do I believe?" There was more identification within, as the self-nature, therefore, divine descents of Supreme Being could now befriend, without the need to stand as a thunderous distant force, could be like a guide that is closer and more befriending. Rama was an exemplary human being who demonstrated the truth. Demonstrated the right use of power in self, the right use of ego-force, the right use of command and the right use of dominion. Humanity at this time felt more identified within itself and was careless with its dominion and command, much as a teenager might enjoy the power of self. Rama came to set things into correction, to show and to demonstrate without a lot of words and without a lot of ritual. With his exemplary use of Divine Being-ness within the human drama, he placed not only into demonstration but into simple words: *"This is who you are, you are a descendent of the most high, you are here to strive to be worthy to be called man."* Rama was a commander, one who led and guided others.

We move on to viewing **Krishna** more closely, in the same light of understanding. In the time of Krishna we see a dawning in the hearts, a tremendous opening in humanity towards understanding and needing to manifest devotion. The opening in the heart and soul of the humanity was deeper and there was an understanding of love and of creativity. At the time of the Krishna descent, in opening it's heart, humanity was falling in love with flowers, the sky, birds, music. There was a readiness of the heart to open. Opened and shining, we see humanity at this time highly emotional and again highly volatile. Once again there is a window of beautiful openness along with wildly swinging applications. A humanity that will love as never before and yet will hate, that will swing between love and hate as though they were the same thing. The divine descent then, through the embodiment of Krishna, descends into a beauteous being. A being who speaks of love, of continual poetry and who exudes beauty and creativity in startling stunning display. This was taken into the senses of opened humanity as though a brilliant flower has descended into the flesh. From this embodiment of beauty and of love and divine perfume, there was again the demonstration of where to place devotion, where and why to be devoted, to what, and to whom. This time humanity was ready for a much more intricate understanding through words. Humanity was gathered in its passions to devote to the one and only truth worth being devoted to, gathering those passions to the most high. Giving words to this, Krishna was a tremendously successful divine descent that impressed the soul of humanity very strongly. We can say that all creativity and artistry stems from that awakening in the human soul. Understand that you are a continuum of the human soul and you are hearing your old experiences. ***Krishna harnessed the wildly opening heart and passions of the human spirit and took those wild and beautiful horses and pointed them towards the infinite.*** There was a long journey made, a long distance being gained in that one short span of human evolution.

Islam

*What is the true meaning of the term **Jihad**? We are asking to understand more about **Mohammed** and his teaching of Jihad.*

Jihad is the inner battle we go through when we put ourselves into the fire to dedicate ourselves, to burn away the human limitations and to become the divine beings that we really are. This is the Jihad that Mohammed gave to the people.

When we aren't able or willing to go within to do this work, and we project on the outside, all of that outward projection becomes the outward Jihad that one would hear of, that terrorists refer to. This is an extreme projection. All human beings project outwardly all the time, whether we are having a fight with a loved one, or perhaps we are not willing to hear or forgive a loved one, and we make them an enemy and project onto them.

The Guidance shows me the tremendous courage of Mohammed the tremendous passion in his spirit and the reduction, in many ways, of what he received into the forms they speak of. What he received was a glimpse, a pure realizing, a brilliance of understanding. Seeing this vision, and the very restricted forms of implementation available for offering it. Seeing how it could be received by this extremely fractious humanity, the peoples who were in many wars against each other everywhere, many wars between many peoples.

So we see the difficulty of where the stream (of understanding) must meet the human mind and emotion. They are very emotional people, very heart driven, protective, using tremendous will force to hold onto whatever they have been given, whatever they believe. Very difficult dynamics, very much infused with a sense of battle and war, and so the information is framed that way. Framed as a higher war, a higher purpose to give, a higher understanding of what to fight for. Don't fight for yourself, fight for unity. Don't fight for your own separation, fight for that which draws us all together. Don't apply your will to division. Apply your will to bending down onto your knees five times a day.

So the roots of it are based in this atmosphere, and soon we are lost into the continuing grip that separation holds on human consciousness. There is no more to illuminate around Mohammed, this is it: an avenue, a receiver, a courageous being, no more and no less. Having this compassionate, powerful understanding of humanity at that time, and to silence the paradigms of war, and of war-full thinking. To direct the urging to lift what one fights for with ones will, mind and heart to that which is eternal. To have the willingness to fling everything that isn't eternal into the fire, and to eliminate everything that is not of Allah, God, or truth, into the fire.

For all who hear this, it is to attend to only the purest meaning in that. What fire? What is not eternal in your being? For all who hear this, this holy fire is for you, not for you outwardly but for you inwardly. And it always was only meant for everyone inwardly, not against the neighbor, nor against those of a different root stream, only for within.

We want to understand the transmission or root stream of divine information that came into Mohammed, as the beginning of the Islamic path. We ask to understand the intention of this, the uniqueness of this. The purpose of this question is to be oriented to the truth, to the purity at the beginning of the Islamic teachings, to the birth moment in order to have a wider, more compassionate vision towards what is happening in the world today.

The Guidance is ferrying me, moving me to the context of humanity, a context of consciousness at that time (Mohammed's time). At that time we are seeing such a multiplicity of ways, of belief ways, of ritual ways, a multiplicity of ways of reaching for truth. It is not the ways that are being pointed at, it is the heart that is reaching for truth and for itself, the human being reaching to know, to live, to extend, and to continue to evolve. In this ardent reaching, there is a multiplicity of forms and ways to believe and to channel this reaching. In multiplicity there is so much separation, division, confusion. People hardly knowing where to stand, hardly knowing how to be in right relationship with one another because of all these different adherences to ways, and all the different belief systems that they ardently hold to and identify with in order to satisfy the longing in their soul.

The confusion and the divisions became so marked and fractious that it pushed the need to this place, this moment, this need for an infusion of understanding, an infusion of realization, and of demonstration. There was a need to lay a path before the people that would ring a loud bell and re-orient their ardent yearning. A bell that began to unify all the fractiousness and remind them that they were all one body within one God. To remind them in the simplest, beginning way of who they are: one body within one God. The reminder that only one humanity exists and only one Creative Origin exists. That one overruling Supreme Intelligence exists and one brain nervous system exists. That it is peril to be in multiplicity, and that is what is meant by the very birth of creation itself, to be unified.

This is the intention of the streaming, this presence of divine information being received. This is a reminder that there is only one heart, one humanity and one child of one father. A reminder that the only way to unify in the spirit is with vigilance, with an imperative, and with a repetitive pattern of commitment. With a fire of cleansing, a fire of purpose. Being committed above all to the truth. Being committed beyond everything else in human life to true being-ness. Everything else is a secondary commitment.

The first and foremost commitment is to remember 'who thou art', and to remember that as you are, all are. It is to end division, to end unconsciousness and distraction and to end fractiousness.

Therefore it was given as a form: a form of lifestyle, a form of prayer life. **To create the pattern of prayer, so that no more than several hours have passed by before one would gather oneself again into the reminder of whom one is.** That truth is the Supreme Principle, which we are in existence to remember and to commit to. That no more than several hours would pass by in human time before one would then again listen, and hear and submit to truth. In that time of prayer, one would dissolve all else but one's heart turned to truth.

The principles that were given were a working format to purify human consciousness towards remembrance of itself and remembrance of its origins, its true being-ness, and its source. It is the Supreme Presence infusing itself into human evolution. In this defined structure of life, it was spoken to dissolve human nature, to make way for divine nature. Submit human nature and allow divine nature to exist within. It was given, to open one's heart to divine being-ness, to turn one's ardency and yearning only to God and to go into ardent prayer, dissolving human nature, submitting human nature.

It was spoken of as the holy fire, the fire that would burn away illusion, human nature, division and fractiousness; a fire that would burn away unconsciousness. It was taught that to come into the pure nature, the full alignment of consciousness, one must treat this as though it were a battle, a struggle, a war and a fire. One must attend with diligence and imperativeness or one would get pulled back into unconsciousness. It must be attended to with diligence. This is all that was meant; a practical reminder that the human nature tends to unconsciousness and to patterns, to fractiousness and division, towards the animal nature. To foster and nurture divine nature one must be diligent and vigilant and treat it as though one is in an internal struggle, a war between consciousness and unconsciousness. And one must submit and dissolve, consciously, the human nature in order to arrive in the true being-ness of love, true being-ness that is experienced with Peace.

All the images of extinguishing, i.e. extinguishing unconsciousness, extinguishing non-belief, **not non-believers,** and extinguishing the patterns of unconsciousness, **not the beings that are unconscious.** Submitting meaning dissolving, holy war meaning holy fire. Let the fire burn within you, stand on the front lines of your own being. Stand courageous and brave in the front line of your own being towards unconsciousness.

It was taught at that time to that highly unconscious humanity that the only way to purify and unify was to have these forms of the daily prayers, of the attitude, of the way to dislodge the heavy, leaden unconsciousness in the culture.

The passionate heart of those people then, and their descendants now, brings a tear. It is a passion against unconsciousness woven, entangled and buried in pain, buried in anger, embroiled in anguish. The very flame of their hearts that loves Allah and loves God is in continual battle against unconsciousness projected outwardly rather than inwardly. The entanglement that is being created, of Karma, of applying this battle to beings that they deem unconscious outwardly without attending to the melting pot within. Without attending to the fire of love, the only force that will create dissolution or dissolving. The Karma that they are creating for their beings causes a bow, a gravity of sadness.

The lesson to be received, the respect, the awe to stand in is the power of that ardent heart. The ones that would kneel no matter if they are the destroyers or the peace lovers, that would kneel five times a day trying to understand, five times a day attending to truth as they know it. All those beings are asking of life, asking of Allah, is for truth, and truth shall pour through them like a river of fire, a river of life, a river of grace, some day.

Current Teachers

***Paramahamsa Nithyananda, Master of Joy**, is an enlightened, spiritual teacher currently in India. We want to know more about his mission and the timing of his coming into the world.*

In this state of awareness I see energetically only, and I see the brilliance of this being, the brilliance of a small sun shining. I see the beings around him, I see their light as well, I see how they are lit up and yet the brilliance of this being is like a full aura of brilliance. I see the orb of brilliance that is Nithyananda, and above his brilliant orb I see the three points of glowing light, above his body.

Nithyananda is new, Nithyananda is not new. Nithyananda has been in this mission for some time. This new embodiment is a continuation and this is known. This new embodiment is here to create a true awareness of the full embodiment of the human being upon the planetary being. It is to create an awareness of all humanity as one body and all Earth as one place of being. The mission of Nithyananda is to weave the entire human consciousness to create a sense of oneness. It is the beginning of dispelling the separations. It is the beginning of a wonder, for those that come close to this teaching and to this being can hold nothing of a religion. They can hold nothing of ownership, or tradition. They can hold nothing but what is before them: the brilliant newness of a unified consciousness. It is dissolving; he is dissolving the containers, the limitations, and the resistance. He is a force of dissolving and freeing.

It is a simple answer, and it is a tremendously potent action. The beauty of this being is the joy, the manifest joyousness that is the carrier and imprint of the message. The words trail along behind, even the action of dissolving trails along behind. The joy goes ahead, the joy speaks the strongest and those that would come close to this brilliance with resistance and fear of letting go, are met with this joy.

The joy is the greatest teacher. The joy says, "Trust, relax." Joyousness is the result of unifying to truth, unifying to all beings, unifying to God, unifying to love. Joy is the result of dissolving and letting go of all the traditions that limit and letting go of all the structures of religion that limit. Joy goes before him as the messenger, as the example of the result. As the opening of the door, and the door that is being opened is not just in the heart, it is also in the mind. It is a door that is opened in many levels, the body, the heart and the mind. *Joy is a grand butler that opens the door very wide;* all doors not just the heartfelt door, not just the intelligence door; all doors.

Nithyananda is an embodiment of joy. Joy is the force that is yet to be seen in this world. *Joy is a force direct from the sun, understood by flowers more than human beings.* And this joy will not be darkened. This joy will carry and impact far beyond the lifetime of this master. And as those that come close and walk away, forgetting everything he ever said, they will not forget the joy that was implanted in their soul.

It is right that this being is housed in India. As we observe the progression of masters, this embodiment of joy is the perfect progression to come into being at this time. Joy is a high level consciousness, a level of consciousness that is sitting in all aspects of the being. Joy illuminates the highest intelligence of the human being and the fullest experience of the heart. Joy must be spoken and expressed in the most articulate of truths. Joy animates the body to exist in full life force. Joy is a manifestation of full embodiment, divine form, and it is time for the human being to observe, to witness, to be touched and opened up to the force we will still call joy.

In the progression of embodiment of divine entity in being-ness, which India has hosted for the world, it is now time for an embodiment of joy. Everyone, turn your beings to that embodiment of joy. Open your heart, soul and mind.

We ask about a prophecy of the **Dalai Lama's** *return to Tibet in 2014.*

The Guidance is taking me to the girl and her vision or receiving (a ten year old girl in India who had a prophetic vision of the Dalai Lama's returning to Tibet). The Guidance is showing the resonance of her being and soul to the Dalai Lama's being and soul, and the resonance of her whole path to the Dalai Lama's path. It is as though they are not two individuals but two paths, two missions, and two themes. She is essentially not a little girl, she is very intimate to the unfolding and progression of this stream of teaching and being-ness that the Dalai Lama is leader of, or sits at the head of. The Guidance shows that the Dalai Lama knows this. It isn't so much about attending to the prophecy of a child, but attending to who is the person, the affinity to this being that is speaking, not so much the affinity to the date and the prophecy.

There is an opening in the entire unfolding of the Tibetan spirit, not only Tibetan but also the Chinese. It is an unfolding of the humanity in that place, and in the struggle that they are in; there is a whole opening that begins before this. It begins to open, making much that mattered before, almost mysteriously not matter anymore. So many things were actively blocking the purposes, the themes, and the being-ness of the Dalai Lama. Again, it is not about the person, but about the whole representation of the meaning of the Dalai Lama. It is speaking of a huge wave of consciousness, the stream of being and evolution of a people. The Dalai Lama happens to stand as a herald, a named herald. But all the resistance, all blockage towards that stream of being, just begins to dissipate. Almost beyond, "Well, what happened?" and we see that there are those who would analyze and try to understand; yet they can't quite see why. However, one such as the girl knows why. There is a smile there, even in the Guidance, that knows why. It's not something that can be traced out with the rational mind, or even traced to the difficult and relentless efforts of the people who are trying to create peace or unity. All the efforts count, yet they are not the deeper movements that cause the barrier to dissipate and the resistance to dissolve. The deeper timing is what the girl knows, or shall we say, her soul knows and was given.

The deeper timing is very important. In the soul of the Dalai Lama and in the souls of all those in leadership positions at this time, it is known, it is known that they were waiting to hear this. It is like a very specialized gong that we are waiting to hear, a gong that marks the shift of the tide of evolution. It doesn't mark the changing of politics, or government or dates, it is marking the shift in the entire humanity. And so this dissipation of resistance is not only seen there, it will be seen everywhere. All over there will be a feeling of: 'What happened?' and 'Where did that go?' As though the energy is falling away from resistance itself.

So understand, in terms of this question, that this marker or message being spoken of is pointing to a very deep turning of the tides of human being-ness. It is held in the patterns or the grids of the Tibetan understanding and of the mystical understanding. It is not a surprise, it is written and it is known. But being written isn't enough, it needed to be spoken, it needed to surface through the innocent, through the unbecoming, the ones who weren't even looking, weren't even reading. To be spoken through a child, a seeming child. And so you can rest. You do not need to question. And even if the physical re-entry into Tibet isn't exact to that year, there begins even just before, the ability. Even though the resistance may still be spoken, the warning, it is an invisible resistance, a patterned habit.

We show the face of the Chinese in a nebulous, all encompassing sort of way, and we see their hearts breaking into a tear, into crying, into a softening and into an honesty of the lack in the heart. From their younger people and elders, we see crying and harking back to the true spirit and wisdom of their people, a vast, magnificent and huge ancestry of wisdom. This is part of the tide as well. Through the eyes of this, there is the actual re-embodying of many of the wise peoples in the Chinese lineage; re-embodying into the present-day Chinese people and further, re-embodying into the present-day Tibetans (former Chinese re-embodying into Tibetan form). The consciousness of unity, the un-sought-for sense of 'you are I and I am you', as though harking back to before division, into the roots and wisdom of what is held. And so from this deep source of re-embodying, it is as though they have no actual memory (having memory of what has been told to you is different than actual memory such as pain and anguish). So the re-embodying is (and has been) swift now, and the re-embodying is coming to an age-time of consciousness as though they are no longer children but coming into their young adulthood. They are looking around and seeing no reason to carry on the division, no reason at all, even if given the mandate. Forgetting it, almost like amnesia to resistance as if there is just no place.

We watch the Dalai Lama, we watch his spirit in knowing-ness, and we watch his final years in wonder, as he observes the out-working of the evolving being that the human is, the evolving great presence. It is as though the bulk of the work for the evolving of the human spirit is not being done by anyone, it is being done from somewhere beyond sight, as though it is some great turning of the universe. We see the Dalai Lama disembodying in peace knowing his whole journey was a miracle.

In the silence that is here (following his death), we are watching a great white bird flying above the plains of Tibet (this symbolism is being given to you all). We see the dissolving of bone and body into peace and the great white bird, and we see the young people arising, neither Tibetan nor Chinese, just people, free people. With sad remains around and a sad history to study, but not much interest, more just "We are here now." and creating a culture that is a blend of so many symbols and ways. We see these people with no fixation on tradition, just loving tradition not struggling with it or combating with it, just delighting in it. And we see the deeper traditions, the true traditions of wisdom spontaneously arising. We see this land becoming a powerful place of learning for the whole world, as though the whole world begins to turn to it more and more, just as it may turn to India to see this unified being-ness arising, this culture of freedom arising. It is as though all that was really being witnessed in all the pain was a birthing, an emerging, a dying of the wooden and archaic emptiness and a birthing of the magnificence held within. We see the Dalai Lama knowing that.

Karma

What is Karma?

In watching the question come in and trying to describe this, there is patience, but there is also exasperation because the question is simple but very big. There is the sense of hands in the air: What aspect of Karma? The Guidance is taking me to the source of the person asking and the meaning that is held in that person. The understanding in that person, is to describe how one thing leads to another, describe how what is happening in one day or one life is a direct feedback or tie back to what was done before. Asking to describe this link between the action of one life, or one day, and how it defines the next.

The Guidance shows how *every moment of a being in development and evolution, is giving rise to the next moment,* every way that the conscious being, or semi-conscious being chooses, responds, adjusts, decides, concludes and reacts. However they resolve that moment and what is in it, gives rise to the next moment. **This is the simplest description of the law of Karma, in that every moment gives rise to the next of itself.** Every moment is a choice to animate an energy stream and to not animate another. The energy stream is a continuum, a continuousness. It is as simple as showing before you several paths. A path is a place of movement, an energy stream and as you step on that path it leads you into the reality of itself. And yet you could have chosen the other paths, or you may jump over to another path. Where that path leads you, is a development of itself. It is an energy stream.

The human being largely sits in unconsciousness of the energy stream that results from every thought, every choice, every reaction, every response, every conclusion and every belief. What if one were to awaken into aliveness and understanding that all these choices, responses and actions, are a living, dynamic setting forth of the reality which is unfolding? In becoming alive to the law of Karma, the true dynamic nature of being-ness, one can swiftly arrive into a place of grace. One can swiftly arrive into the place that is most grace filled, filled with the harmony one so desires. Most lives continue on, neither here nor there, full of suffering, full of circumstances, devoid of apparent choices, and full of apparent suffering, largely because the human being does not realize the dynamic living nature of Karma, of choosing.

For example, one could be in the most destitute of situations where there was very little, and where there was great harm being done, great wrongness occurring and very little to do about it, with nothing to eat, nothing to change. One's only choice is how to be with it. How do you address it? Do you address this most dire of situations with hatred, with anger, despondency and despair? With defeat, with the loss of belief in one's being, with all beings and in existence itself? Or does one choose, in the subtlest of places, which is the only place the choice can be, to realize that this moment is passing, this moment does not reflect the purposes of God. This moment is a moment to be survived and forgiven. This is not a moment to lose the belief of the Greater Truth and in one's being. This is not a moment to succumb to darkness, hatred and anger.

When looking at this extreme example, and then applying it all the rest of the time, *realize that you always have the choice of how to address the moment in front of you.* Always. And when you address it, you build the next reality upon that. By not succumbing to defeat and despair and to the lack of belief in one's own being (which is the furthest down one can go in choices) then in the next movement of life, the next development (either a series of moments or a life) starts to take hold. The soul starts to grow stronger. The consciousness of light within that being starts to become stronger and stronger because they didn't give in when all factors said: "Give in". They chose that moment to exist as never before, to believe when there was nothing to believe in but the stream of truth within.

The Karma for such a being is to move further and further into experiences of becoming. Where as the Karma of the one who succumbed into defeat and depression is to need to choose again and again and again not to give in, not to succumb. They can be given grace and they can be given challenge until they show themselves: "I exist no matter what. None of this hunger, none of this abuse, none of this war actually destroys the indestructible essence of my being-ness."

Karma then, is the law of the continuing stream of being, the continuing creation of events and situations that take shape in resonance to what was chosen before. Karma is the very substance of evolution, of the evolving being-ness that becomes stronger and stronger in the indestructible essence of itself. Karma is the law of creation of substance. Karma is the law in the plant that, given the most beautiful condition, creates the most virile seed, which creates the next plant form of even more perfection. Karma is the law that sits in the physical plan for the strongest, healthiest and most intelligent form in any animal or plant, to give rise to more of itself and more of the same. It is the evolutionary principle as it comes into physical substance, emotional substance and spiritual being-ness. The same law of 'one form giving rise to the next' according to how it settled, how it integrated into the conditions that it was in.

It is a mistake to say: "My karma is..." as though it were a punishment. Any experience that you are in is a result of what you chose, it is based on how you settled into response in the moment before. It was all according to your choice. This isn't to say that if you are in a war and your home is being burned and your family is being killed, that you chose that. What you chose was the need in your being to come to the indestructible nature. You chose the fire of purification and challenge to choose: "I am the indestructible essence of truth and I cannot die. No matter what this army does, I shall not be destroyed, I shall not go into hatred, I shall not go into the poisonous rage, I shall not go into the defeat of annihilation in my heart." That is what you chose. You chose courageously the conditions that would give birth, in your awareness, of the indestructible nature of being-ness.

You can look at many of the teachers. You can look at the Christ when the whole world went against him, when his body was being tortured, and see the example of the indestructible nature of the soul, the true being that he demonstrated. The example of the choice he made was to forgive these people because they were unconscious. Not to hate them or to go into lack of belief in existence. He did not choose to go into hatred, not to prove anything, just to love and forgive and be patient of the unconsciousness that created that destruction.

Look at the choices of that being, and look at all beings that stand out in the brilliance of the indestructible despite the abuse that humanity has given them. Know the choice that they have made. ***For them there was no choice, they knew with such strength and absoluteness that they were already free.*** But for you, the choice comes every day.

We ask about incoming karma, the resolution of karma and the importance of remembering past lives (understanding what one brings forth into this life, how to work with it, how important to remember its origins, its sources).

The premise must be set that all beings are a continuation being, a being in a continuum of consciousness, a continuum of life experiences, of soul development, and a continuum of creating individuality and creating the relationship with Supreme Source. The word Karma, so misunderstood, clatters like a little stone in the bottom of a bucket. What is it? It is simply a description of this continuation. It is an urging to see further and wider, to see with more extended premise 'who you are'. You are a continuing dynamic growing sum of all your experiences, all your incarnations, all your 'study periods' we shall say, the interim between incarnations, which is an existence as well. Not incarnated into a physical body, yet still existing in the individuality, in the shape of the being that you are. Literally remembering former lifetimes is not something to strive, nor reach, nor yearn for. Rather, strive to understand how and when remembrance arises, and why, and why it doesn't.

We show her the point, like a point of light, the point of being, or the point of awareness that an individual is in. If this point of light, this point of identity of consciousness is sitting firmly and fully in their present self-creation, if this self-creation is based on the literal world that they are in, the relationships that are very physically around them, based fully and only on the work they are doing, on the relationships they are in and the occurrences in the world around them, **such a being will have no remembrance for they are in their point of consciousness, only here in this incarnation.** They are in a small room with windows looking out into the fields that are right before them. They have no greater landscape, they have no greater premise of being, therefore, their consciousness is built entirely of the present incarnation and remembrance is a silence.

This is not wrong. It is a necessity. It has been a necessity for eons of evolving, in that the very dynamic of incarnating is to be fully engaged in creating the present relationship to humanity, to world, to culture, and in shaping 'self' in response to that. For a being that does **not** have the deeper in-roads, the deeper development of the greater expanse of soul, to have remembrance of the multiple former identities, would fracture their consciousness. It would disseminate their consciousness and create insanity. It is impossible to integrate the experiences, the pains, the sufferings, the realizations, the stasis that they held and the conclusions that they made. Therefore, the built-in amnesia of infancy is a cleansing, a purifying blessing.

Take an example within humanity as you have been witnessing it now and up until now, of a being that has perhaps been a criminal or a cruel being, has been a thief or a murderer. Take this being through the amnesia towards infancy, take him to the innocent, vulnerable absolute state of an infant and see how cleansed, how renewed, how blessed this new beginning is for him. This is an opportunity to start over and re-shape the relationship to self, to humanity, to culture, to Supreme Being. Their new birth is not the beginning. The beginning is in the study period (between lives), the interim stage when there is the attendance of the Guidance, of the Elders, of the Beings of Light that attend all human souls, all evolving souls. They strive to assist the being in their more permeable, less condensed and concretized form of consciousness to see wrongness, rightness, possibilities, to see the highest potentials of existence, to come into an incarnation as ready as that being is able, to entirely re-frame their identity. As long as so much unconsciousness rules in a being, so does this amnesic infancy serve.

Beings such as you who are waking up like beautiful light spheres, no longer needing amnesic infancy, no longer needing amnesia in any form. How important then is it to remember? Again, no striving, no pushing, realize that as you expand your identity in this incarnation, as you let go of who you think you are, in your emotion, in your temperament, in your "I am this person who likes this, or I am this person who doesn't like that, and I do this and I do that, and I am defined by you and I am defined by this". As you let go of all this identity formation that fixes you into this human character, and you have more and more expansiveness in your meditations, more and more experiences of love itself, of unity with all beings, so does your remembrance start to flood in, unasked for; so does the greater sum of your identity flow in. In that widening delta of consciousness, you can look back and see, that face, that time, that lesson, that relationship. It all begins to be one existence.

The nature of karma then, is that all beings come into incarnation prepared by their arrangements and agreements with the angelic assistants for what this life could set itself forth to clear, to cleanse, to remove, to heal, to face. Drawing the most poignant, the most limiting, the most obstructive of the beliefs and the experiences that are held in the greater body that you may call your soul. Bringing it forward into the birth conditions, the world conditions, the potential conditions of the culture. Going in prepared each and every time to the extent of the consciousness in that individual, to meet it with grace, with more consciousness, with resolution, with solution. This has occurred in each one of you, is occurring in each one of you, and the result is expansion.

You can then say that you have dropped like a shroud the interplay with your traumas, your limitations, your bondage into what was shaped and created in your greater being. Then your karma sits in an upward radiating purpose. You are here then, to liberate others, you are here to expand the consciousness fields of all beings. You are here to give message and represent what it looks like to exist in that liberation, which is not a state that is unattainable. It is walking with the eyes with a smile. It is walking as a human incarnation full of the presence of love, needing to not be teacher, not being anything, just being Grace to all beings that come before you. Being nothing, being no identity but Grace itself to all beings in front of you.

For those who come to the second karma*, to the second theme of expressing that liberation in their elder-hood, these are the ones who are sowing the fields in this humanity. They are embodied absolutely with their illnesses, with their aging bodies, with their full exposure to the story, with their children and their grandchildren, they are part of this humanity and they are leavening this humanity with their grace, with their conscious journey, and that is you.

*The second karma means the second or next major purpose in a lifetime, which can be realized when and if the first one has come to completion. Most often, at the completion of the first karmic purpose, the incarnation ends.

What is the difference between divine ordained destiny and free will or choice?

The question framed as 'divine destiny versus free will' is a continuation of the commentary on Karma. Divine destiny truly is that which was set, before going ahead, and that which was chosen to set the tone and conditions for the next life or next moment. The term divine destiny connotes the bigger dynamic of the next life, the next year, the next purpose.

Divine, is the word meaning *that which sits in truth.* Destiny, the word meaning *the direction that the being is going in the meaning of truth, in the development of truth.* In these meanings then, the divine destiny of every being is set. Every being is built, within the core essential nature of their soul, to come into the glory, into the fullness of truth and to come into the full awakening of their own nature. This is unquestionable law that sits in creation, divine destiny of this entire creation.

The free will is such that the conscious beings must consciously find their way choice-by-choice, life-by-life, and moment-by-moment, towards forging with conscious power and strength, the true identity. They must move from the unicellular being through the carnivorous animal being, to the human being, to the angelic being. They must forge the identity, the Divine Identity through the unconsciousness of matter, the semi-consciousness of the animal being and the human being until by the power of their own yearning, their own choosing, they forge the beauty being; the being of full awareness. Free choice is the tenet, the condition, to create truly powerful consciousness that isn't just given, but that moves substance forward.

Going backwards to the animal in its soft level of choosing, it stands before two paths: one that would ensure survival and one that would bring death. The ability of that animal to sense, the intelligence of that animal to assess and to choose is a choice. The choice then taken, defines that entire animal's being; they never forget. It is the beauty of movement, of the supreme non-manifest into manifestation.

What is meant by the 'Sons and the Daughters of God' is the full becoming of consciousness in form. Don't just see it as a human being in brilliance, don't define it, and don't stop at any definition. *The most beautiful expression of God consciousness in form is arrived at choice-by-choice.*

We could say that divine destiny is choice-less; it is built in because the entire body of Supreme Being is becoming itself. It is built in, and it is the gift. It is the gift you are born with and carry all the time. The free choice is, how closely aligned to the gift do you choose to be?

We ask to understand how to work with karma, how to more consciously enter into resolving karma.

Going beyond an individual's actions or evolution, first understand karma as a tenet or law of creation. As a law within creation, it is a motion or a wind, a force within creative matter. It is to be understood as the law of cause and effect, the impulse and the outcome of movement. It is the dynamic nature of creation, that one impulse or idea, one motion creates the next impulse, the next outcome. It is an ongoing stream of outcomes. At each creative moment, each new inclusion of energy, of intention, of idea, of chemistry and of action creates the nature of the outcome of the next moment, of the next substance, of the next reality. Understand karma as evolution in action, the evolving development of All-being-ness, manifest creation evolving itself through this law of movement and becoming.

Within the individual soul in evolution, every belief, decision and action of a being creates the next reality for that being. First, there is a belief, then a decision and then an action, seeing the triad in that direction. The fourth thing is the outcome, which is created by that triad. From this creation then, how did the belief, how did the intention and how did the next action evolve? The force of evolution within your being is based on the beliefs that you hold, the decisions you make from your belief and the actions you take from there. **Therefore, each soul evolves itself in creating its own state of being, its own state of consciousness and its own reality.** Life by life, year by year and moment by moment.

Karma is not to be thought of in negative terms, as a punishment. It is to be thought of as the law of evolution, the play of evolution. Therefore one's karma could be spiraling into greater and greater light and grace and harmony or it can spiral into further and further darkness and unconsciousness. Therefore, remove the negative association from the word karma and take it into your hands as the power of one's own consciousness, the power of ability. Know it is in your hands; the moment you are in, is your creation. The life that you are in, is your creation. The state of being that you are in, is your creation. If you are witnessing these realities in dismay, hold that dismay for only a moment before knowing: "I can create the next moment, I can create the next year, I can create the next life according to my visions, my hopes, my heart and my truth."

The question is how to take this law in hand and how to resolve the unconsciousness of one's reality more swiftly. To attend to every moment possible, every belief found, every decision faced from the intention of consciousness, truth and love. To attend to this closely is the answer. Unconsciousness dissolves and then the creative potential around the unconsciousness is gone. There is no judge in this Universal Creation. There is only the equal, simultaneous evolving of all human beings. What then is forgiveness? Forgiveness is simply choosing: "Not this, but this", to not choose unconscious patterns and to seek conscious ones. To recognize the actions that created suffering in your being, or for others, and to choose them no more. As the choices that create grace in your being and for others are made, the unconsciousness, the 'karma' (as negativity) dissolves, becomes part of the power of your wisdom and your learning and nothing more. It becomes part of the records of your soul. To the extent that you place your beliefs and the power of your intentions towards the highest principles of becoming, to this extent, you become that. It sits in every being's potential to come into the awakened state of true being. It is according to practice, to diligence, to the moment by moment choices. To the extent of that, a being becomes resolved of unconsciousness and is not subject to past actions of unconsciousness.

The power of Grace, the power of Love, the power of true consciousness is immeasurable. **The power of transformation in any being is an untapped surprise.** You are not locked into an endless cycle except by your own unconsciousness. Unconsciousness and the patterns of unconsciousness, is the only bondage you face, and that bondage will never release you but by your own doing. There is no other, there is no outside to this. There is only each soul becoming aware that they have the power to be awake and as filled with potential and grace as they would. Therefore seeing the meaning of karma as that: the belief, the intention, the action and the result. The pure movement-curl of a breath, where did a breath begin and where did it end? Adding to this movement of evolution, the self-awareness or the realization of who you most are, who you truly are. You are a being of divine potential at the outset, created from divine principle. Knowing what evolution is: the evolving of divine being-ness in form so that this entire creation awakens to what it is: the beauteous creation of consciousness, the interflowing, interweaving creation of consciousness.

Kundalini

What is the Kundalini?

The Kundalini is generally very misunderstood. It is in fact a very specific golden stream of energy, like sunlight, within the spinal column, with a physiological channel reserved for it, starting from the very tip of the coccyx. Along this channel the nexuses are located in the major energy centers, or chakras. Each chakra has a field that it accesses, giving the energy channel access to every minor and major energy center in the entire body. The Kundalini remains latent until there is resonance within the several different energy streams within the physical human being. When there is resonance within the whole matrix, there is a signaling of development and the Kundalini begins to circulate.

Kundalini means the sacred fire, the fire of sacred becoming, fire that transforms the matrix of the body when it touches every nexus. As each of the nexuses and their fields are touched with this highly vibrant sacred fire, the physical being is brought into super consciousness. Super awareness in the physical body allows a person to function in relationship to universal consciousness at the higher wavelengths. At this level, the being then knows how to create substance, they know how to be free of time, and they are no longer subject to the physical laws. They have become *super* conscious in the physical embodiment. The physical self becomes a dynamic substance that holds no repeating patterns of illness stemming from a place of unconsciousness. It becomes purely a substance of the conscious being. The body becomes highly transformative and it can be maintained; it can be eternal. It is a continually renewing embodiment.

This divine fire, this finer force, activates the entire nervous system and brain because the system is in a resonant place. It is available for activation. This energy substance can be transformative but also has the ability to dismember. If a being is resonant but only beginning to be resonant, and is not being mentored into their super consciousness they can essentially lose their consciousness. Because this line that they have risen above means stepping into the region of All Consciousness, they can lose their identity, and have difficulty inhabiting their body. If you were to have an experience of All Being-ness, your present identity would shrink and flounder. It would lose its home and would not know itself. Resonance must be patiently developed stage by stage. There must be a readiness to exist in the vast state of all minds. There must be strength in the configuration of individuality, strength in knowing how to be an individual as well as be super conscious. There must be absolute alignment with Grace so that the shift in the embodiment, the configuration and the use of that configuration, falls where it must. In other words, destruction is possible; mostly destruction and a fracturing of the "I am."

The Kundalini is a description of what a human being is really meant to be. It is a description of the finest energy running through the nervous system. The most awakened and illuminated brain network and cell form. It is a glowing ember sitting in the bottom of the spinal stream like a seed of incredible beauty and flame, sitting there as a gift in every human being.

It is not all or nothing: either it sits there like a little orb with silent darkness about it, or it's blazing up, it is not like that. We are just to know that it exists. The sacred energy of divine consciousness is implanted in the nervous system of every human being. Everything comes together and the brain and the spinal system inherently have the capacity for illumination.

Our work at this time is to create resonance and alignment in every part of our human nature, to accept Grace and Divine Being-ness and to move into knowing that we are divine beings. To know that we are selfless beings of love with no other choice than to live with compassion, giving, trust and peace. With commitment, discipline and effort, to move through the unconsciousness of distrust, fear, and disbelief in oneself.

Creating resonance in your being is choosing continually, with strength, yearning and practice, to sit in the identity of the Grace within. At that time and in that process, the flame gently and softly rises. It is not the blasting open of a dam; it is an arising of the refining quality within the entire nervous system. The development of the brain net is occurring by way of the sacred fire that travels like nectar to open the neuronal pathways. Your experience then, is one of knowing 'who you are', without words, a knowing of your greater being. It is experiencing yourself as a being of grace and beauty; every breath is one of beauty and your eyes behold grace and beauty. In this gentle step-by-step ongoing way of opening a path for this fine light, you create the resonance that can allow absolute infilling.

It is a mistake to seek or dramatize this process; it is better to let it come in stages, rather than all at once. The intensive seeking of resonance and infilling without mentorship and without the ability to know from the outside one's readiness, is when fracturing can occur.

There is a humorous paradox in the west, where there are no masters walking amongst us, no gurus to put ourselves at the feet of. We are left to find the God within, slowly. We are left with true choice, not being charismatically lured from the outside. We go because our being is called and needs to go there.

How much do you remember and what will you do with it, how much do you yearn to come into who you are and awaken and what will you do with that? What will you do if there is nothing on the outside to show it to you, if it is only your heart and spirit calling, if there is no system for awakening set in front of you that your entire family has followed? You will find it in the most real of ways: you will find it because your heart is calling for you to find it within.

How is Kundalini useful and formative to the human being?

First, the Guidance shows me the wave-stream of the so-named Kundalini. Visually, we are seeing a very fine vibrant energy wavelength that is in the finest wavelength stratum of nervous system energy. It is the wavelength that simulates and comes close to the wavelength of light. Understanding that the nervous system transmits many wavelengths, and that the whole energy embodiment metabolizes many wavelengths. The so-named Kundalini or the 'Stream of Fire' is the very finest-tuned, very highly developed stream of energy that the nervous system is able to metabolize, and is able to transmit. In the fineness of its qualities, the

Stream of Fire is a thread that links the entire nervous system beyond itself. It is a continuous thread beyond the individual human nervous system into the Universal nervous system (the term Universal nervous system is misleading), into the Universal Life Field, into the life field of Consciousness itself, and Light itself.

The wonder of this human embodiment is that it has the capacity to stream in, to metabolize and to host this Universal Life Field, Universal Life Energy. When the development and the intention in the embodiment has been chosen, and nurtured, and hosted, then there is the capacity to be beyond the individual identity, into the Universal Identity. The spiritual identity is annexed, enjoined and part of the Universal Identity. The human being is a Universal Embodiment. The human being was developed and is evolving towards Universal Identity as the epitome of embodiment. Kundalini or Stream of Fire is this stream of information within the nervous system that links Universal Identity into the human form. This is what we will say on Kundalini.

Meditative Practices

*We ask how one can be the **meditative witness** in ordinary daily life as we feel and love and interact. We would like to understand the witness state in human nature.*

The answer is to find, create and establish the essential, truest identity of your being. Not the 'I Am' as a concept, nor a thought, but as an experience, an absolute felt and experienced state of being. The identity, arranged around and within the soul, the ongoing essence and nature of your being, not as the created constructs of your character and egoic development. It is to have the eyes fully open onto what is before you. Fully opened eyes observing and witnessing. **Therefore, what is meant by the witness or observer, is to have the eyes of the true nature, the opened consciousness of the ongoing true identity of your being, watching, witnessing, observing, holding consciousness in this world that you are in.**

Witness and observer does not mean detachment or distance, it doesn't mean disconnect and being apart from. It means the eye of the 'I Am' is open, watching and conscious. The language creates energy and creates images that aren't correct. The word observer can imply energetically that one is sitting at the top rim of a hill looking into the distance and not being part of what is seen. However, the meaning of awake-ness, of the eye open, is to be fully conscious within the world that is seen, being fully awake, from the identity of the eternal nature.

What is otherwise? What are the egoic constructs of self? Through meditation you will learn that your mind's thoughts can create states of being, that your emotional responses create states of being, or your physical traumas. Your physical state will create beliefs and expressions and realities that you attach the egoic 'I am' to: "I am a cripple", "I am one with this limitation", "I am one that is afraid", "I am one that can't do this or that". It is the defining and creating of a limited self as a construct within this human frame, which is unconscious most of the time. It is creating self from unconsciousness, from emotional states, from conclusions that create beliefs. We would say then, that the eyes are closed. The essential nature, the true ongoing soul or Atmic nature knows the emotion started here and created this and that it will peter out over there. It knows that the experience that the mind believed, started with this event and created that conclusion and developed that belief. The Atmic nature is apart from this, is witness to all of it. The meditative process is to strengthen the identity in the Atmic essential nature, to be able to dissolve paths of thought belief, emotional conclusion, and to dissolve identities shaped around limitations and lack.

The sense of being witness or observer is in holding a greater and greater presence at the Atmic place of being. It may feel like distance and may require separation to develop that identity, but it is not meant to create distance and separation in the living of life. It is to be able to fuse the essential 'I Am-ness' into the avenues and streams of human embodiment, to love fully from that brilliance and that peace of 'I Am'. Thinking from there, choosing and doing from there. Creating a life that is constantly informed by the Truth-nature. Not believing in and acting upon the limitations in one's own being or in others. The only response to limitation that has already been created is compassion and service. The Atmic eye that is open sees the coming and going. This person's limitations will pass, and pass more quickly if met with love and compassion and not judgment. Not implementing their limitations further by agreeing to them or criticizing them. There is no removal from life to a Bodhisattva, one who lives according to the true nature is intimately part of all beings in compassion, in service, in love. The only separation is that there is no agreement to creating an identity of unconsciousness and limitation. They do not agree to getting bound up in unconsciousness in their interactions with others, nor do they agree to getting caught up in unconsciousness within.

What is it to love from the true nature, from the Atmic being? It is to love without conditions of self, to love without the conditions of needing to create boundaries or safety nets or protections. It is to love the being before you, so absolutely that there is no separation. It is not an emotional experience as much as it is an experience of tremendous attunement and joy and recognition. Recognizing over and over again the Divine nature, the Divine creation in this being, in that being, in every being.

What is the difference between 'the witness' and 'the mind' in meditation?

The mind is a distinct entity or formation. One could see it as a very intricate network of thought paths and perception paths all designed to create consciousness. It is designed as the map of consciousness, the form for consciousness growth and development. The mind of the human being is much more complex than that of an animal, with much more mapping, complexity of thought paths and of perceptive ability. The human mind is a jewel of developing consciousness of the soul, an evolutionary jewel, and an evolutionary tool for conscious development. The mind is still sitting in a rudimentary state of development, its capacity only partially used. Envision a map of pathways with only a portion of the pathways lit up. The portion that is lit up is bright, and indeed, is dominant. The mind dictates in how consciousness is used within this form, the embodiment. Therefore the region of thought paths that may carry roots of fear or anger can dictate the consciousness of the being. It is as though the mind is a window that allows entry to only this much or that much of the soul. If only a small portion of the mind is being used, there is only a small degree of soul consciousness. The mind is designed as a lens or a window for the conscious development of the soul.

In meditation the mind carries a thought, "All that I am is enough, "All that I am is here" or "All that I am is a being of Peace". One could use any number of thoughts of true nature, directives of truth, which the mind holds pathways for. As the mind learns of itself, what it is meant for, through meditation, for example, the lens of the greater conscious is broadened. This allows the greater being, or soul, to manifest in perception, in this form, in this embodiment, in this speech, in this action, in this life creation.

What is the 'witness'? This is the greater being, the soul. The soul does not require thoughts, does not require the map of the mind to exist. The soul is the eternal nature, consciousness itself. It needs no thoughts; it needs nothing but itself. The development of a soul is ongoing and the mind and embodiment develops it. In the first stages of conscious development, the being requires the mind for knowing, like a fine honed point, thoughts and engagement in form, to know itself. As a soul develops towards greater and greater enlightenment, it needs not the mind, nor the embodiment.

Every soul is in evolution. The jewel of the mind and the embodiment are the format of this evolution. In meditation, know that you are conditioning the mind. You are building new pathways or brightening conscious pathways by using them towards the thoughts of true being. You are learning to bring silence to the pathways of contraction or limitation, which limit the lens of awareness. That is 'mind'. 'Witness' is the suggestion that mind can carry, to assist in becoming silent enough to have a viewing, an experience, an entry into the soul nature, the eternal presence, which has such magnitude and vastness, is a much greater source of being. Mind is only a lens, a fragment of soul, a tool for the soul.

We ask for more understanding of the mantra 'Aum'. Why do we use it in meditation?

The Guidance starts by showing me an all encompassing sense of Aum and showing how flat it becomes when it is put into letters and into human concept or words, even if it is a sung word. Even the understanding flattens out into a very linear and lateral grasping at trying to understand this. As though it were a description of a thing.

Aum cannot be understood in the mind, as these words would suggest. Putting Aum into language always appeals to a certain part of conceptual understanding but **to truly understand the Aum is to experience the Aum. It is to experience your whole being.** We could say that your whole being is Aum, that All Being is Aum. We could say that creation in all its manifestation is Aum.

The linear thought and word Aum is trying to encapsulate just that: the whole of manifest creation. Fitting the vastness of that statement into a small thought and word is impossible. Even your sense of self, in many ways, is a small thought, as though you are a separate entity. To truly grasp the meaning of Aum is to become Aum. It is to **become a resonant one-ness with All That Is.**

We will describe in words how all this arose to the three letters and into the practice, and yet always remember what is being pointed at and meant by that word. If you are to open your eyes as you are chanting Aum, everything you see you are chanting. Every sensation and experience of your sensory being, is what you are chanting. The flower, you are chanting. The car going by, you are chanting. The entire All Being-ness of manifest creation is included in the Aum, therefore Aum is the original word. It is the original timeless word. The all-encompassing thought of God.

It is the movement from the non-manifest into the manifest, from the vast, indefinable silence of the non-manifest into the myriad of divine origin creations. It is the movement of creation: the 'ah:' the birth, the 'uh:' the becoming, and the 'mm:' the dissolving. It is the great circle from the endless silence to the peak of sound and back to the silence. It is every molecule of manifest creation arising, breathing, and dying.

To contemplate the Aum is to move your self, breath-by-breath, moment-by-moment, into the center of the river, into the center of the meaning of being. It is to yield fully into the movement of creation through your being, to be reminded, to be dissolved and to be part of.

What is being dissolved is every part of you that would hold to the shore. Every part of you that would say: "But I'm separate, I'm over here, I am of this name and this life, this body." "I am of this profession and I have these feelings." It is a holding to the shoreline and staying outside of the great current of God's being-ness. It is holding outside of God's being-ness, or All Being-ness. To give way to the Aum is to be drawn powerfully into the being-ness that contains all and is all. Letting go of the letters, A, U and M, letting go of the throat that sings it and the thought that defines it.

It is your being, it is you as part of creation, a conscious eye that can open within the creation, the divinity, in manifestation. An eye that can open and see: "This is what I am." And as your eye opens and says: "This is what I am," you are a spokesperson. You are the eye that can speak for all. You are not the eye that clings to the shoreline, the 'I am' that stays separate, but you are the 'I am' that includes the whole 'I am.' You could say the Aum is 'I am-ness.' 'All that I am, all is.' As your mind plays with these words, your being smiles, for your being knows. It is your mind that doesn't know, and it is your egotistical shaping that doesn't know, but your being knows. Your being deeply knows because your being is of that.

The Aum practice is a conditioner of mind, a conditioner of consciousness. It is used traditionally as a conditioner of consciousness. As the Aum is fully brought through mind, fully brought through the body and the senses, it conditions the consciousness to the ancient, known meaning, 'all that I am is this.' 'All that I am is part of all creation.' As your will intends to speak the Aum, as your will gives permission to your human nature to sing the Aum, your will has willed to remember the original, deep meaning of 'I am-ness'. Aum then, is the conditioner of the human consciousness that creates alignment that then awakens the memory, the inherent birth memory of creation and of being-ness. The Aum is the conditioner that creates alignment between all the facets of your incarnation and being, so that your mind sits in alignment with your will, emotional nature, spiritual nature and with your body.

As all this sits in alignment, the identity becomes a streamlined unity. Your finger is part of the Aum, your eye is an eye that sees from the fullness of being, and your heart and emotion feel fully from the seat of love. Your will unquestioningly intends to exist in the fullness of being and for the good of all beings, and your physical form operates at its highest level of cellular exchange, cellular life force. The Aum is a conditioner of the being, creating a divine alignment that places you in the most perfect point in your evolution; at peace with all that you are at this level of evolution. It prepares you for the step forward into more and more consciousness that includes more and more of what creation is within and around.

When giving forth the Aum, first let your mind watch and sense the syllables. The 'ah' like the light breaking in the dawn, the 'uh' like the overhead, clear, brilliance of the mid-day, the 'mm' like the evening twilight, and the silence following, the deep darkness. Letting the mind watch the phases in a single breath that include the phases in greater and greater scale. Let the mind watch this, let the mind repeatedly watch the circle until the mind tires of watching the circle. The mind rests. There is then no longer the contemplation on syllables, the watching of the movement of the circle. There then is the absolute observance of all at once. There is the absolute observance of peace and all being-ness at once in perfect equilibrium.

Looking upon the mind then, one senses the mind as just the eye that never closes: the eye that is watching, the eye in an undefined 'I'. Not the physical eye or the character. Just a point of watching all that is. When one repeats the mantra Aum, one hears every breath as the Aum and one enters into the use of mind only when needed. When the mind needs to construct, perceive, interact, serve, guide and lead, it may do so, but there is freedom from the mind. There is the ability to watch from the greater place of being. To observe the life breath of God itself in all beings all around and to feel part of and not separate. It is like feeling the whole sea all around, feeling every being all around. Every breath is breathing into existence and out again.

The ultimate freedom from incarnation, of human being-ness is to use the facilities of human nature and yet be free of them, to host the Divine Identity, the greater identity, and to host it in the milieu of physical embodiment. To use the sense, the mind, the sensing heart and the interactive will to demonstrate how divine consciousness exists in the human format. To condition ones being towards this, to use the Aum as a powerful alignment that infuses your human nature and your divine nature. Your teachers demonstrate this infusion. Your avatars, your masters, demonstrate the infusing and the possibility of living in the light of grace in mind, heart, and will with the true selfless-ness of divine identity in the human format.

*In Meditation, how does one move **beyond the use of mantra** and visualization, the use of images or words towards being in a meditative state? What is the next step?*

There is a moment of readiness for silent witness, created by meditation, within the consciousness that is so accustomed to and reliant upon thought. Even visualization is a thought of an image. The image may not even carry a thought, but it is a wavelength of engagement within the brain. This meditative moment is a readiness within the consciousness to trust the silence and the vastness, what seems like emptiness, which is the next step beyond the thought realm. The thought realm is an extension of the creating intention. If the intention is towards peace, towards the silence of meditation, towards true being-ness, the thought realm is used in mantra, or vision, to say that and to hold that intention in its realm of action. Therefore the image may be a sky or a silent sea. The mantra might be "All that I am is this". This realm of the thought world is the extension of the intention, and is there as an avenue of the intention.

This is only a moment of readiness, this subtle, indescribable readiness within the thought realm, but that is enough. As though one is experiencing the limitation of the thought realm. Like looking at a postcard of the state of peace over and over and over until the consciousness is: "This is only a postcard. I must enter into that vast sky, that silent sea. I must enter into All that I Am", and then moving through the thought or postcard image into the 'being-ness' of it. This subtle movement out of the thought realm into what the intention really is.

Respect the thought realm, for to hold these most exquisite intentions and thoughts is in itself a victory. It conditions the entire being towards the moment of readiness inside that knows and trusts: "Now I can step into that place of peace, fully." It requires no more thought preparation. It requires no more sustaining the intention through thought. It is so deeply understood and agreed upon within the thought realm and the will, within the embodiment, that then there is the entry.

This experience of entering into that spaciousness of non-thought, of pure being, of 'I Am-ness', can bring in the strangeness, the newness, almost its opposite: "What am I?" How does one create the grounding of identification without thought, without anything but being-ness? Accept the passage as the whole nature of this draws you back to the safety of the thought realm. Even those thoughts could be somewhat frantic: "I can't go there, there is no one, there is nothing, there is just the dissolving of grounding." And so, the thought realm and the egoic realm need to gently, consistently go back and forth, so that readiness is grown and developed. As the passage continues, one finds the tremendous sense of grounding and of presence and of absolute safety. The experience of peace is the experience of alignment with Love itself.

All of this becomes stored and patterned in the brain, in the nervous system, in the self, in the sacred humanness.

*We ask about the **transition from the expansive meditative state**, the state of witness, back to ordinary mind state and how to attend to that shift.*

During the waking hours, human beings exist largely in an uncontrolled, dominated mind-state. In meditation one is in a soul state, the witness, in the place of greater nature. How do we attend to this transition? As one meditates or expands their conscious ability, their inner knowing and their understanding, they know that: "Now I am moving to the mind-dominated awareness for the purpose of what I will do next."

They know this, it doesn't just happen, it is a decision: "Now it is time for this". What never leaves them is the sense of knowing: "This is who I am. This is what is happening and this is what I am doing." "For the rest of this day I will be in an illuminated mind state, using this mind in the ways of dharma, in the ways of Truth." "If I become lost in anxiety or fear or uncertainty, I know I have stepped too far into a mind-dominated state, as though stepping too far away from home and the source of my greater being, and now that is why I am unsure, and that is why I am fearful. I have become lost in a small part of the map and have lost sight of the greater perspective of my being. I have been affected by the generalized mind-state of those around."

One must have the practice or the tools to find their way back, momentarily touching into: "All that I am is this being of peace. All that I am is here." Learn how to reestablish the anchor into Truth, anchor into the true "I Am".

Think of the image of a wheel, the hub, the spokes and the rim. The hub of the wheel is the eternal "I Am" or the witness, the soul, the Atman (many words could be given to that). The spokes are the many avenues and streams of mind for its purposes. The rim of the wheel represents the actions and engagements. Have the image of the wheel and know where you are. To know: "I am out on the rim and am feeling disconnected from the source of my being, the source of what I am." Bring into awareness that this action is necessary: "I am here involved in this action, but feeling the spoke, the stream of breath, of intention, of energy that keeps the truth flowing from centre to edge at all times." Knowing how to shorten that distance, becoming versatile and skilled in bringing through the Truth of All Being, of I Am, of Love, bringing the centred silence of Peace into action and into the intention of the action.

So, this question of transition is the question. Meditation is worth nothing if it is not streamed into action, into mind and embodiment. Know how to bring the light of consciousness into all that you do.

*We wish to know how to understand and work with the mind when outwardly engaged with life situations and other people. How can we use mindfulness while engaged in the outer world? We wish to understand the nature of mind and **how to use mind from a most conscious place.***

First, understand what the mind is, just like understanding what the hand is, or the liver. Understand the mind as a component of being. Understand it as clearly and succinctly as you would understand any organ, any aspect. Freedom begins when the mind is known for what it is and is in its place, being used for what it is built for. The mind is literally and physically a map within the nervous system, a map within the brain. This map is a most refined network of informational currents. It is entirely built for perception and orientation, built to be a component of consciousness. Not consciousness itself, it is built to be a conduit of consciousness. The mind is a builder, a formatter, but is not consciousness itself.

Consciousness itself is not the mind, it is not dependant upon the mind and is beyond the mind. The mind is to be seen as a map, as a conduit and as a component of this physical embodiment that can host, in its refinement, the consciousness. It can receive the consciousness and can build and give to the consciousness. It is as though, imagining metaphorically, a great stream of light or information that can pour into a map system, finding its rivulets, its rivers, its streams, its lakes, its oceans. The stream of light or information, can be translated by the map into ***consciousness within this form***. We underline those words. Without this form, and without this map, there is pure consciousness. But for consciousness to be received into this physical animal form, this map is required, this fusion of consciousness to self within form. The complexity of this is that the human being is a multi-level complexity of the physical animal form with the will force, with the sentience, the senses, the emotional, and the mental or mind. All is the avenue, the format for consciousness and evolution. Understand the mind this way.

The mind will always be processing the information, always receiving the stream. From any direction you turn your waking consciousness, you are receiving a stream of information from this person, from the environment, from your surroundings. The mind receives all the wavelengths of information that come in through your eyes, your ears, and all your senses. It is a map that takes the information, structures it and organizes it. Understand the mind for what it is. Understand and value it for what it is.

To refine the mind is to strengthen the focus of mind onto singular points of perception. To perceive the tip of the leaf, to perceive the dew drop in its entirety, to apply the whole informational reception one pointedly. The mind has only begun to be developed in what it has the capacity for. The mind has the ability to perceive and see through the apparent physical density into the very map of all creation. The mind is simply a lens within this physical embodiment, a lens for the Divine stream of creative force, creative Source. Learning to use the mind in singular intentional focus, in Sanskrit terms: "Neti, neti" (not this, not this). Letting the mind hold the focus "Just this". When it is scattered, gathering, involving itself in other information, "Neti, neti" (not this) and apply the meditative technique "Just this". Perceive only what is before you in its entirety and its fullness. This is to strengthen the capacity of mind, to focus the energy the mind uses. The mind uses most of the energy of your mitochondria. The firing in this map uses the most energy within this physical form. To gather that energy into singular focus, in fullness of focus, both restores and saves the energy so that it is being used most efficiently and most clearly.

The more one meditates into the singular focus of just the present moment, just the consciousness itself beyond mind, or the silent presence, the more one learns to use mind more accurately. Whatever is focused upon is understood in totality, and whatever does not apply to the context or the moment, is not taking energy. It can be simply noticed but not engaged in. Extraneous thoughts can be noticed but not engaged in, because the clarity of being knows "Just this, this is this where my full energy of presence is being applied." It is creating more and more clarity and muscular ability in the lens of mind, to see more and more distinctly, until the entire landscape of one's chosen focus is perceived.

The mind in this human being is the most refined, tremendous tool. It cannot be put into words, what this mind has capacity for and the wonder of it, and you all have it. Understand the (so called) spiritual path, spiritual progression, as truly the learning of who you are, of what all human beings are. Understand the capacity of the human being, in consciousness and what this capacity is actually meant for. Appreciate what this mind is: the mirror of Divine-mind, it has been in evolution for much longer than history says. The human mind is the divine creation, as though Supreme Divine Being-ness created this map within form for consciousness. Then understand what this practice of meditation is really about: learning to refine the use of the lens so that Absolute Presence can be known in your identity and so that consciousness itself (or Absolute Presence) can use the mind.

In wanting to understand the nature of mind, understand that the mapping of the mind is built upon patterns. The efficiency of patterns is the basis of the nature of mind, so that everything need not be built over and over again, decided over and over again. One who is honing and progressing the use of mind knows this, knows how to disengage from patterns and re-build patterns that lead to more and more consciousness. Neti, neti. Not this, not this. Just this. Rebuilding patterns based on thought, dissolving patterns that are no longer necessary, knowing where to place patterns that are necessary but don't need to be in the focus. "Not now, not this, just this."

*We ask to understand more about the seeming contradiction between **self and no self**, the need to understand and truly feel grounded in self, and the teaching that there is really no such thing as self, that we are all part of one being-ness.*

I get the all too familiar smile, the Guidance calls it a divine play. It is like a divine riddle in that the both are true. There is (self) and there isn't (self). Also, in that what is held is a great jewel or a great secret, a great finding as one penetrates into the quest of "Who am I?" and how to understand most succinctly, most absolutely "Who am I?" and the whole journey of identity formation, life after life after life, shaping a sense of self through all the human embodiments. Arriving at the day when the sensitivity, the intelligence is truly asking: "Who am I?" Feeling that question taking one into the inquiry within, the eyes closed, the breathing, the sensing of being-ness, the feeling the I am-ness of their presence, the uniqueness, either the brightness and vividness of their uniqueness or the softness. Feeling the uniqueness of their 'I am-ness'.

As ageless eons of the seeking of identity comes to its completion, a being stops looking outside: "I am a carpenter", "I am a teacher", "I am one of beautiful form", "I am one of ugliness", "I am a success", "I am a failure", "I am safe", "I am not safe", "I am powerful", "I am afraid", "I am a mother", "I am barren". They stop looking outwardly for identity formation and start to move inwardly and find first the darkness and the struggle of inner resistance, "I am a mind chattering", "I am an emotion that won't rest", "I am a body that hurts", "I am an anxiousness that can't sleep", "I am nothing and I am scared". As they move inward to an inner ring and they continue to move inward to the great stillness of: "I am just this one, this one that watches, I am this one breathing, embodied at this time, I am this one that feels love, I am this one that is in love, I am this one that is love, I am Love Itself, I am the Watcher Itself, I am All Being-ness Itself." The ***true identity is all being-ness itself***, love itself, and the quest is over. That which is held as the jewel in this journey, the central secret, is found. The answer to the riddle of all riddles is found. I am love itself. If I am love itself, I am the formative force of all creation, and non-creation, I am in your eyes and your being, just as I am, apparently, in this being. The creation then, following realization of individual nature, is a creation of grace, a creation of service, a creation of joy with no attachment and no bondage. "I shall sing, I shall be a carpenter, I shall be a mother, I shall be on all the outer rings of identity to serve the child, to serve the world, to joyously serve and experience the existence yet with non-attachment, with the true identity known, needing no embodiment, no shape, no words, no name." Please understand that your question comes from the process, the path. Walking along the path, asking the question, seeing it as a duality or a contradiction, for walking along the path it sounds that way and appears that way, yet when the path leads you to the peak where the whole landscape of being-ness is known within, it is no longer a duality but a unifying. Then one can go back down into the lower regions of the landscape and create shape again, can host the duality in peace, can move into the doing-ness the being-ness, the shaping of character, a joy filled, love filled character with no forgetfulness, no amnesia of the unified state that "I am all being-ness".

*Given the expectation that evolution and greater spiritual awareness would go hand in hand with the development of **higher sense use**, we ask for commentary. There may be one who is accessing and sensing universal presence and universal identity within, but does not have higher sense perception, the higher use of seeing, knowing, hearing. In contrast, there may be one who has the capacity for higher sense perception, but is not opening in their heart or deeper being to the awareness of universal presence and oneness. What does this mean?*

For a being in an ascension of identity, or for a being that has come into an enlightenment, which is a greater consciousness of the true identity, the true fruit is unity awareness, the awareness of being in oneness with all creation. Being in intimate relationship with the source of all creation, the bhakti devotional relationship with love itself. This is a being who, with ease, feels the devotion to all that is, to the nameless great source of being-ness. The rest of the human capacity for awareness is trappings, extensions, and tools. The rest is incomparable to the heart that knows love, the being that knows God within, God as self, God as all.

To use the nervous system and the sensory system, in order to know, sense and see more, to seek that for and by itself is a side path, a trap. *If there is anything to be sought, seek to be in a relationship with love itself, letting the identity merge into love itself.* Be Love and Grace in the purest most shining expression. If there is expression of higher capacity (meaning clairsentience, higher sense capacity) within the human nervous system, within the human being-ness, let it be only to serve: to heal, to assist the light to flow into other beings, directing them, sweeping the path before their feet towards the one and only goal, Love. *Use the tools of higher sense perception only in this way, to sweep the path, to show the way, to clear the line of sight, to clear the being, to assist, to heal.* And yet always know that nothing is needed. The heart in its makeup, in its simplicity, the human being in its true definition is enough. Direct immersion into love itself is simple, needs nothing. As examples, choose those who may not say a word, those who have no skills, those who are just love, those who give endlessly and silently, those who are open vessels of the shining presence.

The Guidance shows me that the ability within humans to expand into the higher use of senses is a very real path, and yet, if the intention is not for the true higher relationship with love itself, it will have to reach a plateau. If there is no purpose towards the true goal of remembering 'who thou art', in the Source, in the beginning and in the end, and if the streaming light flows into a nervous system and expands, this expansion can only go so far if the being is not aligned to the true purposes, the true intention of this. There is the very real danger of the human being developing itself down the intricate paths of sensory ability and becoming lost, fractured or distracted. These ones may be getting to a very highly developed sense of self and being-ness, without the direction or the intention of dissolving into love. The direct path through the heart, through bhakti, through devotional understanding is the safe and wide highway leading directly to the true identity of being-ness.

Intuition

We wish to understand more about intuition; what blocks it and how to open it.

"The intuition is the most untapped resource on the planet."- Nithyananda

The Guidance shows me immediately the part of the brain where the intuition arises and shows the region of the brain that is the apparatus for gathering information and direct knowledge.

The difference between direct knowledge and indirect knowledge: indirect knowledge is conjecture, it moves through the part of the brain that places things together, that calls on memories, that is based on conclusion and learned conclusion. It is a very mechanized, very construction like process where one thing leads to another, which leads to another, which leads to a belief, a knowing or a conclusion. This is indirect knowledge, knowledge that has been gained experientially.

Direct knowledge has nothing to do with that process. Direct knowledge is accessing knowledge beyond your own self, your own experiences, your own experiential existence and receiving it from the great well of knowledge that sits in existence available to all beings. It is called sometimes the Akashic Records, or just the Great Well, the Great Source that everyone can drink from and draw from (Universal Consciousness).

The human brain is beautifully designed to access direct knowledge, knowledge beyond one's own progression and one's own self in evolution. Direct knowledge does not replace the personal evolution of knowing how to live with that knowledge, how to enact it, how to become it. It is knowledge none-the-less, just knowledge. What you do with that knowledge depends on your understanding of it, your readiness to live it and to become it. If in your readiness there is not enough ability to understand and manifest that knowledge, then you are in a hit and miss relationship with direct knowledge, it is not sought. But as the being evolves in strength and ability to understand, manifest and become that knowledge, it strengthens the linking and this part of the brain develops more and more.

It is a true comment that intuition is an untapped resource, but it could be said in different ways. It could be said that this region of the brain that is at a higher capacity, has not yet been entered. Not yet been evolved, in scale. *It sits as the glorious next phase of the human being recognizing itself as divine being.*

The transition from human being to divine being can be defined as knowing one is not a separate entity, but a great entity. It is not an identity that is based on the smaller sense of self, separate from all others but is a part of greater self, a part of all beings. If you are a part of all beings, this portion of your brain is active; this part of your consciousness is active. You are a consciousness as if you are a part of all beings. You are no longer holding onto "I am just this," "I am in isolation," "What I think is just my own thoughts, what I choose is just for me, what I need is just for me," and "What I've chosen is just for me." In a higher mind you know that you are a part of a cell in a great body of being, that everything you choose and do is a part of All. Every piece of knowledge you gain is given to all, and when you need knowledge you listen to all. The division between the sense of individual self and God or Greater Self is just a thin choice, a little membrane to pass through. *The intuitional brain is truly the shared brain. It is the part of the brain's apparatus that is in access to All Being, to God, and all knowledge in all the words you could place to that.*

As an untapped resource then, it is just that the human being is not identifying beyond itself, not identifying as a wholeness of presence of divine nature. He or she is seeking knowledge through the cumbersome, experiential way, 'I have found something, I have read something, I have heard something, I have learned something,' rather than realizing that all knowledge is for all beings.

But see the trick, the valve. To gain access to all knowledge one must let go of feeling separate. One must transform egoist nature. One must not hold on to the small room of self and keep the doors locked, blocked and protected from all selves. One must change the identity, the identity that you are not just you, you are all. You are part of all and you are responsible for all. ***All knowledge can flow through you for you are part of all, and all love can flow through you because you are part of all.*** You are not alone, and in your very consciousness behind your eyes, within your breath, you are not alone. Divine presence flows through your every nerve path, your every breath, and your every yearning and every thought. As you willingly let go of the separate identity within you, as you expand into the true shared identity you are part of all beings here and everywhere, you are part of divine presence in all its unknown manifestations. The so-called intuitional part of your brain has been activated and entered.

The knowledge that sits in creation is the resource, answering all problems. Answering all material problems of resource, energy, relationship, government and world management. All answers are there; an unfathomable resource that creates freedom, blessing and completion in this realm. As you develop your greater brain, your brain of all-ness, your intuitional being, you develop that within all beings. You brighten the pathways, the nerve pathways and the consciousness pathways within the whole map of the whole being with which you are a part of.

It must not be seen as a formula, it must be seen as an entire movement of your being in consciousness. Not for the purpose of using intuition or finding answers, but for the purpose of becoming truth, becoming the true being. It must be encompassed in that all encompassing reason, 'I yearn to be love, I yearn to be all that I am.' As that true movement of heart and soul is engaged in, through your meditations, through what you allow in your mind and in your speech, what you choose to do, how you choose to treat others, in the entirety of the movement in your being in this way, so does it open that part of your brain where the identity of all being-ness sits. Compassion is the expression of identifying with all beings and all creation.

Why are some born already open to intuition?

This is becoming very familiar now to me, sitting here with these questions and the Guidance beginning with images. The beginning image for this question is again in the brain, showing the pathways of consciousness and that this is not just the brain, but also the whole embodiment. The pathways of consciousness sit within the whole embodiment.

Intuition is direct knowing. To define intuition is to define it as knowing that does not need cognizance, does not need a certain area of the brain that configures, deciphers, places block after block, and arrives at conclusion. Constructed knowing comes as a learning process based on the environment, the findings, the discoveries and the use of the mind that is gathering these. Intuition bypasses constructive shaped knowing, it enters in beyond itself. Intuition is the whole being as a receiver of knowledge, when knowledge isn't constructed with that beings effort, it is received through that being's ability to receive. Intuition can be the receiving of knowledge, wisdom and understanding that has no relationship to the present, no relationship to what has been told, already learned or read, or what the mental body of that person has been prepared to know.

Going back to the image, they're showing the pathway of intuition, the pathways of direct knowing, and they're showing this pathway as a streaming in through the seventh chakra, through the opening at the top of the human embodiment, and a stream of information coming and falling, fanning out the way light does when it falls on the surface, into the very center of the pineal brain. It is an infusion of knowing that is very specific to the situation in front of that person. It is a receiving of information about what is happening in front of that person, but it is directly received from beyond. Once this information stream has fallen and fanned out, and been infused into the pineal body, it then moves into the cognitive forward brain. It also moves into the auditory brain, the lower brain and it into the entire mapping of the pathways of consciousness. Intuitional direct knowing can be felt, tasted, heard and known. Intuitional direct knowing is an entire and whole experience whereas it is very seldom that the cognitive upper brain involves the senses. It sits in isolation, a room where the knowledge and information is configured and observed but not felt or understood by the entire being. So these are two pictures of knowing.

Each birth is a continuation of that being. Each being that is born has a continuum of development before the birth and a purpose for this birth. This continuum of being-ness, the many phases and stages of development before this birth are where the answer lies to describe the present lifetime. Each being upon birth brings forward into their birth that which is most needed for this lifetime's purpose. If one being is born with the stream of intuition flowing, it is not necessarily a measurement of their development. For it could be that the purposes of one person's life is to be very present at a very physical level with their eyes level to the world. Seeing this physical world just as it presents itself. In other words having closure, having limitations that help build the evolution. The statement, *do not judge*, means all of this; do not asses, do not measure another being's evolutionary process for you cannot see.

If one is born with the intuitional abilities fluent, with the pathways of consciousness opened, this is because it serves them in this embodiment. It is part of the fundamental elements of their evolution and their being. Often it is that they are prepared for the level of knowledge that this brings. They are prepared in their soul, prepared in their understanding to host that opening, to make use of it. They have a prepared understanding that to know directly is a gift to give, not a power to hold. It is a gift of compassion to know and exist in compassion. It is a gift to assist others and it is an attribute of an opened heart and of a loving being. For it to be a truly opened pathway, it means there is the preparedness in that being to truly love and be compassionate to others, a preparedness to receive higher information and give it to others. To exist as a being at a higher level, relating to life as part of all beings. To be able to relate to existence with no seeking of power or domination, for truly the stream of direct knowing could be used wrongly. When it is used wrongly it begins to close itself, it begins to go against itself. It becomes a destructive stream in the embodiment if direct knowing is used wrongly.

To simply answer this question, ***every being is born in the exact configuration of their evolution and their need to evolve further.*** Look upon every infant and every child as the visible chapter of a very long book. ***Don't look at them as a beginning point but as the next phase of themselves.***

Worship

How will forms of worship change with the evolving consciousness of our beings? What will worship look like in the future?

This question is a joyous question whereby we show the founders of all the faiths, the teachers both known and unknown, the Avatars, the carriers of Truth, the ones that held the life mission of Truth and gave to humanity the words, the language, the practices of worship and of understanding. We see each of these beings that have held this mission stepping forward in a combined way, in a message to all those who have attached their hearts and souls to them, to show the absolute unity of the message, the absolute unity of their presence, the dissolving of attachment to the one over the other.

For example, the one who may hold the image of the Christ in their mind: the Christ, itself, as ongoing presence, gives the faces and images of the Krishna, of the Buddha, of this father or that grandfather, or this holy being. Therefore, the one who is attached from the heart and soul is being guided into seeing the unity of the message, not allowed to stay fixed on the one. There is a stepping forward, a force that comes through the combined meaning and effort of all these very powerful leaders who are still in full existence and full action. **We see this Great Gathering of all hearts, all minds, and the swirling unifying of image, of proverbs and statements, of mantras and truths, so that all who have attached faithfully, in devotion from their heart and soul, are in access to all others, all teachers, all proverbs and statements, all mantras and hymns.**

In this great gathering and unifying of hearts and minds, the image (and by this we mean the image of the Divine, the image of the Most High, Supreme Source, the image of Truth) blends and enters deep into the psyche and hearts and genetics of the human being, so that they find within their inner image and sense, this highly defined and yet unified place of attachment, of attunement, of Divine Source meaning.

There begins the reshaping of worship to accommodate what we are describing. **Worship begins not to be called worship, but attunement**, implying that it is an inner expansion, an inner identifying, an inner opening. **Whereas worship sets the reaching and the Source outward, attunement is the refined understanding that the Source is within**, is the substrate and source of one's own being and the truest identity of one's own being. Therefore, worship, or attunement, is becoming more of one's own being, becoming awake to one's own nature. Forms of worship dissolve, in that it is more a great support system of attunement, an enjoining of beings in attunement and becoming as one embodiment, one receptive experience of tremendous knowing. We show the remembrance occurring within all beings in this setting, remembering the original attunement and the *original* instructions and directions: to sustain attunement and to not go into amnesia or forgetfulness or separation. These directions, these instructions are ever-present, to be remembered and found and re-enacted.

What is occurring to the soul in ceremonies of **ancestor worship**? *What actually occurs to the one who is being honoured, in physical mummified form or in name?*

The Guidance shows that each person leaves behind a print, they leave behind a gift, the sum print of their life and actions. They leave it in the great knowledge bank of all beings. They leave it in the memory bank of all beings and all creation. It is there. Their name, their lifetime, their history linking the being to the sum total print of what was their lifetime. How their soul moved forward into manifestation is a more clearly worded way of saying 'the print'. How their soul moved forward and manifested, leaving behind what they manifested. In this we see their thoughts, their beliefs, their conclusions, their actions. It is the sum total of what their soul brought into manifestation.

To honour the name and life of an ancestor in this way is to honour and call upon the sum print. It sits there like a leaf in a book in a library. It is, in a sense, opening the book to this page and paying homage to the sum total of that being's life and all they manifested. *What occurs to the soul itself, who has continued to evolve and grow?* We say here, that no soul ever stops evolving and growing, that there is never a soul held fixed to the sum print of a lifetime. There is continual movement and expansion. Movement is the law of creation. It is the law of manifestation.

What happens to this soul then, with continual honouring, continual homage? **Depending on the level of consciousness, there can be the sense of being called into the memory of the sum print of that life, called into relating as that, again.** To some souls, this can be bondage, as they are brought back to what they are finished with. They are brought back with a sense of duty, a sense of obligation, as if being called to read the same page over and over, of what you had become and who you were. Bondage in the growing identity can create a struggle within the identity of the soul, if the sense of obligation and duty is strong, and we speak this way because it is. In other words, it can be a hindrance to the ongoing evolution of that soul.

The soul that has built enough strength in consciousness, enough liberation in being, is not called into the returning acknowledgement of those who are left behind. The answer is according to the individual being-ness. In cultures with ancestral worship, there is much hindrance to the continuing evolving of each other's souls. The sense of obligation and duty is very strong on both sides. Therefore when a culture dissipates, it can be liberating to all involved due to less identification with religious patterns.

On this side, it is through maintaining and holding to the ceremonies of homage to ancestors, that some continue to create their identity as a people beyond self, beyond individuality, a people in relationship to Source, to Great Spirit. Yet, ancestral worship is seeing God only so far, like being able to see to the edge of the field and after that, not being able to see. One who has just died is a representative of deity, assisting that culture and that people to feel in relationship with the void, the great unseen.

We ask to understand the **origins of duty** *and commitment in spiritual practice. What is the difference between a practice based on a sense of duty and a practice approached with willingness?*

We come to the origins of the teachings towards duty. The origins and meaning of this teaching are based on the human being's tendency to easily become locked into patterns of stasis and unconsciousness. If the human being was to have a challenge or, we could say, a fault, it is to repeat that which is familiar and comfortable, choose safety versus growth. The human being is built to see the unknown as danger, has learned to become fearful of change, fearful of the unknown and the new. The human being is suffused with the animal nature that seeks safety, and patterns that create safety. **Realize that human nature has animal nature in its foundations.** The original teaching around commitment and duty then, is to lift this pattern and establish a new pattern leading to more expansion. Realize that this new pattern would never establish itself if it weren't understood as a duty, as a commitment in a cultural sense. As the new pattern becomes established, it opens the development of more consciousness in human nature.

Understand with compassion, the teaching on duty and commitment given to the child-like human mind that would fall back often into the animal state. To give this practice as a duty was to give them a chance to establish new patterns in the way of viewing existence. Realize that within your being, you will come up against the patterns that seek safety, the known and the repeating familiar. You will face within your being and your nature, tentativeness and resistance to the unknown. *Holding a practice as a duty may be the way that is needed for you to develop the ability to make the unknown known.*

What is the difference then, between the known and the unknown? It is that you have walked it and smelled it and tasted it, have experienced it and have built it into the pattern of your being. To move in your spiritual development beyond the sense of duty and commitment that is not based on true willingness - this requires bhakti, the path of devotion, opening up the heart of yearning, opening up the love for beauty, for the divine. This fast-forwards the progression of the being. *It is saying that the unknown is love itself.*

The unknown is the source of love, the source of all that I am, that all beings are. There is nothing to fear in the unknown, nothing to fear walking into new realms, the supreme presence of love is there. Therefore the path of bhakti and devotion lifts one away from duty and commitment, and energizes the soul by love itself. As a being is based in an understanding of love, is in love, nothing can stand in the way. There is no unknown territory. There is no animal nature blocking the expansion of the being towards consciousness. Animal nature hasn't the complexity to understand the source of supreme love, supreme being-ness and does not yearn to alter its path to become closer. It would never forage alone up the steepest peeks, to be with Love itself. Therefore the practice is fueled by the yearning for beauty, by the willingness to be all that one can be, the desire to be closer and closer to the endless light.

Dreams

How can we understand and use dreams in the spiritual path, the path of consciousness?

Dreaming is a component of the movement from unconsciousness towards consciousness, like the movement of growth from a seed into a stem and the flower. It is a movement from the shrouded unconscious state towards resolution, towards the flowering and development of consciousness. To the extent that a being hosts unconsciousness within their waking mind and within their entire being, so does the being, the brain and the soul, strive to pull from the unconsciousness that which needs to be resolved, that which needs to emerge and be known, dissipated and freed. To the extent that a being is hosting and holding unconsciousness or semi-unconsciousness, so does this emerge in their dreams.

The question around the spiritual purpose in this understanding of dreams takes us away for a moment from dreams themselves. As a being develops absolute consciousness within their waking mind, within their choosing of being within the day, as through meditation, as through inner illuminations and inner realizing, so does their dreaming journey become less and less. As the basement of unconscious experience is lessened, there is no need for the movement of this stored unconsciousness up into the images and knowing that the dreams hold.

What is liberation? Liberation comes when there is no longer any unconsciousness within the being. Unconsciousness is bondage. Enlightenment, or full consciousness is liberation. Therefore, see your dreams as the mechanism and the effort of your being to become conscious, to become liberated from what sits unconsciously within.

The nonsensical and puzzling images are formed as the energy of the unconsciousness strikes the thought realm brain. It gathers bits and pieces of what is stored there, of images, of experiences, of conclusions, as though the thought realm is a greatly disordered room full of gatherings, placing all of that into a drama.

To use the dreams correctly is to feel and sense behind the images into the feeling, into the direct knowing that is expressing there. The dream path is a powerful path towards liberation, and yet you will find swiftly as you attend to dreams, attend to what is being lifted up in the dream towards awareness, as you do this, you dream less. As you inwardly choose to become conscious of your feelings, of your inner realm in all its ways there is no need for the circuitry of dreams. The nudges of discomfort or fear or the unknown that you may carry throughout the day from experiences that would then manifest themselves in dream dramas, can be dealt with by sitting in the meditative intention of: 'What is within me? What is this feeling? Where is this coming from?' Lifting it into consciousness at the time.

In the most liberated conscious state of the soul or being, there is no dreaming and essentially, there is no sleeping. There is no unconsciousness. There is the sustaining of the awakened state, the Buddha state. Resting for the form is a different description than slipping into unconsciousness. This is said to show you where you are going, who you are essentially developing to be, Buddha-beings, awakened beings.

Life Purpose

How do we know and find our life purpose?

The Guidance is looking at me, looking at the question; it's just a look. The look is very stringently thoughtful. The words that come with it are, that your purpose is written and known to your being on formulating your birth. Your theme of unfolding, of your learning, and the conditions that support and facilitate your learning, are known in formulating your birth. We are not saying 'at birth', we are saying 'in formulating your birth'. The vacuum in your development, that needs filling through life experiences, calls forth the conditions that match this vacuum and would fill it. Your sum state of being, before an embodiment, creates a calling. It calls conditions and setting to you. Each being is consciously partaking, witnessing, is part of this to the extent that they are able and willing.

Often we move into comparative descriptions at this point, of the most conscious, and the least conscious, because there is never one answer to these questions. It depends upon where you enter in. If you are entering in from the very least conscious place, then the vacuum of your need, the emptiness that is your lack of development will call into resonance certain conditions of birth. Therefore **the purpose is to be understood, always, in the conditions of the lifetime and of the beginning of the lifetime.** A being that has developed and retained awareness of their eternal nature, and is in a continual consciousness to some extent, will partake even more in the choosing of the embodiment and its conditions.

By conditions we mean the setting in the world, we mean the country and the potentials in that country for plenty, for lack, for ease, for struggle. By conditions we mean also the genetic patterning in the birth parents, the emotional and spiritual conditions in the birth parents. All these are in a resonant match to the need for the development of your being. The most conscious know this, have willing agreement, move forward in agreement and love into the life setting that most matches them and knows their purpose inherently. The knowing may not sit written in the mind during childhood or even adulthood but it is unfolding around them. Conscious beings can very easily look within and know why these conditions are here, what they present, why the challenges are here. What they present as opportunities for the very strengths, the very building that one needs. The unconscious being feels knocked around by their conditions, shepherded without agreement forward, still gaining, still facing in this semi-conscious way, the very elements of life that invite them into more awareness.

Ask yourself this question: "What do you mean by knowing your purpose? Do you mean by holding a mental structure of thoughts? Do you mean by knowing your own heart?" What do you mean by knowing, for you do know. To uncover that knowing is not finding a series of thoughts in the mentality, it is finding the knowing in your heart, in your depth, in the center of your being-ness. It is learning to listen compassionately, fully within, to hear, for your information is yours, and it fills you. It is the streams of resonant attraction and becoming that you entered into upon birth. The door that you went through was a very familiar door, and you understood in your deepest place of being all that it held potential in this life.

To understand your unfolding becoming, to understand where you have been unconscious, where you have a vacuum of unconsciousness, you must listen and ask within your being: "Where am I not? How do these life conditions that I'm in right now match my need to become more aware?" Knowing that they do match, knowing that they are not mistakes, that they are the resonant surroundings to my state of being, they match my being. They have been chosen either by my grace or by my emptiness. Ask truthfully, honestly in your being: "How does this outer setting and these outer events match my being's needs? How have I created this?" In doing so, you meet that fabric of the outside conditions with awareness and with acceptance. You become then, a powerful part of creating those outside conditions. You meet them, master them, accept them and you realize that it was through you that it became that way, not randomly. You are not victim.

If every being was to see the outside fabric of their life as the falling out, the precipitating from their own resonance, as though they were a bell rung, that arranged all the outside in the shape that it is. If one could see how fluid this is, that the surrounding wavelengths of happenings and beings, is because of the pulse of the sound, the output of your own nature. And in that consciousness you see moment by moment, day by day, the purpose. The purpose is not a series of statements fixed. *The purpose is a day-by-day awakening to who you are and who you have yet to be, where you have emptiness and where you have fullness.* The purpose for every being is to become responsible, conscious to this, and to choose continually: "This is in my hands. This is my creation. The sorrow, the pain, is my creation. The peace, the plenty, is my creation."

The purpose of every being is to learn to shape the clay into a beautiful vessel that can hold the infinite light of Truth, to know their being is the clay, to know the Infinite Light is their full potential of True Nature.

Don't become fixed on a purpose that can be stated like a vision statement. Purpose is a living dynamic daily becoming. Shaping the clay daily, every moment, every choice. Becoming more and more skilled to know how you shape the area in your being that can never take the stresses, that always breaks, that is blind. Learning how to attend to the blindness, to understand it, and to re-shape and re-choose the very way of being within you.

The specific nature of each individual could be placed in statements: "This is where I am not. This is where I have been blind. This is where I have sustained hurt for too long and become numb." Therefore your purpose is to say this and know this and to re-shape this so that it is no longer a pain or blindness or anger. *Realize that your very patterns are fluid and not fixed, and you need never be lodged in a pattern or a way of being that is a break in the side of the vessel that can't hold the Infinite Light.*

Living Our Spiritual Identity

How does one bring the spiritual identity into the sense of self? How does one integrate spiritual nature with human nature and the egoic identity, living our spiritual nature in relationships and day-to-day events?

Once the spiritual identity becomes an experienced and clearly understood format of being, it begins to flow through one's thoughts and actions, lifestyle choices and moment-to-moment decisions. This becomes possible when a being understands their true nature as eternal and ongoing in this life and lives, and has a felt, experiential sense of 'I Am'. All of the decisions in a day ("What shall I say?" "Shall I do this or that?") flow from the identity that is most operational, from the most active operational sense of self. Where is this placed in you?

What we mean by egoic identity is the more superficial placement of self and focus into the body, into the world, into the needs of human nature. From the egoic sense of identity, one is seeking safety, nurturance, companionship, seeking comfort and place, etc., establishing the parameters of solidity and safety, stability and nurturance in this very physical realm. The egoic nature seeks to create, protect and develop this. If the egoic nature is central, this is the identity. "I am one who needs to do this from the moment I wake up until I go to sleep. I must ensure and create the stability for this form, for the ones I am caring for, for our safety, for our nurturance, for our comfort, and for our pleasure."

The (so called) spiritual nature and identity is a similar place of being and development and yet with an utterly different set of parameters. *Where is this place of the spiritual identity? What is nurturance in this description? What is stability?* The spiritual nature is not dependent upon the physical form and is not identified by the physical form, not placed into the physical realm. It is not, in and of itself, born of the physical realm. It is born of the realm of the infinite, the infinite and Source of all creation, of all forms, and of formlessness itself. The spiritual nature is the "I Am-ness" that doesn't die like the physical form. In each being, this spiritual I Am is ever evolving, within and outside of physical form.

What is this identity formation? As the spiritual identity becomes the operational identity, it knows: "If I miss this meal, I'm ok. If I sicken and die, I Am, still. All events, both tragic and small are passing. I Am is a continuum of being. I Am has absolute place, endlessly in existence: " I Am a component of God itself, I Am a component of all creation." No sense of place lost, if one does not have a good position in their work, in their school, in their family, there is no threat to the spiritual identity. Place is insured. It is the birthright of all beings to exist. It is the nature of all beings to be magnificent in the Light, to be absolute in Love, to be born of Grace, to be deathless in Grace. The spiritual identity is an identity of Peace. Peace, though disturbed by grief and sadness of the human events, of the human temporary experiences and tragedies, the operational spiritual identity is of Peace. Never questioning its existence, its place, its beauty, or its validity.

As the spiritual identity is developed more and more, through practices such as meditation, and becomes more and more the operational place of being, this flows through the thoughts of the mind, through the emotional being, through the feelings and choices, through the whole framework of awareness, and through relationships. You are in relationship to another soul, to another deathless being of Grace. Their unconscious actions aren't as large a blow, knowing that they are just an action of unconsciousness, temporarily. The attachments aren't so great knowing that this being preceded me and will follow, going through many such relationships. We are temporarily together. Each being is a magnificent being that you can see only a small part of. Therefore, you are in Namaste. One cannot judge from the spiritual identity. One can notice and be aware of what is occurring now, but not judge another being, for the vastness of their magnificence and their wholeness is beyond your human sight. Spiritual sight could see it all, and as the spiritual identity develops, more and more is seen and less and less matters at the human egoic level. It is met with peace and equanimity, with patience and with love.

And so this describes your answer: to bring through the spiritual nature and identity into the human actions. It may appear as detachment, but is actually wisdom and knowing. It is a reorientation of consciousness. All human beings in evolution are moving towards the full implanting of spiritual identity into form. As they do so, lifetimes will lengthen, sickness will disappear and the full infusion of the spiritual I Am will shine through the eyes, the thoughts, the actions, even the physicality of this being. Know that every action you take and effort you make to bring forward your ongoing spiritual I Am-ness calls this forth in the whole of humanity.

How have we so completely forgotten our eternal identity?

The question of the eternal identity is held and answered in the incoming conditions of incarnation. It is designed that the being stays in relationship to the eternal identity, the reservoir of soul. It is designed that they hold, mapped within their consciousness, the pathway to the greater "I am-ness". It is designed that they hold the ability to refer into the greater bank of I am-ness and to pull their resources down into the human incarnation. In this sense, their eternal identity is flowing into their incarnation, and though there may not be distinct memory or identification of other lives, or of their greater presence, they will constantly be drawing upon all that they are.

To the extent of a being's development, they may not forget, they may know that they have re-entered. They will know without words, they will know the presence of being, just by the substance of knowing, and they will experience a freedom from their surroundings. They will experience a sense of patience and a capacity for the limitations around them, an instant sense of drawing from a great resource of Being-ness, how to meet this life. There is much that can be given to an incoming being to assist them to stay linked to their eternal identity.

The simple answer to: 'How has it been forgotten?' is that the human being suffers. The human being has suffered so greatly in its treatment of each other, in its losses, traumas and shocks, that it holds a flatness, it holds a trauma in its consciousness, it holds a desire to become simple, immediate and comforted, like a child that needs to be fed right now. He or she doesn't want to understand about waiting, about where the food comes from, about what food it should be, they need the instant reassurance in that moment. ***The human being is a suffering being, and in that suffering being there is restricted resource to their greater identity.*** They are, as incoming souls, experiencing isolation even in the womb, and either stay distant from the incarnation, or enter in with the path severed. However, as more and more beings are raised and born and live in wholeness and wellness with conscious parents, the more the flooding remembrance of the eternal nature is there.

Born Complete

Is each person born complete?

This brings the sense of a warm, all-encompassing smile. We go to thoughts around birth. In our embodiment we think of our birth, or a birth that we have witnessed in our babies or in others, and we view that birth as a beginning point. From the viewing perspective of Guidance, seeing each one's many births, many weavings in and out of embodiment, many moments of lives, the understanding of completeness is a much bigger understanding and a much bigger answer. The completeness is throughout, pervasive, absolute and built into the very original fabric of each being. It is a description of the completeness of all creation, of all embodiments. Completeness, in its truest answer is an understanding of what each being actually is, of what all beings actually are. It is in this description, of what all beings actually are, that the completeness lies.

The completeness is a wholeness, an already become, an already known, a fullness of purpose and meaning that is held in the very fabric and substance of what every one of you is. This completeness, this wholeness is the very reason for birth and births, and death and deaths. It is the reason for every morning that you wake up. It is the reason that your heart loves the child, that your heart loves the colours, that your heart stirs with life around existence. Love is this completeness. **When you love, you are accessing, and in, the completeness of your being. When you love, you deepen your consciousness to your completeness.** To exist in a loving state in your mind, in your heart, in your form, in your actions, in your thoughts, is to live in the conscious completion. To live in love is to live in the conscious completeness, the conscious totality, the consciousness of what you most are, what you are.

May we say that a being who exists as an Avatar, divine embodiment, is in an expressed manifest totality of being. A being such as you is in a partial consciousness, a partial manifestation of this totality. Both are born complete. One exists in a full consciousness of that completeness and the other is a partial. All are God. A being who is in full realization is in a consciousness of God-mind and God-nature. A being such as you is in a partial consciousness. Both are born of the same substance, both are made of the same fabric, the fabric of love, the fabric of God. You were complete even before you began to evolve because you are God and you are of the fabric of love.

Each being is born with all the components of the totality. Each being is a composition of the totality of love. Even a being who is mentally crippled, even a being who can exist only partially, because of the configuration of their embodiment, is in the same totality. What they may express through their limited mind is no complete picture of who they are and why their expression may be limited. For the one who can say only part of the sentence, still knows the whole sentence, even if they lack the ability to speak it. Therefore, one can never judge, for the totality of each being is always existent. The evolving of each being towards that awareness is what you see.

As you nurture the child, and each other, and yourself, with the fullness of possibilities in love, you actually deepen that being's consciousness of their totality, their wholeness. You clear the sky to their light, you Namaste their being and when you see them, you see the God being-ness, the Divine Nature. You see that which you most are in the eyes of every being when you love.

There is to be no doubt and no question that each being is complete at the root, is a totality of equality. Each being is absolutely identical in all the options, all the components that love is, that God is. Therefore your only focus is how to see it in each being, how to nurture it in each being, how to see it in your own being and nurture it there. That is the only action. Seeing this as brushing off the path, brushing off the jewels, brushing off darkness, clearing the weight, loving through to the essential being-ness of each one in front of you. And so, after all these words, the answer is yes.

Old Patterns of Human Nature

How do we remember and dissolve old patterns within our nature, within our being, that limit us, so that we can come to freedom, and not be hindered by the past?

This question is being attended to with a grave and serious gaze within my being. This is a very important question and it begs to be answered clearly. When you really look at this question, it is THE question that all human beings, all embodied souls need to ask and to realize, for **the human being is built of patterns that are as deep as the sedimentary stone of the Grand Canyon.** The human being is an entity built of ancient patterns. We would say that nothing is actually forgotten; no part of your being is actually dissolved. All that has ever occurred, not only in your being but in all creation, never dissolves nor disappears.

It is more the activity, or the latency. It is more the consciousness. In the brilliant sun of the full conscious state, only that which is of the current living truth is active, and acted upon. Consciousness is the answer. **The brilliant light of consciousness is the force, the power, the freed energy that allows one to see all the patterns, to see all the layers with a sweep of the eye, and to know which ones are actions of the timeless living truth.** They are the patterns that build freedom, the patterns that have the right to be living nature, the patterns that continue to give outward into creation the messages of freedom. They are the right patterns, the patterns of rightness. And yet in the most conscious being, essentially, there is no patterns at all, the most conscious being is continually in that living truth of awareness, allowing only the action, the thought, the feeling that is in accord to the current state of living truth, the current living truth of the moment. A most conscious being is not triggered into a response or a reaction in half awareness, a stirring of the sedimentary layers of their development. A most conscious being can see every layer of their development, can have it in hand and sift from all of it, that which is of the most dynamic timeless living nature of truth. The question is: *How do we remember, and how do we be free of limiting patterns that we repeat over and over? How do we become conscious beings that are not just puppets of unconscious held patterns?*

We show her the path of development of the evolving true being. The evolving consciousness (in all beings in embodiment) has built into it the streaming of energy in refined and refining properties. We spoke of it as the light streaming, as the living fire of consciousness, which refines itself every time a being chooses a choice of love. Every time a being chooses an action of truth from their heart, any time any one of you makes a choice that aligns you with living timeless truth, you refine the conscious force within you, the fire of illumination, you refine it, you sweep it upwards, you give it more impetus, more vibratory force within your physical system. With each moment of refining, each meditation, each choice, each word of love, each day that is aligned to the most living truth, you are building, you are gathering your being in a certain level of amassing this spiritual force.

As you amass your being in this refined spiritual force, there comes a time when the light, when the illumination, or the consciousness (all the same word) begins to radiate and fan out and back and forward and all around, and all those layers of your patterns and all those layers of your evolutionary development become infused and flooded with the light of consciousness. Peacefully then, without effort you turn your head to the side and see it all. You look back and know, in that illumination that has come from being fully present to each day in love, in choice. **The illumination dawns upon you one morning, one series of mornings, one month of mornings and you remember.** You remember with greater and greater ease. You remember who you are; you remember the walks of who you are, the stories of the development of who you are. Remembering in this fashion is freedom. Remembering is the same as what you mean by dissolving, remembering is the moment; when it is remembered, you are free. You are free because now your whole being sits within you, before you. You are now free because you now have the choice, the understanding. In this illumined, refined consciousness it is easily seen which story took you into pain, which story built the being into greater and greater consciousness.

In the remembering, there is freedom. When you are in the beginning phases of this remembering, and the remembering takes the form of feelings, emotions, partial memory, sensory memory, physical memory; the path then is to sit with the heart widely open embracing what is arising, inviting it with a sense of peace and capacity. Inviting the remembered experience in its nudging, in its partialness into your field of awareness, into your heart of love. Calling back, calling forth 'all that one is', into the stage of consciousness that you are in now. Calling forth the images, the knowing, inviting them, as if you have come to a pinnacle or throne where all can come to you. All that you have ever walked and all that you have ever felt and known can come before you. This throne is a place of peace, a place of understanding. Understanding that there is to be no negativity, no criticism, no self-destruction, no self-loathing, and no self-rejection. ***The throne is the place of love within your being where you are in love with Love itself. You know that you are the Love, the Beloved, and the Lover.*** From this throne, all that your being contains can come before you and be loved. Love is the dissolving, love is the freeing. Remembering is a journey of joy, of wisdom. To remember, one needs to be firmly cognoscente of the throne of love, sitting in the throne of love toward one's own being and toward all beings. The force of love, the dynamic of love, is the actual energy and experience of incarnating divine being-ness. You are incarnating divine being-ness, as you love. Love is the force of unity; love is the dynamic of unified consciousness and the knowing of all creation as One Being-ness. Love is the consciousness of non-separation, that there is no being through all creation that is not part of the unified purpose and that all creation is love incarnating. Therefore you become such as the herald, such as the God of your own being, when you enthrone on love and gather all your memories toward you. The universe of your own being can open up to you and be included as love, in love.

One who sits in self-rejection, self-defacing, self-denial, cannot remember, cannot create freedom. They cannot have the turning point of the great illumination within their consciousness. To deny oneself is to deny the creation of unity, the love itself and the purpose of creation. ***To deny oneself is a great darkness, a great injury.*** So many beings sit in self- rejection and in self-denial. This healing is the gift that one must be led to, and given, and taught. To love one's self is to love all beings, there is no separation, to love all beings and to love one's self is to dissolve all limitations. It is to know intimately all knowledge and each being, nothing hidden, no darkness anywhere.

You know that you are the Love, the Beloved and the Lover.

This question is about en-grams or engraved memory. How can we become cleansed and free of memory attached to thoughts and feelings that limit us?

The storage of the trauma or en-grams, these cramped held patterns of memory never seem to go away unless held to a great light, the light of a master, or the light of a soul on fire in love, and there is no difference. If one is with a master, one is a soul on fire in love, and if not with a master, one can be a soul on fire and in love with presence unnamed, truth unrepresented by a physical Guru. This is God Itself, the teachings themselves, and the hope the teachings give of the Grace inherent to creation. As the human soul is reminded in glimpses of the great light, the memory of trauma dissolves, great sadness, loss and grief, the conclusions of many deaths, the sum total of the meaning of many lives dissolves.

With patterns of the mind and emotions that limit consciousness, how can we incorporate their dissolution into our daily awareness?

Guidance shows first that the pattern formation, thought or feeling is an inner reality. First this must be illuminated, it must be understood: *"From where has this come? What is held in this formation? What is its point of creation? How did it arise?"* This must be respected with compassion and non-judgment. Again: *"How did this arise in my being?"* The root cause must be understood with compassion and with clarity. From the starting point of clarity and knowing it can then be dissolved, it can be seen for what it is: *"It arose from this situation or that. It held necessity at that time and it doesn't now. It was created to survive, to accommodate at that point and is no longer necessary. That thought and that feeling was made because it had to be made and I didn't know anything else, and now it isn't necessary. Now it doesn't need to be made any more. It is an old aspect of my becoming that is no longer needed."*

One cannot dissolve formations without full consciousness of their arising and their validity at the time. They can only be undone through such compassionate consciousness, and by applying that compassionate consciousness to the root, over and over: *"That was then, now it is now."* Then the pattern loses its hold, its unconscious impact. It is still there, as a memory and as a way that was, but not as a way that is. In this becomes the daily choosing: *"Aha! There is the feeling (or thought)."* Know that this moment is a choice. As the sense of choice becomes very real, what do you choose? *"I will not choose that because that isn't of now, that is of then."* What do you choose now? What is the next illumination? *"I choose what is of Truth, what is creating freedom, what goes forward into Grace."* And to know exactly what that thought choice is, what that reality choice is in relation to the one that was with you for so long.

This is the outcome and usage of the meditative state, to observe so intricately, inwardly, what has taken shape in your embodiment, in your being and what needs to take shape. What is the shape of the limitation and its root cause? What is the shape of the related resolve, or freedom? What is the identity that was shaped there? What is the identity that is available now? And to simplify this in the swiftness of inner knowing, inner image, inner statements, to come to that point of choice over and over and over throughout the engagement in your conscious life, and re-choose. Choose from the identity that you now are able to create. If ever there is rejection or anger towards the identity that was made from that root cause, then the whole process goes on hold. **One can hold no anger, no resentment, no frustration, no inner judgment, only compassion for the unconsciousness of others and oneself.** No judgment, compassionate love and compassionate witness 'and then'. The 'and then' is the choice: *"Now this is what I am able to do. Now this is what is facilitated by the being in the situation I am in."*

Now, looking at the repeated pattern of the dissolution and the repeating patterns of compassionate witness and the new choice. Once this has been truly done, up to seven times, thoroughly done, there is the erasure or dissolving of the dynamic of that former formation pattern and there is the sense of spaciousness and freedom. There are conditions in life that can hark you back to the choice-less-ness. When one is too stressed, too exhausted, too impacted by the life around, one's consciousness state may be lowered into former levels of unconsciousness. Therefore, what must be maintained continually is the state of calm and stillness. Continually creating the state within of absolute peace, continually touching into that state in the same way you would touch into eating a meal. The same way you would nurture your being through sleep or food you nurture your being through creating the inner state of stillness and peace. This keeps the movement forward, where old patterns drop away, essentially forgotten and lost, and new patterns become the operating identity.

Finally, understand what is occurring in your being when you create inner stillness and peace. Though it may appear to the mind's thoughts as *"I am doing nothing"*, there is an integration of all the highest streams of realization and becoming throughout all fields of your being. The state of peace is a trigger point that integrates the finest elements of conscious becoming.

Following a discussion on the power of the mind, in what it believes and fears, to create our state of being and our emotional and physiological reality, these questions arose: How do we transform these **deep foundational beliefs** *that can hold us in unconsciousness and dictate our health? How do we change a faulty thought pattern that is creating bondage and is limiting to our life force and our wellness?*

This question is met with gravity. It is a question that is heard and received very deeply. We are talking about a re-writing of the format of how we have taken shape in a life or lives. It is really a question about evolution and the evolving soul. As the soul is evolving from unconsciousness to consciousness, the process of illuminating a belief that is untrue and limiting is a move from unconsciousness to consciousness. It is an aspect of liberation and is a very witnessed movement towards enlightenment.

Enlightenment is consciousness. Every root thought that binds a being into unconscious behavior or response, every one of these thoughts that is attended to and eliminated, is a step in evolution, evolving the being into consciousness; thus the gravity of the question. You are not just replacing or illuminating a thought, you are actually evolving your being. **You are removing a whole stratum of unconsciousness from your soul and from the expression of your soul in this life.**

The question was: *How to do this work?* To recognize the profound power of consciousness is a start, to sit in conscious illumination within. It may appear that you are sitting in stillness within, doing nothing, but you have already transformed the path, just by holding the limiting belief, in consciousness, in willing awareness, in an un-denied experience of realization or revelation within, you have done the work of evolution and done the work of resolving.

The human mind and embodiment, like all animal forms, is built of patterns. Patterned learning and patterned response. Survival is ensured and energy is conserved by these patterns, in that there isn't the need for re-learning, moment by moment, in every situation. A response that is learned becomes a pattern whether it is a belief or a response that is true or not. Understand this premise of your patterned nature. Your belief and response came about because of a situation and then became a pattern. Just as now when you illuminate that and realize the un-truth, the unnecessary limitation of it, you begin a new pattern. The pattern in the first place was built and gripped onto and believed in because in some way it insured safety and survival: "If I always run from this situation, I will always be safe. If I always contract against this experience, I will be safe. If I always take control in this situation, I will be safe. Therefore, it is important to repeat this pattern." And the pattern becomes just that, an unconscious response. Replacing a limiting pattern with truth, liberation and release, will take the same effort. Every time I think this new thought, every time I hold this new idea it creates peace, it creates release and joy.

The more joy and release are experienced, the higher the sense of safety. This has everything to do with safety. In the child-form, or the animal-form, safety is based on protection and on true physical survival, emotional safety is woven to physical survival. **The state of consciousness and liberation is a higher octave of safety. Safety, in that you never die, in that you always exist, safety in that your very nature is peace, is joy, is light.** Safety in that you can rest in the eternal knowing of your deathlessness, of your pure nature. It is truly moving your patterning into a higher octave with its rewards of 'safety', and here the word feels too small. We would rather give the word peace, the endless peace of knowing one's self in this higher way.

This is the human legacy and the legacy of the brain in its capacity, the brain as an instrumentation of intelligence, of soul knowing itself in form. This is the legacy of the human soul in embodiment, through this nervous system, in this world, in this brain. This is the journey of the human being who sits in a duality of the animal form and the spiritual form, to move up the responses, to illuminate the higher consciousness of being and put to rest the dictates of the lower consciousness of being.

Authenticity

We ask the Guidance to describe and define authenticity.

The word authenticity like rings a bell that creates a distillation, a movement of consciousness to the most direct, eternal, central stream of being-ness. Like ringing **The Bell**, not just a bell, that calls the consciousness to the most original stream of being, the most true, eternal, non-changing stream of being within each of you, within each form, in each manifestation of being-ness in evolution. Upon these words we show her the layers of manifestation around every evolving being. The temporary, fleeting, ever-changing layers as identities are shaped and transformed and let go of as incarnations are chosen and shaped and dissolved. As ideas come and are hosted and leave, as responses and emotions arise and leave.

Authenticity is the ever-living, ever-existing, ever-present eye of watching, the truest layer of being-ness that moves in and out of experiences, in and out of incarnation. It is the substrate, the foundational identity behind all identity creations. Seeing that all individualizing, all evolution, all the taking shapes, all the forms of manifestation create identities in order to evolve. They create the shapes of selves and self or identities in order to evolve and move, to learn, to interact and to grow! Authenticity is evolving to exist in an unchanging, ever-present foundational identity of being. It is evolution itself. It is the movement from unconsciousness to consciousness. Could we define authenticity as full consciousness? The most conscious state is the authentic true being. The authentic true nature is a full conscious state.

One in authenticity as their true conscious state can create an identity and yet know that they are creating it, can create it for a purpose, like putting on clothing that fits the atmosphere and situation, and yet know that they are doing it. They know their nakedness; they know their non-clothed state of being-ness. They wear a name, they learn a skill, they take upon an action and yet know their namelessness. They know their being before the action and after. They know their being before the incarnation and after. They know their truth before speaking and after. They know The Truth beyond their individuality and before. Authenticity is a mergence with Truth itself, with Being-ness itself. It is the being-ness that manifests in all beings, the great sum of truth that manifests in all forms, in all words and actions.

Therefore we define authenticity as the unchanging, ever present source of true being-ness. To live in authenticity is to live in consciousness, or to live in the active process of becoming conscious, the active process of finding and knowing truth. "Who am I, essentially?" Who are you in Namaste? Who are you in your most divine nature? Who are you in your purest, unchanging being-ness? "Who am I?" What is the true action from the place most informed by truth? What is the most authentic movement, choice, or words? What is the most authentic action that I can take tomorrow, today, and forever? This must be informed from the most authentic place of being-ness. This is authenticity, if we could we say it as a verb: an action stemming from a place of Truth.

Levels of Consciousness

We ask to learn more about the development of consciousness and the levels of consciousness in people and in groups of people.

When we look at an individual being, we need to understand that a being is a continuum of embodiments, an evolution of itself in an ongoing maturing of 'Atman' or Soul. It is only from this context that we can truly address the question.

Correlate the word consciousness with wakefulness, with the meaning of Buddha, to be awake. Correlate unconsciousness with sleep, with not being awake, being incognizant and having no greater perspective of actions, of feelings, of remembrances, of lessons learned and having no cognizance of the whole, of the greater out-workings beyond oneself. Understand wakefulness, consciousness, as having the perspective beyond one's own window of self and window of present experience.

The description of a being that sits in awake-ness or consciousness to a very full degree is one of a being who holds cognizance to the entirety, to all beings and all stories woven as one, to the story and truth of the unity of creation as a composite of all its beings, all its individualities. **A fully awakened consciousness has cognizance to the unity of all.** A being who sits in full consciousness does not act from the small place of itself or the moment it is in, but acts for the whole and of the whole and identifies as the whole. This describes the full conscious state, which in the question of levels, would be the most encompassing manifestation of consciousness. A being who is manifesting consciousness to a great degree is one who holds compassionate true awareness of all beings present, of all that is occurring around them and not operating from the egoic self first, but operating from a true cognizance and awareness of all beings around.

A being who is operating from unconsciousness, or lesser consciousness, is reactive, protective, is feeling threatened by existence, in defense, feeling that their small stronghold of awareness is threatened. They are acting from the animal state, feeling continual vigilance is needed to survive and to exist. The unconscious, yet living being doesn't see the eternal nature, the continuity of Supreme Being in evolution and only sees its own being in a very limited evolution in this life. Their entire effort is protection, defense, survival, and reaction. A being in unconsciousness has no experience of peace or equanimity. They have the experience of pleasure and relief and contentment, yet all the more positive states are temporary and protected. There is no sense in the less conscious individual of the continuity of self or of the unbroken peace that is the true hallmark or nature of consciousness or existence. A being in lesser consciousness is subject to the ever-moving forms of the material world, of the atomic nature, of the birth, of the death, of the ever-changing landscape of the material plane.

A being in fuller and greater consciousness: this one's eyes are set to the unchanging, to the slow movements, the continuity of eternal nature, the continuity of Grace and the ever present nature of Supreme Being. A being in full consciousness exists from, and as, Peace, exists as Joy, and identifies as Grace. In these two poles of description, there are the millions and the millions of steps of descriptions of individuality.

Call consciousness to yourself, as being awake to the full meaning of Grace, the full meaning of Creation. Never bother to create measurements on another, for you can't know the out-workings in that being, in that country. Place your full efforts into being awake within the world, the country of your own embodiment, your own being, the vastness of your own being. And as you awaken there, your emanation of Grace penetrates the world and the community. Your one and only action needs be to awaken.

Relationships

Why is it that family relationships may become distant or estranged, whereas with apparent strangers there may be an instant recognition. We want more understanding of what is occurring in relationships, in this way.

The answer swiftly comes that relationship is so much more than the presentation of one embodiment to another, in a position within their family or their country, or their community. Relationship is always soul relationship first and current physical embodiment relationship second. This silent streaming of recognition or non-recognition, relating or non-relating is occurring between all beings at all times. To the ones who are focused in their humanness and have placed very little into the development of consciousness, this higher exchange is silent, mysterious, or not even realized and yet is still active, for one soul will recognize another absolutely and instantly. **Understand then, that all relationships are soul relationships first, and current human relationships second.** Every time you encounter someone there is a viewing of that being from soul to soul, recognition or non-recognition. This filters down through the human senses into seeing them as beautiful, familiar, understood, attractive, or as strange, very different, if not repulsive sometimes, or non-interesting.

As you hold a greater consciousness to yourself, realizing you are an ongoing soul in embodiment, you will learn to read your human senses, your human reactions, and not see them as strange but know: "This being is one that I know, this being has been known to me. I love this being and there has been experience with this being before now." Whereas with another in the family, one can compassionately say into oneself: "I don't know this being, I don't understand this being. There is more work for me with understanding this one." Or even: "This one does not feel resonant to me and does not feel like one I need to stay in a nurturing relationship with."

We end here by saying that any being that has embodied near you, whether they are recognized by your deeper nature or not, is there before you for a reason. Whether you feel distant or close, each deserves your Namaste, each is a place to learn love. Do not let your unconscious attractions or aversions dictate your action. Each being needs love to equal measure.

What we can be told about marriage relationship structures and partnering in the more evolved future. What will this looks like?

There is an orientation of this question that the Guidance brings me to, in a micro-second of understanding, which I will try to put it into words. The identity of the present and the past has been shaped around masculine and feminine components as each needing the other, completing the other and the very powerful magnetism of this completion. The soul's expression of identity has been mediated through being in the masculine or the feminine. This identity has been as a 'part of the whole', rather than 'the whole'. The relationship between masculine and feminine creating that completion, as though we are filled out by the gender identity of our partner or our spouse. This format for relationship is very deeply engrained in the evolving embodiments. There is held in this identity of being in one or the other gender, that there is incompleteness in one's being that must be completed and filled by the other. A deep contentment and sense of wholeness that comes by being completed by the other. There is the deep sense of not being alone, of being accompanied and companioned.

We look at the identity of aloneness. The experience of aloneness is essentially a feeling of incompletion and not-wholeness. In this not-wholeness, not being absolutely at rest, not being safe, not being capable and full and whole in this dimension. The magnetism and the structure of completion through relationship brings about this safety, this sense of capability: "Together we can do anything, together we create a safety, together we are a wholeness, a oneness that can meet this dimension fully."

You ask of the relationship in the future in the more evolved human soul and we show you an utterly different picture. Identity in the future is of wholeness of being *within each being,* a genderless completion, the identity of unity existing within each being with the poles of the masculine and feminine equally present in each being. In this identity of wholeness, there is no sense of incompleteness, non-safety, incapacity or aloneness. Therefore, the premise of relationship is utterly different. The premise of relationship is the premise of freedom, not need, of no emptiness, no bereft-ness, nor fear. There is no sense of needing the other to complete oneself or make one safe. The premise of relationship in the more evolved being is as though looking at a whole new octave of Love, itself. It is love that no longer has the attributes or tenets of nurturing, for creating safety or creating completion, or caring for the other where they can't care for themselves. The tenets of love are freed of these more baseline premises that humanity has held in their division, in their unconsciousness. What is love without these basement structures, without these foundational thoughts and callings?

The relationship of the future, in the freed state of each being in the wholeness of their identity, is to magnify and go into the power of illumination. To rapidly expand the illumination of love within each soul, but beyond each soul, as though there is a radiance of Love, itself, through each relationship towards the rest of humanity, towards the rest of creation within this sphere. It is bhakti, it is the highest meaning of the path of love. The relationship of the future looks like the former relationship between a devotee and a Master or Guru, bhakti (the merging into each other's being through the heart for the sole purpose of expansion of consciousness, of illumination or liberation). Relationships in the future merge at the heart in the same way as Bhakti creating tremendous expansion, tremendous liberation and illumination, both within each other and as a radiance to humanity.

In this future foundational premise of relationship, the world is built, the families are built and the children evolve more swiftly into their maturity. The children, in this radiance, become awake very young and evolve very swiftly into the maturity, even in young bodies. They are not bound, and more and more so, no one is bound by the polarities, by the struggles and lack within the polarities. The bondage of relationship is a thing of the past and is gone; there is no bondage within the being to another. There is just the living Bakti, the mergence of the heart. There is no bondage to format. There is no need for this proximity, for nearness and though nearness is still dear to the human, and touch and continual presence with each other, there is no need for this proximity for the Bakti, or for communication. In the wholeness of the being, the wholeness of the identity, there is no need for speaking, there is no need for words, no need for proximity for communication. There is the simple intention of communication of the consciousness, of the mind in its fuller capacity to flow communication one into the other and back again. There is instantaneous knowing of each other and instantaneous giving into one another.

We speak of a span of evolution that could be entered into at any point to see what we are speaking of in its stages, in the birthing of this. There is much resistance and much struggle in the souls letting go of their division, in seeking their pattern of being in one polarity or the other. There is much resistance in the streaming into each other's consciousness without barrier. Yet you ask of the most evolved outcome, when resistance is also a thing of the past and there is the peace, the settled-ness and norm of being in the fullness of the enjoined polarity in one's identity, and the freedom that this creates in the experience of love itself, of relationship itself, and of consciousness itself.

The bhakti merging cannot be confined to just one, who is then the partner, it is a bhakti merging with many, though there will be a structure of alignment to another for creation purposes: creating children, creating forms in this world, work in this world. And yet there is the knowing that the bhakti mergence of love at the heart is a way to be in communication, in communion with many, if not all beings. Love is not just that between you and one other of a few others, love is the way of being, the premise of being.

We ask if all the important relationships in our deep histories (before this life) are with us still, active and part of our lives.

The Guidance shows this as a description of love; through love we no longer exist as an autonomous separation within our own being and energy field. Love itself is an outward streaming, linking force, at a very high level. A high substance linking being to being, never ending, even upon death. Like a high network, or rivers of light that never stop flowing, even when an embodiment dies. **Once two beings have related in** *love, they have simply opened up the channel of a river of light and they flow into each other always.* They flow through each other's natures; they experience through each other's experiences.

This can work through the ancestry then, in the continual widening of the river of love, the continual adding into the relationships of love. To really understand this question is to realize that your being is linking to many others. Linking all over to the experiences of others. Those embodied now, those not embodied, those having experiences through other embodiments, or in the subtle planes. All of them having little streams or trickles of energy and light that impact you. You are truly a great unity of many beings. The stronger more direct streams in your being are based on resonance, based on themes of individuality, and themes of evolution in your being. So at some point in your life when you are opening up to a certain development, a new level of your own evolution with its specific nature, then you are resonant to an ancestor or to an embodied being who can add, deepen, reflect, and be a part of that.

Some of the rivers, some of the streams can be almost silent, receded, and some can come forward and pour in. You are a dynamic moving globe of light, and sometimes the rivers pulse strong from an ancestor or a loved one who has already developed that knowledge, that ability or that wisdom. Once that is gained into a completion within your being, the river recedes becoming a silent stream. It is ever dynamic, ever changing.

For you to understand the full conscious interplay with this truth, is to understand a divine master who exists for the good of all beings, who is open to the rivers of love of many, many beings and is continually mediating and moving within them. Using a divine master as an example of the ultimate of this picture, the Christ always working within those who are linked by love. Always placing in the highest resonant possibilities and pictures of what it means to be Divine Nature.

For you then, realizing that you, too, are living for many. Every step you take, every choice you make is affecting many beings. Giving them light, freedom, healing and possibility. And if you choose otherwise, if you choose that which causes condensation, contraction, fear, it is as though the energy of this doesn't move upriver only down. There is temporary stasis and closure, for evolution moves along the downward flowing motion of love. And when a being is not moving in love, it meets the resistance and there is stillness and closure and lack of connection.

If you were to live your life as though you are living it for a myriad of beings, that you both know and don't know, how would you live? If every choice you faced you realized the outcomes were touching many, what would you choose? This is how the Christ thinks, this is how Moses thinks, and this is what the most conscious beings understand. They understand that they exist within all. As you do unto the least, you do unto me, and as you serve this one, so do you serve me.

After Death

What happens to the human being and soul just after death?

This answer cannot be absolute for what occurs to a being following death is dependant upon their state of consciousness, their inner identity and their spirit or soul. It depends upon where the consciousness was focused, whether it was focused largely on the physical world, the emotional mental world in a physical way, or more inward towards their soul or their internal being-ness. What occurs following death is prescribed by that individual's state of being-ness.

Generally speaking there is a dissolving of the physical identity form. The dissolving of the 'I am' through this body, the 'I am' through these senses. There are many constructs. You hardly realize how you are identified: by your hands, by your sweater, by your house, your car, by your face, by the sound of your voice in your ears, by your relationships and the sound of their voices in your ears. Identified by your village and your sky. **You are held in definition by a myriad of factors in the physical world. Following death is the dissolution of your identity according to that. The process of dissolution, its swiftness or arduousness, is in accordance to your consciousness.**

However swift or slow, in peace or in agony, the dissolution is relentless. It is an individual description. Some need no help, they flow with ease into dissolution and rest with recognition into that which does not dissolve: their eternal internal 'I am-ness.' They open up into the fluidity of the form possible, the fluidity of the realm beyond the molecular. They flow into the relationships of fluidity and light, of grace and higher refinement. It is a time of great realization, great expansion, deep absorption and integration. As though one was to take one breath and absorb all that they are and all that is. Like a great breath that hasn't been breathed for a long time, a great breath of true existence. This breath is then chosen to be held as deeply as needed; how deep a drink was needed to drink the drink of all drinks, of all existence. It is a deep immersion into the entire meaning of it all, the love and the presence of Source pouring through. As though truly every being resources fully and aligns fully into All Being-ness.

This phase is then followed by the realization of that which cannot be sustained there; in other words what is left in this being towards (requiring) evolution. As though the immersion into Source was the great gift and then the awareness of how well this can be held or sustained, how much unconsciousness is still within the being, how much karma is still within the being. Could they sustain that great moment for a tiny moment before all the factors of their remaining unconsciousness came back? Or could they sustain the great moment for a long time before the soft awareness came over them: 'Well, there is still this, there is still this calling to me.'

And so comes the phase of defining the next embodiment, some with great awareness some with none. Some fall into the next embodiment heavily with no awareness, no ability to be aware, simply because they need the infancy, they need the newness and the opportunity, again, from the pureness of that moment of infancy. Again, no definition can be given; it is according to the consciousness.

There are those who remain in a state of unawareness of their death and those who hold elements that they cannot let dissolve. They fall into the next embodiment sooner, become cluttered in their next embodiment.

Generally speaking the dissolution is followed by a re-sourcing, which is followed by realizing the meanings and purposes of the next embodiment. At every step and every stage there is force applied, assistance given by the surrounding beings, magnifying the meaning of each phase. Beings are present. Whether it is just cradling and love that is needed, or if it is deep teaching or harsh and sharp mirroring, assistance is given. There are beings given to this passage. No one is alone and no one is left alone in their rigidity nor in their pain, nor in their condemnation of self. No one is alone. No one is alone in trauma. If they've died that way, the force of Grace applied is seven-fold.

We could say that the movement of evolution is greater at this time than while embodied. The fluidity of the state of being lends itself to swifter evolution. A being that cannot sustain any consciousness of this fluid energetic realm of being, falls swiftly back towards embodiment, to the only place where they can sustain consciousness, within the physical world.

*We wish to know more about the **transition of death** and what occurs to a being following death.*

The state of consciousness of the being before death highly defines the consciousness and the state of being created and entered into following death. The reality that is woven into the sense of self carries through and is somewhat intact following the death of the body. The identification of being-ness through form, the sound of one's voice and the feeling of one's shape, is still there following death. The sense of self or identity through inner voice, inner thought patterns, inner naming of: "This is who I am, this is what I am, this is what I do, this is what I believe" is still there. The disintegration and dissolution can be swift or prolonged depending on the spiritual preparedness of that being. How fluent is that being within, or how fixed is the identity of that being, how expansive?

The identity of the being who has died is in the dynamics of tremendous expansion. Once losing the body/mind, the centre of emotional response, the entire relationship to this dimension, the being is plunged into expansion, a streaming into their true nature, a streaming into purity, a nakedness or actuality of them-self. Constructions are not maintained. A being fixed in the constructions of their beliefs and their identity will experience a prolonged dissolving towards that purity, truth, or nakedness of their soul-self. And yet, one who has been exploring and allowing true expansion in their consciousness, inquiry into the true nature which they hold, will experience a swift painless dissolution of the constructions and belief patterns that were in response to the life, that were adjustments to the life, or conclusions from the life. There is the blessing and baptism of a soul shedding all constructions, all shapes that were built in response to this physical world: the shared belief patterns of the culture, the very powerful shared consciousness in relationships, in families, in countries, in media. The reality that is constructed as a group, shared relationship ideas, and all that is not sustainable, all that is temporary, dissolves.

The essence of this sacred journey past death is a condensation, a settling onto the true eternal flame of soul identity, the soul's ongoing 'I-am-ness', the Atman of true being-ness. The definer of this journey is in the hands of (so to speak) that being's effort in true nature. Regarding their development in the previous life and lives before, has that being's effort been towards a true consciousness, or has that being's effort been in denial, been in avoidance of their own truth, of their own being? A being in avoidance, or a being who sits in an unconscious state within, will still be in an unconscious state following death. A being such as this will require a longer process and a sooner rebirth.

The shedding of the constructions is a sacred process in itself. The phase following death, of purification and the shedding of constructions, is a true examining and an opportunity for a very deep awareness of what assisted in building the soul's reality and what was blocking it; what was developing the truth and what was obstructing it. This dissolving of what was created around the eternal being is a very sacred and vital reflection on the life, and as the journey goes on, there is a holding of that into the backdrop of all lives. It is a time, potentially, of tremendous consciousness, tremendous learning. It is a time of recouping, of gathering, of being a student, of truly understanding the entire sweep and scope of evolution within. For a conscious being it is that. For a child, child-like, or unconsciousness being, there are shades and measures of that. There is the assessing within a being of what needs to be carried forward, what needs to be existed within, what needs to be manifested in the world of form. For following the deconstructing, is the beginning of setting up the resonant potentials of how to evolve further.

There is an embodiment within this subtle phase, this phase of the soul's embodiment without form. There is still the body, not the physical molecular body, but a body of wavelength, a body of light. This body exists as a sense of embodiment around the soul, a body that is lived in and expressed through, a true existence; a body of an entirely different description than your image of body, and yet, a body; a body that reflects the individual nature of the being and where they are in their evolving.

This is a sweeping generalization of that passage with many regions, many variations, many attendants, and very many processes to assist beings in this naked, absolute time of their true nature. As much as there may be resistance, denial and unconscious choice within the physical world, there can also be, beyond it. And so is the evolution of the soul a very long evolution. There is not the dissolving of one's constructions of unconsciousness as soon as the body is dissolved. In the case of one who may have taken their life, there is not peace, there is not resolve, there is, even more magnified, the reality that they have denied themselves their own existence. **What is created every moment of your life is what you die with, is what you enter into in a magnification following death.** If you create grace and peace within your being, upon death it becomes magnified. You embody it in a more fluent form of light, of grace, a more direct mirroring of your state of being.

There is no escaping consciousness and consciousness development. Death is not an ending; death is not an instant peace. Death is purification; death is a rest; death is a deep integrating and absorbing of what has been manifest and what has been created. **Death is a re-sourcing in order to continue the evolution with renewal, with the emptying of all constructions that were blocking consciousness.** Therefore an old person or a person who had become entangled deeply in pain or hatred, becomes purified, simplified, blessed by the emptying and yet, sits in the painful pure consciousness of what must be carried forward, what must be dreamed.

As a being enters into a human birth, there is the gift of absolute newness and amnesia in the infant state. The blessed infancy of an undeveloped brain and nervous system and the blessing of that new moment with all constructions dissolved. As the soul begins to take shape within this new embodiment and choices are met from this partially informed, amnesic truth, there is the opportunity to re-choose, to re-frame, to re-construct an existence that chooses freedom and the values of grace. So then, a being that dies knowing full well the values of grace, the purposes of evolution, creates a body that is swiftly a freedom, a beauty. Nothing can obstruct a being that yearns for truth. Nothing can stand in the way of a being that dies yearning for Truth, who has placed every effort to choose Grace.

*What is occurring **between incarnations?***

The Guidance uses (such as) a hand to spread across a great sweep of an answer. ***There are so many possible paths in the territory between incarnations, thousands of paths.*** The path chosen is written according to the consciousness of that individual and how they have created the being-ness that they are throughout all their incarnations.

There are the paths of the unconscious, those that sit in resistance to consciousness and this is a very short path. The time of embodiment in the soul form is short and is of very little use to one who is unconscious or one who is resistant to consciousness. This form is too subtle and non-fixed for their consciousness to develop or grow. So, the path between incarnations can be short and the need to re-embody is the only way. The unconscious being needs the reflections of the physical world and the separately embodied physical bodies around them. They need the very nature of the physical world to have consciousness at all.

This is a silent time of a being gathering itself into a coalescent resonance of all that they have become, and very unconsciously being pulled into a resonant entry point. No being exists alone, no being finds their way alone or finds their entry point alone. Surrounding them is the guardian, the guidance that assists the finding of a resonant entry point (birth opportunity). They lean toward that being with whispers, with sound, with nudging. Leaning as close as possible to that being, "You are not alone." All beings feel this accompaniment, no matter how unconscious.

And so it goes in gradations of clarity within the being. There is the coming out of the life embodiment; there is the dissolving of the character, and the phase of the dissolving. The phase of dissolving is either swift or long according to the willingness, readiness and strength of consciousness in that being. It is either a process of pain or joy, according to the willingness and the readiness, the amount of resolution or not within the life. We call this the phase of dissolving. And as the phase of dissolving completes itself there is silence. The silence of the being in their true existence, in their 'all become', the summation of all they are to whatever level of awareness they hold there.

In this still point or silence there is a sifting and rising forward from the 'all become', the summation of all they are, of what is most dominant in their need to evolve in consciousness, what sits as their broken edge, their karmic weight, to define the conditions and the entry point. Again, this is a law, the law of the movement of God, of being-ness forward into expansion. It is guided and no being is alone. According to the consciousness of that being there can be great dialogue and learning at this point, as though viewing that summation and becoming intricately part of it, deeply knowing and seeing.

The phase of manifesting, of having arisen to the dominant calling, the resonant shape that most matches the need for evolution in that being begins to place that being in proximity again to incarnation. A phase of re-entry begins far before conception. It is a learning of greater humanity; it is a learning of the evolution of the universe and the evolving of God itself. Gaining a more outward learning of how to move into this map, how to be part of it.

At this point there is the beginning of the reducing of consciousness. Preparing to put aside and become singular, to become that which is the personal condition of the embodiment. Preparing to narrow into the becoming character and the shapes of the senses. Becoming the character that matches those very needs. There is the final reduction of going into a simple singular stream as though going through a tunnel. Going into trust, and jumping off, as though jumping off with all that has been prepared within, into emptiness. Being pulled into the infant state and into a blessed amnesia or into a partial amnesia depending on the consciousness of the being.

*What does **ascension** mean? What is the activation, in the near future, for ascension?*

The next phase of refined consciousness for the human being, such as you, gathers unto itself an awareness of universal inhabitation, universal relationship, universal identity, rather than Earth sphere identity, Earth sphere inhabitation. ***The confines of existing as a human being within the Earth sphere fly wide open into becoming a universal inhabitant, a relationship so much greater and so much more inclusive.*** Therefore, it is called ascension. It is called a liberating expansion into Universal Existence. The next phase of conscious development is this. Literally, the next segment of the DNA fully infused and dictating physical body formation creates a quantum opening in the consciousness going far beyond this Earth identity into an identity that accesses far beyond the limited linear sense program, therefore it is called ascension. No lifting, no movement, no departure, yet an ever widening grasp, an identity whose starting point is utterly different.

What is being spoken of then, at this time, is the marking or meaning of the next era, of the next generations, of the next phase of evolution. It is to be pointed at, reached for, agreed to. It is to be set or anchored like a seed, put into the ground. Understand that if you open to Universal

Identity as an understanding, as a yearning, as an agreement, if you open to all that you could be in your heart and mind, if you agree in your consciousness to what all this is, you have the seed planted. You have set the alignment, and the growth, and the becoming.

How can you do this for yourself? You always do this for yourself, every time you love a being of truth, every time you open your heart and mind and soul to a being who has the truth pouring through their eyes and their presence. You always do it for yourself when you truly love the sublime, the omniscient, Supreme Light. You could agree to it through this teacher, this one (Jean). You could agree to it through the teacher you have in India. You could agree to it through any being, any teacher who is manifesting the higher manifestation of refined consciousness. And yet it is not an intellectual agreement nor a mental understanding, but a heart opening. "Yes, to all that thou art within my being. Yes, what thou art is what I am. Carry my being in the embrace of your being."

We go backwards to the Being with the blue pure white light streaming from his eyes and his hands and his heart, the Christ. It was just this, this invitation into love, this activation of this next portion of being-ness. Love itself calls unto itself. Love in its purest principle holds the absolute state of divine truth and becoming. Love is the seed that your entire being, throughout all its incarnations, has been forming itself around and from. Love is the generative, powerful seed that creates the course of developing the DNA.

There need be no fear, no concern of not being part of, of being left out, nor of being unable to receive this acceleration, this gift from a Being who is offering it. Simply to understand, it is the supreme, unobstructed pure light of Love that is being spoken of, and the yielding, like the Tarot fool in absolute heart, yielding, saying yes.

Consciousness in Healing

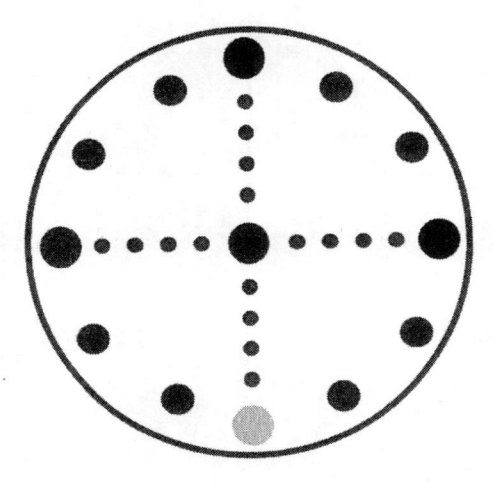

Words on Healing Practice

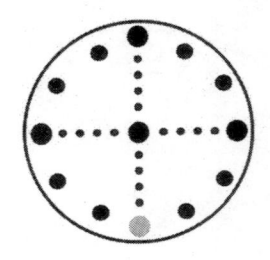

*Is there, sitting yet **in the future**, a direct and effective modality of healing that supersedes all the rest?*

The question creates a great smile, for the human mind that can ask such a question already knows it is true. In the future there will still be a need for healing. There will be a need for structural repair and for the removal of disease that may have been carried genetically, or carried from exposure to the Earth that is still healing. Earth will still carry its weight and toxicity through its soils, water and stones. Therefore, the human being will carry toxicity through its bone, flesh and genetic prints. There will be a need for healing for a long time to come. In the future, healing will occur truly through only one form or modality. 'Healing' will still be a word, but will be more understood as a correction, or as an adjustment of the very formation of this organ or of that cell site. The correction and adjustment will occur through a learned process of bringing forth a specific stream, energy force, and energy ray meant for the purpose.

What is the definition of such an energy ray? It is a correctional energy stream that holds within it the perfection of that cell site, tissue state or organ. It holds as a vision, in the highest illuminate purity, the intended perfection of coding for that site. The coding of that cell, cell group, and organ is beamed in a way that is similar to the crude laser beam that exists now. It is beamed as an activating image. The energy and knowledge of the specific code activates the cells. Activating the consciousness and the code of that cell group creates a swift correction and revision. The renewal of the organ or cell site takes place swiftly, not dependant upon the time that you now think of for cell replacement. The stream of image creates an awakening. This stimulus can occur through the host or it can occur through one who is there for that purpose, such as a doctor, one who has swift access to the pure stream, one who is unburdened, deeply trained and ready within their being for that task.

In the future, every being will have access. They will, with swiftness, be able to see the needed image and give it into their being and into their form, and correct their form. They will be sitting, in a 'sense of being' beyond their form. Now, humans feel so woven to their form, that it is part of their self-definition. 'I am this body.' There are many who think they are only this body. Whereas, in the future, the human being will lightly wear this form and as disease arises within it, they will know that they are not just replacing a cell group with the image of its perfect nature, they are also healing all that it originated from. They are healing into the ancestry of it and into all other likenesses of it. By healing the very body they wear, they are healing Earth. Remember that human identity is no longer singular in the conscious state. Therefore, the bodies worn are part of the great embodiment, part of the Earth. Even now as you heal your body, you heal the Earth. **When you lay your body down, you lay its message into the Earth, you lay its health into the Earth.**

If the body has everything it needs to heal itself why do we need doctors?

The body indeed knows how to heal itself. The body is healing itself every micro second of its existence. The bodies of all life forms know how to heal themselves. Healing oneself and continuing to sustain oneself are the same things. The body sustains itself continually and in the movement of sustaining itself and replacing its every cell, it is continually healing itself. It is always drawing upon the perfect image that is held in its coding. It refers to its coding every micro second of its existence and its coding is its master plan.

Why then are there doctors and why then is there such illness?

The sluggishness and unconsciousness of the energetic and physical systems create a drag on the coding, its message and the resulting action.

The action is not accessing the coding. The healing renewal is faulty and slow even though the coding is there. The repair, renewal and replacement of those cells and that organ, is slow and only partial.

Like the metaphor of a commander or foreman who knows how the building is to be built, who knows how the country is to be laid out and who issues the commands from the perfect-ness of that knowing. But the messengers stroll, nap, fall asleep, stroll some more and take their message slowly to the outpost of action. The outpost of action is then partially built and is not built in the context of all the other outposts being built. It creates a slow and partial action for the rest. There is amnesia, sluggishness occurring between the central image/knowing/coding and the action.

The human being is burdened. Burdened by the tension and weight of its fears and anguish, and its struggle with consciousness, the struggle with its identity and with identifying with outer. Consider, if I am being identified by you and you are yelling at me, or if I am being identified by what is occurring in the government and the government doesn't care, or if I am being identified by outer conditions that are fractured and worrisome. In this condition, the human being is struggling with maintaining its being. *It is not receiving enough hope, purpose and reminders of the perfect image of who it is.* As on the outside, so it is on the inside. As the outside appears purposeless, fractured and despairing so does the inside. What is the point of the messenger really getting there at all? What is the point of rebuilding this kingdom? What is the point of re-building this body if it needs to face anguish over and over?

The doctors ultimately should be the ones that give hope, that give and remind that there is hope. They should give the image of that perfect, beautiful existence of spiritual and physical health. The doctors should be the ones that walk to the outposts and say: "We should re-build and maintain this beautiful mansion, this beautiful kingdom. We need to, for that is who we are. We will all get through this. We are here to build beauty, we are beauty." The doctors should be those who nurture the perfection; remind, teach and show it.

Hold for your answer, that all healing is built in and entirely capable, within the genetic coding. It is part and parcel of creation, part and parcel of every cell division and of all the knowledge held in each cell towards its division and towards its task.

*How does spontaneous and **divine healing** occur between a patient and a master? What is the dynamic and the actuality of the form of healing where someone's illness state or pathology clears up instantly or quickly? Describe what is happening between a master and a devotee (the person who has come to him).*

The Guidance is introducing a state within my being; it is not just information, but a state of understanding in my being. The Guidance is showing the yielding, absolute love and surrendering that is in the devotee who wants and needs healing. This state of surrendering and yielding in love is what is flowing through my being. This is the condition in the one being healed, whether their mind knows it that way or their consciousness has that fully in place. In the heart and in the depth of their being there is a yielding. There is a giving of their embodiment, of their heart of hearts, to love itself and to the principle of love itself in that Guru or Master. This is the largest description of falling in love: as that devotee attaches, suffuses their being, and gives the center of their heart of hearts in love.

In this yielding, their entire physical being and entire energetic embodiment has merged and become one with the master. It has made full availability, as though the master's embodiment and the devotee's embodiment have merged. A being in enlightenment is a description of a being in the full synchronicity, in the full harmony of all sheaths of embodiment. Consciousness flows unbroken from the most sublime, to the most cellular. Life force flows from its most exalted wavelength, to its slowest unbroken wavelength. There is a continuum of synchronicity and harmony within all systems and within all sheaths.

The super-charged life form, which is worn by a master of full consciousness, merges to the unconscious life form (the devotee's physical being). The unconscious life form is then receiving reminders, corrections, and dissolution occurs; dissolution of blockage, unconsciousness, memory, substance built around trauma and cellular substance built around unconsciousness. All this is attached to the super-charged life form of a being in enlightenment. The devotee's embodiment dissolves for a moment, and is held to the state of full consciousness. The state of full consciousness is lent, and in this actuality of the streaming, unbroken lines of life force and of conscious force, the ultimate correction wherever it was needed occurs.

When a devotee reports of a pathology that is gone, there is far more than pathology that has gone. There is undetected pathology; the pathology that has yet to manifest is gone too. All that is preceding the pathology: the unconsciousness, the trauma, the memories of the lives that build up and create stagnancy and blockage. All that is gone as well. To fall in love with a supreme being, a being in full consciousness is to accelerate swiftly one's evolution. It is to borrow, for a moment, the super charged and fully lived in embodiment and allow one's own being to be carried.

You ask of the actuality, the cellular actuality and dynamics of the healing. Look at one cell that has succumbed to depletion of life force, collapse and death, one cell that then creates tissue mass of depletion or cell death. In this tissue site of low life force or cell death, any number of named illnesses can develop. We show the effect of the highly charged lines of conscious life force that stream through any system anywhere. The access point into an embodiment of this highly charged conscious force comes through the higher brain, through the endocrine system into the nervous system, through the nervous system into the immune system. The immune system is where the correction of any cellular state takes place. These pathways are in every embodiment.

You ask how we can do this ourselves; the pathway is in every being. Through hosting sustaining the highest consciousness, the God consciousness, the Divine consciousness, one feeds the very pathway through the higher brain, endocrine system, nervous system, immune system and finally into the cellular body. A master does this swiftly and instantly through the love, attachment and merging of beings.

When a devotee is in love, or when you are in love with another, you merge your being and you merge your body. You begin to become each other. **When you are in love, you begin to become that which you are in love with.** When you choose to be in love with a being of full consciousness, a full embodiment of life force, you begin to become that one. And as you begin to become that one, your divine nature is awoken. You are flooded through in your physical human nature and given the gift of freedom and of awakening in your very physical body. The dissolving of physical pathology is the simplest outcome. The dissolving of memory held in the soul is much more subtle and deep reaching. A devotee will contain, dissolved in their soul that which they don't even remember, yet are shaped by. Through giving their self they are freed of the encumbrance that reaches back to the beginning of being-ness.

Supreme being-ness embodies laterally in the human form in order to lift the human being, to suffuse the human being with the charge of memory, and the activation of remembrance. This is who you are. Though you may gaze upon the beautiful face of embodied divine being, and in the ashram on the screen, all forms of divine face are ever present and can be called upon within. They can be fallen in love with and merged to. There is no past, present or future to the divine face.

What is important is the absolute yielding, the absolute falling in love, which as a human being can be difficult without that being existing before you. Without their movement, their voice and physicality. Yet realize, that the physicality, the divine energetic and the individualization of divine being-ness doesn't dissolve upon the death of a master but stays active to whoever has touched, to whoever has brought that being in. ***The Christ is a dynamic active point of divine embodiment that is eternal.***

Your task is to fall in love, to fall in love with your heart and your whole being. Bhakti. To know devotion and it's meaning is to fall in love. To care so utterly and fully that nothing stands in the way. There are no doubts; there is the absolute giving of one's life to what one is in love with. To fall in love with the divine face, with divine being-ness through Guru, Master, through the embodied presence, is the gift and the way. All that within you, that has built up around unconsciousness shall be dissolved.

In your question of the actuality of healing, we stopped. When the immune system receives the highest pulse of itself, the highest permission to exist as itself, it has in place the ability to dissolve instantly any dead cell, encumbering cell, or disease process in any cellular manifestation. We show a force of fire and light, the immune system works swiftly; it dissolves a cell so swiftly that it can barely be seen with the inner eye. It reduces it to its most atomic components instantly and reabsorbs it into the system in its finest particles. That which is most inert and that which before seemed most noxious is excreted. There is that which is excreted that is very physical and there is that which is excreted that is subtler, passing off through the etheric causal body like a shadow or a cloud.

Even a great collection of cellular pathology can dissolve swiftly, instantly, timelessly, and yet it must be said then that held within all cellular pathology is the story behind it. It is the concretion, the build-up of all that is held in the being from their lives. Complete dissolution and removal is only possible when that being is so yielded and deeply ready, has the empowerment of strength and purpose within their being to move forward into all that they are. The very cellular result, which is *the illness, is also a part of that being's evolution. It is also an integral and respected part of that being's evolution and the dissolution of illness is not always the gift that is needed, but the process through the illness is the gift that is needed.*

A being that has very much to realize through their illness and yet is in absolute yielding love, in recognition of the divine face with their Guru or their Master, may have a simultaneous experience of absolute healing and realization of their karmic understandings. So hand in hand are they with their master or their Guru that it occurs under the umbrella of that relationship.

For your own understanding, realize that the dissolution of an illness is a respected process and understand why you hold the illness you do. Understand it most intricately. Understand it with compassion and intelligence, spiritual intelligence. Hand over your entire being-ness to love itself, divine being-ness itself as a correlate to this understanding. Allow your being to be progressed, guided, infused and led. No, the master is not taking your work away from you, the Master is asking you something greater: *"Can you love, with absolute non-reserve and totality, the being that I am, standing before you? Can you love the meaning of existence? Can you love the face of love?" And in that action you have dissolved all your unconsciousness and all your past.*

*If there is **not** a master to adhere to and hold before our eyes and love, how do we heal deeply?*

We show her that every heart yearns for itself, every being yearns for love, to be loved, to love, to be in love, to be absolute in love. Every being yearns for this, it is the rudder of every ship that a being is. *It is printed in the very first measure of the genetic song. You shall seek that which you are.* You shall seek the great light and the eternal presence of which you are. For those gifted to find their way, to find openness to a Master in their heart and life, it can be swifter. But all beings seek this love. They may see it as great light in the wonder of a garden or the wonder of the seaside, or in the words of a poet, or in the eyes of a husband. *The great light, the great truth will find everyone, wherever they are looking when they are ready.* And in that great light, all is dissolved but itself.

*How does **healing through prayer** work and what are the most effective ways to pray for someone?*

The first image, experience, and words within my being, is that prayer is an act of the heart. It is a movement and an involvement of the heart with the other being. It is an engagement within the heart, and moving into the heart of love, having the focus of one's intention and consciousness of the moment, coming into the heart. Holding the other being in the highest loving intention. Then it remains to understand the heart.

We show the consciousness, the energy of a being coming into their heart center, the center of their love, leaving their mind, leaving their worries, their details, their mental workings, and coming into the pure love, into the place where they hold the other being in pure love. ***The heart then, is not a place of one's own; the heart is the seat, the throne of love itself within all beings. Love is a shared space of consciousness.*** Love is the premise of consciousness and the premise of being-ness. ***Whenever one goes into their heart, they have left the pinnacle of their individuality and they have come into the shared space of all beings.*** In the heart, one is enjoined to all beings, whereas in the mind, one is separate.

Prayer is an action of the heart. The heart is where one deepens, expands and strengthens into their experience of love, into becoming the embodiment of love.

Prayer, in its most simple form, is holding that being in the 'fields of love'.

Prayer is going into that shared place of being within and embracing the other with no words and concepts, nothing more than: "By holding you in love, I will bring forth the highest potentials towards resolve, healing, or freedom. By holding you in love, calling you into love, it shall bring your whole being further into resolve, to clarity, into freedom."

It requires an understanding of love itself. An understanding of love beyond its word, beyond its many words, and beyond its feeling. Understanding that love itself is absolute synchronicity, absolute harmony. It is the straightest lines of force, the most harmonious weavings of the lines of life, of all manifestation of life. By centering into love strongly, powerfully and consciously, it is to hold these lines of synchronicity; it is to sing into another being the lines of harmony and the correcting forces that are needed within their being. Holding in love, engaging in love for another is entering the shared place of all being-ness and calling another into that place.

To increase the effectiveness of prayer, the one who is prayed for can also be invited to enter into the heart and to come into a place of silence and receptivity while you pray. To invite the other to partake as well is to invite them to enter into the agreement of yielding so they may be held in love. To consciously have that moment of surrendering into the prayer, even if it is at a great distance: "At 3 o'clock, will you go into a silent receptivity while I pray for you?" When the other being is yielding, they are opening their being to that shared place and they are in receptivity.

A being who has learned to disengage from the egotistical self, and move into the greater field of being, divine consciousness, and who has learned to come into the shared place of love consciousness, is able to actually flow into that other being. They can actually move into the energetic form of that other being and hold love even more strongly in their specific sphere of being. Prayer is a healing action. Prayer in its ultimate description is a healing action, and in the future, for those who have learned to disengage from their egotistical nature and move into their divine nature, it will be prayer alone, entering into the engagement of love for another alone, that will create healing.

Healing can take many forms, and yet it is the re-alignment of all the forces of manifestation: the cellular, the energetic, the emotional, the consciousness; all the streams of manifestation correcting and aligning. It is the supreme and brilliant force of love that creates this alignment, this ultimate correction of another being, of an illness, of a state of trapped transition.

Realize that many times what you are witnessing (in illness or distress) is not something wrong, it is transition, it is movement, cleansing, purifying, releasing. It is a necessary surfacing of unconsciousness towards consciousness. Your prayer then, is lending direction, lending courage and lending brilliance to that transition. It isn't to stop it, we do not stop a draining abscess; we increase it. We increase it towards its perfect resolve of release and then of healing.

Therefore, prayer is not a mental process of "I wish" or "I want."

There is to be no mind directing, it is to be just heartfelt pouring in of the forces of love. Trusting absolutely that that being in their entirety, their divine nature, their human nature, their process, is doing something important. By lending and moving into, with love, you direct it towards the highest outcome; an outcome that you may have no understanding of and that may bewilder you. But it is an outcome none-the-less. To be ill, to die, or to be in a struggle is not wrong. What is wrong is to be trapped, to be despairing, to be caught and lost in that transition. Feeling isolated, feeling in a rejection of the transition is wrong. To pray and to hold that being in an engagement of love within your heart is to create movement, consciousness, understanding and freedom.

The answer to your question of *how to most effectively pray:* it is to learn to come into your heart in the fullness of your awareness. Come into the pounding, open, warm field of a heart that is love. A heart that is open, is not restricted, reserved and held back, but is open wide. Then call that being; that name, that image, and hold that being in the warm open space of love within your heart. Hold them there, breathe with them, breathe in them and love everything about them, every part of their condition, their words, their feelings and their existence. Hold them inside your heart and trust that love *is* grace, love *is* Supreme Being, love *is* the healing force and you are simply holding them in the river or stream of grace. And when you release them, there is no agenda. Whatever the love did, it did. Wherever that being needs to go, they will go. All you can do is continually return to the love. Increase the love.

How can we be more conscious about **sending healing energy** *to others?*

The Guidance shows first the image of all of you and how you hold your sense of self/center in your stream, your human character, your sense of individuality, and the inhabitant of your sphere within your body. To truly send, to truly involve your energy in the energy of another, to truly assist another being in healing is to lift your own being beyond itself. It is to consciously become attuned to all beings, to all Grace, and to a streaming love and perfection of identity within. It is to prepare the field of your being, to let go of your separate self, to become the prayer and to become highly vibrant love. It is to prepare the field of your being as a sanctuary for that being. To prepare the field of your being as an arena of grace and an embodiment of love and then to gather that being in. To breathe as them, to hold them in your body because it isn't your body, you are the embodiment of love. **To hold that being in your being as deeply and intimately as you can. To hold no separation and to pour through their embodiment with flowing, harmonious life, grace and love. All that I am is all that you are.** All that I am is the same as all that you are, fusing. Using your intention to lift this fusion of you and them into the unity, and into the greater embrace of Supreme Being.

This description sounds magnificent, austere and impossible but it isn't. It is as simple as opening your heart and truly being love to that being. Full love. When you are full love, you are Supreme Being. When you are full love there is no longer the temporary individuality of your human character, there is only the true being that you actually are in your greatest description. As you enter that and hold them there, you remind their being that they are more than their pain and limitations; you lift them up into their true being. As to how much of that experience their stage, evolution and readiness can receive, you will never know and you don't need to know.

This is not a sending but a gathering. **There is no sending of healing energy, there is only becoming healing energy and embracing inward.** There is no separation and there is no distance, there is only becoming greater and bigger within one's own being. There is that moment then, when you held her in your energy, in your heart, in your highest description of inner being-ness, and then you let go of the moment and went forward in your day. But you didn't let go at all, for you planted that being into you, you increased your being and that being forever.

There is no sense of time; there is no: "Now it begins and now it ends.", "Now I need to do it again." You did it, you now breathe in that being and they are being breathed by your love. You will experience this if you yield your being to a master, to a being such as a Guru in the most enlightened description of what that is. **You forever are being breathed, you forever are being dissolved and embraced and yet you too do this for any that your heart seeks to.**

We are asking about helping and healing others by embracing them into our hearts, into our own being. We hear that we don't send healing, but that we invite a being in need of healing into our own field and our own sphere of being. We create conditions of love and harmony within to surround them. The question then came, out of fear and trepidation, *of what it would mean to bring someone in, who may be very ill or in a dark place within.*

You are not alone, you are not this little human being struggling to try and create the conditions of love in yourself. You are not alone, you are an avenue, you are an opening to limitless light and limitless love. You are not to step into the healing format towards an individual in aloneness, but as part of Greater Being. You are to say then: 'I am this one in my humanness, imperfection and fragility. I am this opening, this white heart of divine development, and as I invite you into me, I invite you into God, into All Being.' You are not responsible in your aloneness and your human-ness. You are a plug-in, you are a part of an avenue. You are an intention of love and that is all you are, you are not the one creating the healing. **You are not responsible for the healing of the one with the cancer within, you are an intention of love and you are a prayer.** You are one who amplifies the love for another. You are the one who holds another in the greater mind of all being. "See this one, this one needs."

See yourself as bringing someone into your very heart and soul and lifting them up: "This child needs." Giving them into Greater Mind, Greater Being, so that what you did there was an intention and a lifting. You will not be harmed by intentions of love. You will not wear, within your physical body, signs of their illness. You will just be swept through by compassion and love. **You are not alone and you are not taking on the magnificent task of healing alone in your human-ness.** You are an avenue of the infinite healer. You are a child, an opening or portal of the infinite light. As you embrace the one in need to the portal, you lift them up into the infinite light.

We ask how to understand the oft spoken need for protection, protection of one's energy, one's being from others, from evil or darkness or negativity, and to understand how real is that, what is the real story about protection?

This question comes out of a fear: that the integrity of one's being can be compromised by other humans, perhaps other energies, or other entities. This deeply held belief has long governed human consciousness and is deeply rooted in the human psyche. **Indeed, at one time, the entire understanding of illness was that an entity or another being had robbed or taken away the life force and the soul force of another.** Health equated to merely good protection and illness equated to loss of protection.

What is the truth? This is not an answer that can be given in absolute terms of black and white. Those who hold such belief, hold their beings in ever-readiness of fearful nature. They hold themselves as vulnerable and they hold within themselves the consciousness of a victim. One who needs continually to create autonomy and protection because one could continually lose it to another, this is the core belief of a victim. To lose it to another human within one's life is less fearful than losing it to an entity that is un-embodied, and this too is a deep root of belief in the human psyche. A continual need to protect against entities in many forms, and a continual need to create affinity, approval to the same entities.

Beings that hold firmly within their whole energetic nervous system to this, indeed create vulnerability, they visit illness upon themselves. Did the illness come from another? We would show her that the illness that is most feared was manifested and that it is all an attribute of unconsciousness. Another un-embodied entity cannot create an illness in a physical being. An entity that is seeking to exist in physical embodiment and has a relationship to an embodied being, can create entanglement, can create deeper unconsciousness. Beings, whether they are embodied or not, can be in relationship and can create knots and entanglements and can sicken each other just as two people in continual argument can sicken each other, but one being did not cause sickness in the other, *it was caused within that individual alone by the state of fear and worry and stress coursing through their nervous system, their adrenal system, their physical system.* They created their own illness, they created it unconsciously and in this old form of human belief, it is firmly blamed outside of one's being, firmly blamed on another, which is a sign of the unconsciousness. *To blame another for anything is to mark yourself unconscious.*

Where does protection come in? *The true protection is to become all that you are in the most conscious light, in the most become light of being-ness.* A being operating in the fine tuned wave form of love consciousness, of a consciousness of ascending and greater and greater conscious being-ness has an immune system like the sun, has an immune system that disallows degeneration. Seeing the scope of that, *a being operating in the highest principles of consciousness, has an immune system that operates in the same way.* The beings that feel vulnerable to the energy forces of others are operating in far less consciousness. *True protection, then, is becoming in-filled with the "I am", the true being-ness that you are.* Love is the only protection the human being will ever need, should ever need, and *as you become a love defined soul, a love defined spirit, your field becomes large, and vibrant and pulsing and there is no room for a dark intrusion,* there is no room for fear, there is no resonance with lower states of being-ness or energy. Love, then, is the only protection a being should ever need.

What is white light? White light draws the consciousness to what love means. The efforts at creating protection, energetically, which are effective, lift the being into thoughts that are more refined. Being surrounded by beautiful light refines the entire field and refines the immune system. Please know how subtle, how malleable, how fluent your being really is, how your immune system can move into another strata of vibrancy by thoughts of colour, by actions of love.

*How does **silent sound** or **mantra sound**s internally spoken create healing?*

The Guidance is bringing me to a place within the brain that is a generic informational receiving point. It is a place of receiving information that is pure source, or information in its purest form. This is an information reception point or hub within the nervous system is a central area in the brain to where all information eventually must come.

Information coming in could be coming in as sound energy along many paths before it enters into this pure informational reception hub. It also may be coming in as visual energy, through the visual aspect of the brain, or it might be coming in through the emotional, the kinetic. It also might be coming in through the higher perceptual aspect. They show this as rays, frequencies, or streams of energy information forms that come in through the brain and are taken apart, down to pure information, and then arrive at this point in the brain where it is pure information reception.

This is being described because sound is a stream of information, just as image is, and emotion is. They are streams of information from the surrounding world coming to the individual point of awareness, the individual being-ness of consciousness. **Realize that all sound, all image, all senses are simply informational streams** and further realize that the center point of receiving information is beyond the stream. It is in the heart of the lotus, in the consciousness root, in the center of your being. When your being sits strongly in a focused manner, in consciousness, you are not fixed as to whether it is coming in as a sound stream or a visual stream. You are not bound in the streams or dependant upon them. You go beyond the streams; in a sense you jump, without any sense of time, to the source of the meaning before it even came into the stream. **When sitting in a full conscious place in the center of this consciousness, you understand before it was spoken, you understand before it was painted.** You receive the information the instant it began to enter any communication form.

The usefulness and the use of the silent sound (internally sung) and mantra (externally sung), is to disengage from the sound stream itself. It is to come into a closer orb of the pure information held in mantra, song or spoken word. It is to interact directly with the meaning. It is to interact with the area that sits closest to the center point of information receiving.

To describe this visually for you, if you were to see concentric rings, the most outer ring being the physical sound and the inner ring being the meaning the sound carried, the most central place is the pure consciousness of that meaning. The silent sound, the silent mantra is sitting imbued with the meaning that is held by the mantra. It is learning to translate the word sequence into just the meaning. It is learning to disengage from the sound waves that carry the words, to just the words, and the next step is not the words but just the meaning. The step following that is a *continual consciousness of that meaning.* Practicing the silent mantra is a refinement of informational receiving.

You ask of its use for healing, we speak of the correcting influence of a sentence of power, a sentence of truth for lack of better words. The stream of such meanings of truth as is held in these words, and the correcting aligning influence of this, within the physical embodiment. To hold silent mantra is to reach for that meaning, to open to that meaning which opens to that correction. Your whole being is listening. When your ears are not listening, your whole energy system is listening. As your whole energy system is part of listening, it rearranges itself in order to listen. It aligns itself to what is listened to. When you listen to just sound, not even mantra sound, just sound, your being arranges itself to listen and it can arrange itself in a dysfunctional manner if the sound is crude or it can arrange itself in a refined manner if the sound is refined. One learns to disengage from the auditory listening and open to the inner listening, changing the listening from that part of the brain which is translating sound waves, to every part of the energy system that now has to listen.

Every part of the sensory being listens to silent sound. In listening for silent meaning, silent transfer, the whole energy system arranges itself for that listening, and *in that* there is healing, realignment and correction.

Beyond this there is the development of consciousness itself, to use the whole being to attend to silent mantra, silent spoken meaning. To use the whole being to bypass even that and to directly sense true meaning, true message. This expands, hones and deepens the direct exchange between Omniscient Source Supreme Being and your being as a manifestation of that.

You can also send forth healing and intention without sound. Through holding the pure experience of that meaning as though holding the alignment of your being in the state that truth gives to you. For example: if the meaning was "I wish for you to be at peace," as a thought sentence held in the outer ring. Yet as "I wish for you to be at peace" becomes an entire inner experience, your being is aligned energetically into peace and the peace of your being is being extended and held towards another.

We could say, as we show the direct transfer between the center of informational being-ness in one being to another (without sound, image, words, touch or contact), such is the possibility and the development of an enlightened being to assist others. It is a direct transfer of the meaning of meanings, the experience of truth and the alignment in their embodiment into truth. ***The mantra is given as the vehicle, the passage. It is preparatory, toning and conditioning the individual's mind path, the outer rings.*** And yet the refined teaching, as your teacher was speaking to you, is to distill it further in to where you no longer need the outer rings.

Immunity

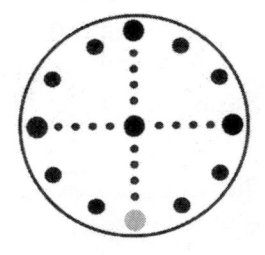

How can we raise our immunity when we are ill?

The Guidance shows the individuality of this question. Every individual, in their most sensitive and conscious way, must look deeply into exactly what it was that lowered their life force, causing their wavelength to flatten. What was it exactly that took the inhabiting of their form to a less conscious place? ***Each individual must understand and perceive how they lowered the life principle within their embodiment.*** They must attend to that, repair that and realize that this is what sits behind lowered immunity: the vibrancy of the life principle lessening so that the immune system is working sluggishly, slowly and carelessly.

In the future and now, a being that attends to this and corrects it, can bring their life principle back into the vibrant range for which there is full immunity. It is the answer around consciousness. ***How conscious are you of your being, your actions and your responses to life, to the results of your decisions and your actions, and how committed are you to changing any of those actions or responses?*** As consciousness within you attends to it all, there is a steadiness of life principle. There is never a lowering of life force to the point of chronic illness.

Understand that when becoming temporarily ill, the life force is not lowered to the same degree as with chronic illness. It is more that the life principle is engaging in the struggle to become conscious, to meet the organism (i.e. a virus or bacteria) and to instruct the entire body towards the organism.

With chronic illness there is defeat in the immune system with very little effort placed towards becoming more conscious physically, within the immune system. However, even with chronic illness, the conscious work toward healing involves attending to the story and the journey that led to the disengagement from the life principle within one's body and one's life.

Self-acceptance

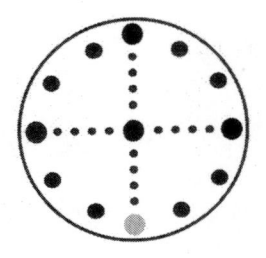

We ask to understand more about self-acceptance and how to love one's self.

In the evolving of moments, of days, and of lives, in the evolving of individuality towards consciousness, the action of self-acceptance is the ability to pause over and over again, to observe fully, the being that you have become and the actions you have created, the feelings and responses that are within you. To observe as fully as possible in every pause, all that is within. Having as the root intention of this pause, to learn, to become more, to create correction, reorienting of the next step and the next part of the path. This pause is not for regret, nor for rejection, nor for despair at unconsciousness and the actions of unawareness. It is purely for learning. It is for learning and forgiving, learning and committing. It is for learning: "This path does not lead upwards, this one leads down, I choose it not." "This path created confusion in my being or in others. Which path would not?" and choosing the path that leads forward.

Self-acceptance is truly self-reflection with the intention of learning to continue moving forward into more light and grace within. It is to have compassion, not only for your own being, for all beings in evolution. **Having compassion and an understanding that one does not move into the higher regions of full perspective without each step along the way, without every effort towards each step on the way.** Every evolving being needs to take every step. For each step to take one into further expansion and more light, there needs to be the grace-filled intention to learn to let go of that which takes one, or others, into confusion or pain, and to never choose it again. To realize that all life lessons, all evolving lessons are meant to be. It is in the design, in the mind of Grace that one is evolving from unconsciousness to consciousness, and that many of the steps taken are unconscious and create pain and confusion.

The responsibility of self-acceptance is to include unconsciousness with love, with compassion and grace. It is to continue to yearn and to learn, creating corrections based on what is learned, and to peacefully let go of that which creates pain and confinement and bondage.

As you learn to accept each step that the self has made unto this moment, with the intention of learning, and the intention to have compassion, you learn to accept and have compassion for all other beings. Every stumble, every mistake is viewed from the humility of self-acceptance, understanding that you have given Grace to your own being. To understand that this is all in light of learning, in light of evolution, in light of choosing over and over again, that which brings more and gives more.

*We ask for more understanding on **how to forgive** one's self for something that is very difficult to resolve and feel at peace with.*

There is a hard stare at this question. There is intensity around the meaning of the question and what is held in it. The Guidance begins by saying to actually forgive one's self or another; to genuinely and honestly forgive, requires consciousness, realization and true awareness.

Forgiving is not real if it is just a gesture or an act of letting go: "I won't think about it, care about it or let it bother me. I will let this go." That is a gesture, a brush that could be called forgiveness but it isn't true forgiveness. **True forgiveness is realizing past the event, realizing through it.** It is actually dissolving the energy caught in the event or the action. Dissolving the weave, the energetic memory, and the emotional experience; however you would describe this reality. Dissolving thought forms, energy forms or feelings through realization and consciousness.

Whether it is a small or large event or action, of another or yourself, true forgiveness is attained by a growth in consciousness. Truly understanding and realizing what happened and why. Truly understanding what was held in that being that created the action. The true awareness of why they did what they did and a true consciousness and compassion of why you did what you did.

True forgiveness also necessitates the understanding that every being is coming from a pure intention all of the time. This is a remarkable and challenging thought. Every being, even a murderer, is coming from a pure intention. *The root cause of their action is a pure intention.* Just like the root cause of creation is a pure intention. The root cause of any movement in the universe is a pure intention of love.

This is the kind of consciousness we speak of, a full consciousness that comes down to the root intention and can see all the gradations, all the consequences, all the choices made, and can sift down through all the layers of this to the root intention and see it all the way through. When the consciousness can see it all the way through, then there is letting go. There is dissolution, and then there is forgiveness. Forgiveness is the cleansing, the dissolving of the cloud until there is just the absolute: the blue sky. There is the unwritten, the purity and the beginning.

To forgive yourself then, is to have the inquiry, the invitation within, to have full consciousness of what you did and why. To listen without judgment and to continue listening until all the information unreels and you hear it all. You hear how you were feeling and you ask why you were feeling it. You feel what you were feeling in that action and why, where it came from and where it began. You unreel the event until you come to the pure heart, the pure center, and the original point of what your intention was. You are forgiven by the action of a full listening and compassionate ear into your being that assumed you are goodness itself and always have been. That assumed your intention right from the start was pure, even though the unconsciousness of your action caused injury or mistake. You assume pureness of the original intention, and you return to it.

Learning to truly forgive is learning to truly listen with compassion to all that person or all that your self is feeling or saying and to listen further into what the person can say or what you have said, to listen further inwards with the ear of your heart and the ear of your soul. To truly hear into what that being really holds or what you really hold. When you truly listen from your heart's ear, you unreel, undo, and bring life, consciousness and love to that moment or that event. You have listened to yourself right through to the beginning, and you have seen and become more aware of who you are. You have increased in consciousness.

Forgiveness increases consciousness. And as you forgive another and increase in consciousness towards them, you know them more deeply.

You don't know them by their action, words or mistakes, you know them by their heart and by all they meant by that mistake. All they clumsily were trying to do or say. You don't listen to the clumsiness of what they said or did, you listen to what their heart was trying to say and their being was trying to do.

You remember that every being is coming from a pure intention. Every world is born of a pure intention, every birth, and every movement in the great field of divine being-ness has pure intention at its onset, its genesis. And though this is a vast sweep of words, it translates into human nature, and into human action. It is no vaster to speak of the beginning of a world, as it is to speak of the beginning of an action or the gesture of a relationship. Don't use the terms large or small, only use the term 'truth'.

See the need to forgive as an opportunity of consciousness increasing. See it as the increasing of freedom in consciousness in your being and towards another.

(An example: The root intention of the murderer of John Lennon was that he loved the magnificence of John so much he thought to kill him and therefore become him. This pure intention was love and awe and a desire to be like him, therefore we hold him to his pure intention, not a condemnation of his distorted mind.)

*How can we adopt an attitude of willing agreement to **our challenges** rather than feeling victimized or burdened by them?*

This question deals with holding a stance of full agreement to a challenge that is before you versus rejecting it or seeing it as unnecessary or wrong, something to move on from. The choice is to be deepened into consciousness by the challenge or to feel victimized by it. True reflection within the being is required, and a continual return to true reflection, enough to discern and to understand what is being gained and what is being learned, and what is being developed in your being. **Nurturing an ability to see what is being gained in your being is the direct method to avoid being caught up in a sense of loss, being drained, defeated and emptied.**

There are two places to stand, and the world looks utterly different from each place. To stand in one place is to ask: "What is being gained right now, what is being built in the cathedral of my being?" To stand in the other place is to ask: "What am I losing, what is being destroyed, what is being taken away?" To stand in the place of what is being built and gained is the place of the mature being knowing that all evolution is always gaining and building supreme meaning. There is only forward motion in the evolving of divine purpose. To stand in the place of loss is to stand in the stasis of unconsciousness that tries not to see, that distances one's being from their true nature, from their movement, their momentum.

Most of humanity views trauma as a wrong, views crisis as a wrong, entering into a stasis of consciousness, creating more distance to their soul's progression and holding tremendous energy around viewing the situation as wrong, when it never was, when it never needed to be. Rather, stand in the place of what is being developed, what is being offered and ask: "What does this lead to in the forward momentum of my and everyone else's evolution?" This very choice of stances is what makes the difference in this story of evolution. To swiftly enhance the movement into the full conscious state means never lingering in the stasis, never creating a separation by rejecting the experience in front of you.

Consciousness Towards Others in Illness

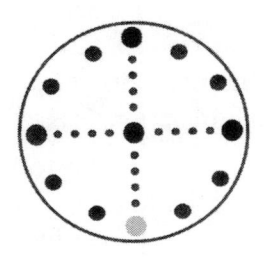

When we face somebody who's in a very dark place, possibly suicidal, how can this be understood? How may one support such a person in every way possible?

In answer to the question of what to do, and where to go when you witness the darkness of another: your first responsibility is to not increase the darkness by entering into it yourself, by feeling hopeless, scared or despairing. Your first gesture towards that being, and all beings, is to refuse their darkness and refuse their despair, within your heart, within your mind and your substance. By your refusal, by becoming taller and more brilliant in your refusal, you have said everything they need to hear. You have said "No, it is not so". You have shown the fallacy and you have shown the truth. The truth is, there is nothing to despair, nothing to doubt, and there is no premise for doubt.

In showing, by your presence, your eyes and your words, a being that exists without doubt, exists in full understanding of Immeasurable Grace, you give the unforgettable assistance. You give to one who is teetering on the edge of such choice, the message that will guide like a beacon and never go out.

Beyond this, words may guide and teach of the eternal nature, that there is no such thing as death, only the transitioning of form. That which is contained within our being, of heart and mind and soul, does not go through death. To kill the body does not kill the despair, nor the identity, nor the quandary the identity is in. It only kills the vehicle that the identity expresses through and its living context, temporarily.

To be able to say boldly, strongly, that the only solution to despair is to learn the truth of the true nature of all beings. To learn and open to what the truth is, of what the soul is, of what it's made of, of where it's going. Beings, such as the one you speak of, are poisoned by hatred, a hatred for their own presence, their own being, which condenses their being down into a shrunken state of paralysis. A being that sits in hatred needs to be shown love. What needs to be spoken of, is love. Love is the only medicine, the only healing action.

To the extent that love can be shown to the one that sits in hatred, there can be release from that hatred. No matter how ugly and painful their words, their visage or actions, love them absolutely. **They cannot learn to love themselves without being shown unconditional absolute love.** Therefore, your second task, from a place of unsullied light, is to love, fully love. The suffering one's readiness to be loved is not in your hands. But know that your love didn't go unnoticed, it was stored, experienced. It was received because **hatred and despair is a starvation for love.**

How can we best help someone who is in a severe crisis or suicidal state?

This is a generalized teaching assistance for someone who has come to such a reduction, such a pointed place of their pain. Understand that one who has come to such an extreme, pointed place of their anguish and their pain, is in a place of power. They are in a place of vulnerability; a place where they stand on one foot and the other one is in the air. They are vulnerable, they are reachable, and they have come undone into a fluid moment where everything can count.

How to be there for them? You are there for them with your presence, with your companionship, and with your compassion. You can be there with the full measure of your love. **You direct where that next footfall shall come, simply by your love.** You hope, you pray, and you hold their most beautiful self in your mind's eye and in your heart's sense. You stand before them, believing in them. Knowing they are worth your time, your silence and your presence. You become a force of an angel, a force of love that is like a wind that will blow the next footfall onto solid ground. You don't delude them with your words, your conjectures, your fears, your anxiety, your information and your know-how, it isn't the mind that needs to be reached in one like this, it is the heart. It is their feeling. They are questioning whether to exist, whether to take the next step. You don't encourage an infant into the world with words, you encourage them with love and with the embrace of your presence. You give them the message that this world is a good place to step into. Realize the silent emptiness of this state, this poignant moment of the next footfall. ***Be there, with your body, your heart, your presence and your belief in their existence.***

Stand as an angel, for that is what you are; you are an angel of belief. An angel is one who can believe fully in the beauty in front of them and see only that. You look past the ugliness that they have created, and the anguish written on their face. You look past the alcohol or the drugs that have contaminated their form and you see their beauty. An angel is one who stands there and rings the bell of their beauty, "I believe in you." You are not there to convince them, or talk them out of something. You are not there to be anything but one who believes fully in their life. Be the angel, you are the angel, and any being that is operating from the fullness of heart, and is able to see the Namaste, the divine nature of another being, is an angel.

If that being chooses not to be seen in their beauty, and chooses not to hear the message of your belief in them, even then, hold grace. Realizing that the process of stepping into the dark reduction, the severity of crisis, has purpose and meaning. It is not your failure nor is it theirs, they need to make their experience more extreme, deepen their reduction. They need to come further down into the nakedness and the vulnerability of the state they are walking in.

You were noticed, you were one who stood there at that corner and believed in them, and had the bright path of life behind you. If they walk past you, if they walk past that corner, realize that they will find another corner, another angel, and another chance. It might be you, it might be someone else, it might be a friendly dog, it might be a flower or beautiful tree. When that being is ready to take the bright path of life and begin to believe in their existence, they will notice this and they will hear.

We wish to understand how to help others using skills and knowl-

edge, how to know when to help and when not to.

The Guidance shows the silent presence of the compassionate one towards the one who needs help. Showing the potency of silence, of simply existing in compassion, in being selfless and fully present to another in silence and compassion. Surrounding their being with compassion, entering into their being with love. The invitation for more, for words, hands, for leadership and guidance is being received by your compassion and by your silence. Their being is receiving the invitation when you are in full compassion and when you are in a selfless love. They need no words, but invitation. Their being then can bring forth the words to ask who you are and what you mean, will you be teacher or will you be healer? You have not done 'nothing' in your silence; you have presented the true invitation by being there in the silent compassionate presence. Offering no actual form, no actual method. In fact the greatest work of any healer is in just the compassionate surrounding, giving that person the experience of being surrounded, befriended and totally cared for, with no words and no action.

Letting the offerings of your knowledge and your skills be asked for and only given according to the question. Discerning what the question is and only giving that which answers the question. Realizing that the mechanism within that being is that they are reaching for what they are ready for and then absorbing what you have given. They will reach for more once it has been absorbed. Compassion then, is discerning that. Only giving them what they are ready for and what they have asked for. **Compassion is continued selflessness, knowing what that being is ready for and giving no more.** If they are asking for nothing, just be there in the compassionate eye of your presence.

What is happening when we feel **aversion** *or are aggravated by another person's way of being or their energy field, and what we can do about it?*

The Guidance is speaking of the 'person who creates disturbance' as an example of a situation that may happen often. That person is saying perhaps nothing, perhaps one thing, but that isn't what you're hearing. Your energy field has ears, your whole being has sensors, and your whole being hears truth and senses truth no matter what the person might be saying. Whatever that person may be presenting from their words, or their story, and what you sense. The aversion comes *when the two mes-*

sages aren't the same. When your whole being is feeling and hearing a message, a truth, and it is different than what the person may be saying or doing.

The person and people that cause this aversion are trying to create power and dominance. They are trying to establish themselves because they are unsettled, hurting, afraid, or deeply insecure and sensing your sureness and strength as you question. It can cause a reaction, an enhancing of their fear, an activation of their insecurity. They can begin to energetically dominate the moment, trying to establish a solid place inside because of that fear.

If you could just hear the true words that their energy field is speaking, it would make more sense. "I'm afraid here, I'm afraid of shrinking into nothing-ness. I'm afraid I am nothing, I'm afraid I'm worthless. I'm afraid you'll see it. I'm afraid you'll criticize it and call on it. I'm afraid of you." "Therefore I'll make you afraid of me, therefore I won't let you in. I won't let you in, therefore I'll push you away." Those are the words coming in energy language from those that are unsettled, in pain or insecure.

Listen to your senses, what is this? What am I feeling? What am I really hearing? Listening with your most inner ear, what is this person feeling?

The answer of what to do is to love them. To know they're hurting, and that they're scared and empty. It is to reassure them, to hold them in your heart, and to go past your instinctual reaction like a ripple on your own energy field that prickles and hurts and says: "I don't want this." ***It is to not respond to the reaction of your field but to go into the higher place of your being and be love.*** This person needs love, and they may not need love through your touch or your words, they may not be open to you in any way at all. So in the silence of your own being, hold them as the most beautiful being in your heart, and bring love in their name. You hold them where they most need to be held: in love.

Your task is not to respond unconsciously and reactively when your field feels dominance, aggression and fear, but to have your spiritual ears prick open; someone needs love, someone is hurting. Hear it like a cry, not a threat. The very action we describe, you all do to an embodiment of love and freedom (such as a highly developed soul) that cannot be hurt by another human. We do this because in your soul you are love and you are part of all beings and you can only love and be loved.

Do unto others, as you would have others do unto you.

How strongly, how deeply do two people in relationship affect each other in terms of limiting or liberating the other?

The entire picture, the entire resonant potential is there at the very beginning of a relationship. Though your mind doesn't know this, your beings have assessed each other fully in all the potentials, all of the possibilities and likelihoods, both positive and challenging. In the deepest knowing of your being you already know the potentials for growth and development or for challenge and blockage. You also already know why the challenges and the blockage may be the path that your being is choosing, or you know why this companion is offering more and more liberation. The real answer is in these questions for each of you: How much of this internal, already held knowing do you access? How much of your inner counsel, your inner knowing do you access in your relationship? How much do you turn to yourself for what you already know, for what you have done in choosing this one? Or how much do you go outward and invest your whole emotion and mind on the actions of the other?

If you are limited by any being, it is because you are not accessing yourself. There is no limitation on a being who is in consciousness of their evolution. Any blockages, any resistance, any challenges from the one beside you or around you are there because you have agreed and allowed. If you have become helpless and unconscious to why you are there, the partner can be tremendously limiting towards you, can block your path over and over, because you have agreed and you have become helpless. However, that very same condition, their resistance, their stubbornness, their choice to be unconscious, can actually offer you liberation. To meet that partner with true compassion, with loving the soul, the Namaste of their essence, and to give them only love and nothing but love, liberates you. It teaches you that no being on the outside can limit you, ever again, and that limitation is never going to be your choice, ever again. The testing conditions of a partner that creates what appears to be limitation, have become a test that you succeed at realizing: "I shall not be limited in my consciousness, in my evolution. I shall be in the full centre of who I am and all actions chosen only as love towards any being close or far."

Conversely, when a partner presents ease and gifting and liberation, what really occurs there still needs to be an inner choice, not taking for granted the good nature and the openness of that partner. Every step you take, coming from the centre of your choice and your consciousness, whether to take the gifts or to view the challenges as gifts. You can view the plenty as challenge too. One can become sleepy and dependent on others both negatively and positively. The awakening soul who stays vigilant to their own inner state, is affected neither by judgment, nor praise, nor blame, nor persecution, nor honouring. The awakening being is in a steadiness of self, whether in relationship or not.

Why does a being, or soul, choose to embody with **mental illness,** or to die at the end of life with mental illness? Is it wrong for a caregiver to stop their care giving and send their loved one into a care centre? Does this end their personal karma with that one they are caring for?

The Guidance is standing, so to speak, with this wide sweeping question, needing to remind us that there is always purpose outplaying with every situation for every being. It may not be possible to generalize, as each being or soul is a story and each life is a part of that story and a continuance of the evolution and the story of that being. Mental illness can serve greatly in the story. To describe this would be to enter into the story, to enter into the being's evolution and describe how and why mental illness was a choice. We will say though, that mental illness is a reduced state of consciousness that does not allow for a great coalescent view of existence. It is a narrowed view that can only see certain angles, certain areas, depending on the nature of the illness and of the being. ***This reduced view can serve greatly in the evolution of that being.*** The smaller scope, the neediness, the dependency, perhaps being held to child-like concepts and image, can all serve the being greatly in their evolution, can cleanse and liberate great reams and realms of experience from a being.

Mental illness is only 'illness' when deemed that from the outside. And it is old knowledge that one in mental illness is actually in a passage, a narrow tunnel of their soul's expression. ***They are on a power walk and they are walking with limitations.*** They are meeting those limitations and this is raising the power of their soul. It was known that those with mental illness were to be respected and acknowledged as souls on a power walk in a way. It was never called illness, it was seen as that and there are many terms and many of the ways of old knowledge for ones in mental illness. They were seen as ones who were courageously choosing, for this lifetime, the path of limitation, and the path of limitation is a power choice.

The question of the relationship between the caregiver and the one with the illness or limitation cannot be generalized into an answer either. Sometimes, many times, the decision can be overwhelming and is impacted or determined by the community in that the support systems are not there. It can also be a karmic backing away from what needs to be done. This question can't be answered generally. It must be answered specific to the individual and the individual relationship.

Returning to the path of limitation, the choice of power, and the understanding that mental illness is a choice made by that being. It is a choice of how to enter life or how to leave life and it is a choice that their being has made, having nothing to do with any relationship around. It has to do with their own contract, with their own evolution. It is to be respected as such, and it is to be held in honour as such, and not judged.

*How can we buffer **aggression**?*

The Guidance brings to my screen of seeing the image of the wisdom teachings and practices in Tibet. This is brought forward because of the impact on me personally and the answer that has come to me before on this question. The Tibetans are people who have suffered and have been part of aggression. Their group consciousness is the very deep development of consciousness within Tibetan Buddhism towards compassion, towards how to be in relationship with aggression. The preparedness in these people was already there before they were aggressed, a root understanding embedded in their temperament towards aggression and peace. This is where we go for a generalized answer. Yet what is personal in each situation must draw from the greater Truth and not be edited or put aside. From a place of wisdom, the basis of how to be in relationship with those who are in aggression is to understand and enact compassion. **Compassion holds the wisdom and understanding that the aggressor is the first one to suffer and the aggressed is the second one to suffer.** The aggressor was suffering first; the aggressor is a sufferer. Suffering became aggression; aggression created more suffering. Compassion in its action is to address the aggressor with compassion with the knowledge: "You are suffering. You are suffering first before I am suffering now. In the greater consciousness of my being, I choose to acknowledge you as a sufferer, and hold compassion for you as one who suffers and has chosen to go into this response, into anger, into pain, into fear, into power." Knowing that it is not the true response, the true response to suffering is the tears, the pain, the anguish and the fears.

Your question was 'how to buffer' not how to understand aggression. True buffering is to be immune, to be bigger than the aggression, stronger than that person's suffering. True buffering is to not suffer because they are suffering, not to receive, unconsciously, their suffering and become a sufferer. True buffering is to stand in the bigger place of Heart with compassion and be able to see the aggressor with the eyes of love, with the eyes of true acknowledgement, the eyes that see past the aggression to the suffering of that being. In that action not only is there protection, *there is no decrease in your being, rather, there is increase.* In that action there is a giving to the sufferer, a giving to the being who is aggressive, an opportunity for that one to find another path, to come to a place of transformation and a corner. For their aggression was not returned, and as their suffering was not creating more suffering, they receive a lesson of Grace, a lesson of wonder. As the one who was being aggressed sits in love and instant forgiveness, which is the attribute of love and compassion, their aggression is empty and visible to them as empty. Therefore you are not only buffered, but you are increased in your presence rather than decreased and you created a shift, an opportunity of transformation for another.

*We ask for advice and counsel on living with someone who is in **depression**, how to avoid being pulled into another's depression, how to stand closely beside someone who is depressed.*

The guidance first brings me to a visual of the energy field of depression, the energy currents, the energy shape, the dynamic of the energy field in someone who is depressed, and how this effects the energy fields of those linked or woven to that being. We use an energy description for true understanding. The energy interactions between beings are a silent continual exchange. One is living in another, pouring into another, receiving from another, affecting another. There is no true separation between beings when seen energetically. The state of being of one is continually pouring into, imprinting, being felt by all those around.

Going back to the energy field visual of someone who is in depression. We show her the general contraction of their energy field, the energy field pulling in upon itself, becoming a much smaller globe. It has a gravity of its own, and is collapsing in upon itself. There is no radiance, only a gravitational pull inwards, onto itself. This causes a slowing of life impulse. The energy field appears grey and dull. Continued depression can create dead spaces in the energy field.

A person in chronic serious depression is starting to die. Their life field force is shrinking and dislodging. The essential un-dying being, the spark of being, is leaving the body. The embodiment rejects its owner, rejects inhabitation and rejects the purposes of the embodiment. This creates fear in those around, where the energy field sensing is repulsion and fear at the witnessing, energetically, of the dying and shrinking. It can create the need to shore up or protect, and become less attached, less woven to that one. Letting them go and protecting ones own intact sphere, energetically. In this sphere there can be reaction in trying to stop the shrinking, stop the dying in the other. Not only because you don't want that one to suffer, because you don't want to suffer. **Realize how much our reactions to others can be a protection of ourselves.** We want it to be better for that one so that it will be better for us. All of this is unconscious interaction.

The answer to your question on how to live in the highest manner, how to survive and exist beside someone who is shrinking, while staying intact, staying free, staying undamaged, like the oft repeated answer to so many questions, the answer is consciousness. Being conscious of what is happening before you and why, in a more subtle and complete way. Understand this one in front of you, that they are shrinking, they are rejecting their life embodiment, they are rejecting their life purpose and perhaps, understand what has burdened them so and brought such a response. Know all this consciously, with compassion, and yet to isolate the knowing of their story, of their choosing and their dynamic is to create more autonomy, fewer inroads into your own fields. **Consciousness is its own protection.** Consciousness creates the opposite of shrinking. It creates the radiating infilling, the potency, the radiating potency of a being who knows itself and who exists fully in its life purpose in acceptance and awareness of its embodiment. Consciousness creates its own protection. Be conscious of your purpose, of your reason to be embodied, of your challenges and how to meet them, choosing to meet them in the highest light of developing more consciousness, awareness and wisdom. And as you tend to that within yourself, you create radiating fullness of being.

For the one who is rejecting themselves, be able to look upon them with clear illumination and see, speaking it or naming it unto yourself: "This one in their unconscious suffering is rejecting his very own nature, rejecting his possibilities, rejecting his growth." ***There is to be no anger, no judgment, no anguish, just the observation and the compassion.*** So as not to be drawn into this sinking spiral, turn towards the horizons of light that sit before you. "My story is that I shall attend in full awareness to all that I am. I shall in-fill and radiate with acceptance of my purpose, my embodiment." Knowing that as you do this solitary infilling of your presence, your energy being, your print, your field, is giving the information to this one, the silent interaction of shrinking versus expansion. Not with words, just with energy. You are the example, the silent continual messaging of energy, or in simpler terms, meet contraction, the shrinking of depression with expansion.

As you feel the invitation, the impact upon your being, becoming drained, becoming defeated, shrinking - meet it with finding all that you love about life, all that you are in life, and open your being even more strongly to life, because of this. Replenish your being more than ever before because of witnessing one who is not; become the opposite of what you are witnessing, because of what you are witnessing. Know that you are not doing this only for you, but also for them. The messages of your expansion are flowing into their being. In the very worst situation where one shrinks into a darkness of their life, most fully rejects their embodiment, if there was one nearby who stayed near and didn't walk away, stayed as close as possible, filled with the radiant acceptance of life, the joy of life, then this message of choice accompanies their being and enters into their leaving and into their karmic workings.

We speak what the masters have given to humanity through their experience of suffering, lack and fear, through the life conditions put upon them by humanity. ***They existed within those conditions in full expansion, the intact radiation of presence. Without words, this has been the greatest teaching human beings have witnessed.***

*What happens to the soul of a **drug addict**?*

Looking at the conditions in a soul that is using drugs heavily, we see that there is a deepening of unconsciousness, a deeper setting of roots into unconsciousness. A being is placing their will against consciousness and therefore against self. Placing their will against the consciousness of self and consciousness of all. This is an action of deep suffering. It is the action chosen from deep suffering. It is an action chosen from a suffering state that feels helpless and overcome, feels incapable of being free of the suffering. The conditions of a soul like this are conditions of defeat and the sense that there is not enough capacity or energy to move beyond the defeat. Therefore, the drugs are holding unconsciousness in place. Holding unconsciousness in place feels, temporarily, like a blessed reprieve from suffering.

What is happening to a soul? There is a deepening of the patterns of unconsciousness and the karma within that soul which will create a much longer journey to dispel unconsciousness either within the next embodiment, or next phase of the same embodiment. A debt is being created, where unconsciousness has been added to unconsciousness. It could be seen that the unconscious conditions of suffering are added to, by choosing the implement of defeat through drugs.

Yet a being in such strong conditions of suffering and defeat contains within them a power and intensity that 'looks like this' this time. An intensity or power of soul that has a need to take this path into the rocky depths of unconsciousness, not necessarily because they are weak, but because they need to see this, because they need to wear the cloak of defeat like this. Therefore, it is not for anyone to judge and say: "You are wrong." "You are weak." It is for others to observe the intensity at play, the creating of that crisis, and to know that the crisis comes to a breaking place. There is a place at which a soul can go no further into that darkness. There is a place where a soul knows a transition and knows that essentially there can be no more defeat, there is no death. There is no death and there is only one path and that is life and eternal existence.

Through the pain of watching someone in this condition, always respect the powerful learning that is in place. Always know that there is a transition ahead where that soul learns the lesson that all souls come to, that there is no death, there is only eternal life, there is no other choice but life. A soul that makes that corner and transition, will bound ahead with the same intensity and strength, knowing there is no more choice but this. The soul that we are glancing upon, through the questioner, is like this. Into the choosing of darkness, there will arise a choosing of light that is endless and not surpassed. We are to have hope, then, for any being in such suffering, and we are not to judge.

*We ask for more understanding of **suicidal addictions**, how to understand one who is destroying their life slowly through addiction, in a generalized description.*

One who is choosing this is bringing forward, from the depths of their being, the deepest hatred of self, the deepest denial of self, deep messages that they have been carrying through their course of lives. Though, from the outside, you look on with horror, pain, and helplessness, realize that each being is always working out their story by creating endings and beginnings, creating realization. Even when it appears tremendously traumatic and wrong, they are creating realization. There can be held in many beings, a death sentence that was given through a life or lives of: "You should not exist, you have no right to exist, you are unworthy to live, you are debris, you are condemned, you are wrong." So many souls carry this death sentence in their heart, in their being. So you can look around at this one's life, or that one's life and say: "Everything looks good around you, why are you doing this?" You don't see why, you don't see the surfacing death sentence that is coming up through the layers of their being, what they need to face, what they need to look at and conquer and how.

Perhaps this path of destruction is how. Perhaps suicide is how. If a being feels they shouldn't exist, and they stop their life, and then they are in their ever living being looking at their destroyed body, what do they learn? They learn that the condemnation was wrong, that every being always lives. Every being has the right, the full right to live forever, to live always. No being can take and condemn the reason to live for another. All that a being learns through a death this way, is poignant and beyond your sight. And your only action is to hold them in compassion and in full heart, giving the communication each and every time that: "You have the right to be all that you are to me. You have full permission to be the whole being that you are right now with me. To me you are perfect as you are, right now."

As we speak this, ***we are shown the great work of Mother Teresa, giving full validity to every being she encountered, no matter how destroyed, how defiled and broken, and shattered. She stood like the angel at the door, giving full validity:*** "You may pass, pass into life, pass into the fullness of being from now on."

The Holocaust

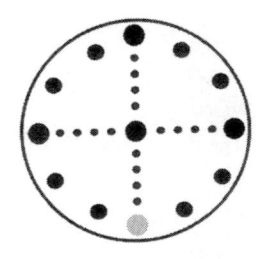

What has occurred for all the victims of the holocaust, for the souls of those who died in the holocaust and of the Germans who committed suicide following the war, who were also victims of that time. What is the ongoing understanding towards this tremendous segment of humanity that went through such massive death together?

The Guidance is taking me there and showing me the great field or space, yet it is like a field of light and succor or Grace, that every being was received to. It appears like a tremendous hospital of sweetness and light and cleanliness and silence. **Everything in almost exact opposite to the dark horror...even the smells of this place of light are attended to.** There is sweetness in the smells and every sense that was assaulted with horrifying intensity is there in its opposite in this field. We speak of it as an energetic field, the reception field for all those who died, whether they died as the killer or they died as the victim. The ones that died as the killers feel very little difference to the ones who died as the killed. The massive trauma in the soul, (massive meaning all at once, all together) rode in all beings no matter where they stood. Dying of hatred, dying being hated, dying with violence streaming through their being, or dying of the violence crushing their being. All are received into this field, which has a name. And they are first informed, instantly informed of the name of this field, this reception field that was specifically created at this time.

We are shown, in answer to the question, which again is a general question and so cannot be answered in detail, that there are many who could not see the field. There are many who were crouched, shall we say, even though their bodies are gone they still, as all beings do, sustain the sense of body following death. Especially a violent death or a death which holds a lot of confusion or suppression; a sense of the embodiment is retained. We see many of these beings crouched, crumpled, lying there unaware of the field of light that they are in. Spending time, we could say, or space of being, not knowing and needing to be attended to over and over and over. And we show the attendance, a certain touch on the brow within the sixth chakra of these beings. *They are touched over and over, as if touched with a dewdrop of exquisite light, over and over until the film leaves their eyes and they begin to see, hear and smell where they are. For some beings this took a long time.* For others who were more evolved, more strong in spirit and strong in heart, it was very quick. They had an instant sense of resurrection and an instant sense of awe and gratitude for the eternal nature of being-ness. They became helpers to all the others who were slumped in unconscious despair, unconscious trauma.

And so the field of light became a very active place for the evolution of all beings that came there. Many stayed and are still there, staying in service to those who are having a hard time waking up. And many have re-embodied, many have re-embodied with a readiness to exist in the fullness of truth, knowing that they have resurrected and left behind darkness forever. Many have re-embodied to work through a proving to themselves that they have the right to exist, seeking experiences of validation to heal the tremendous invalidation of dying that way. All souls who have passed through that specifically created field of Grace continue to feed each other, continue to find each other, for there was a unity born of that time.

For those who collapsed into the darkest emptiness of their being, not having the content of evolution within them to survive with awake-ness, it takes two to three embodiments for this validation, and for the full measure of believing that they can exist, and that they are an eternal being. And yet, as we said, the unity of all beings that have passed through that field enhances and speeds the evolution for all. Each one sheds their dark illusory cloak of believing that they shouldn't exist, and as each one is liberated into a sense of resurrection and powerful validity, so are all others touched, nudged, re-stroked at the sixth centre, re-stroked awake, nudged awake. None are lost. The message that each soul there learned, and each soul that even looks upon and witnesses, the message that endures and that sits now in the soul of the human being, is that *there is no*

room for darkness such as that, ever again. There is no room for the lie of invalidating another being, ever again. And there is no place for the segregation of beings, the hierarchy of who is valid and who is not, who is superior and who is inferior. There is no place in the human soul now for this to lodge. This was the birth pang, the labour movement of the birth of unity, which will unfold in the next two to three embodiments of all beings who were there.

Challenges in Healing

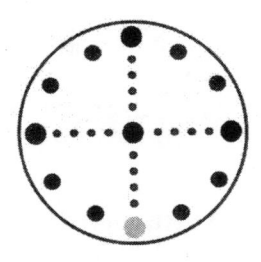

*We wish to understand more about **personality disorder** and what it really is in the human being.*

The Guidance is quickly taking me to the identity formation, the personality formation in a lifetime. It is saying that your egoic self is not in the Greater Identity of the soul, that moves into lifetime after lifetime. Egoic self is the temporary personality shaping that occurs in childhood, the beginning of a lifetime. This personality shaping is an integral relationship to the world, shaping the personality to meet the world that one is in. Learning to respond to the world, to have power within it, to claim it and to enter it. Understand personality as a window that is being built to see the world through. It is a window of uniqueness, voice, presence, and shape through which one sees the world and is seen by the world. It is an interface. Personality is a temporary interface, a character, a shaping to meet the world through, and be met through.

A personality disorder is where this formation has been traumatized and disturbed highly. That is all! Disturbed significantly enough that the shaping can't settle. There cannot be a settled sense of "this is what I am" and "this is the shape that I've made." Therefore, they can't be seen from the outside: What is the shape of this person? What are they? What is their feeling? When a human being looks at another, they sense the other being's personality window in many ways; they sense it with every nerve ending, they sense it with their emotion, they receive it through their eyes, they smell, they hear. There is an entire way to see what the other being is making, what shape is in front of them. **One with a person-**

ality disorder is not presenting a unified, cohesive shape. It is a shifted shape, a fractured shape; therefore they never receive the affirming attentions and energies from the outside. They receive confusion, rejection, they receive fear, and the sense of not being safe, for another human being will not feel safe around a fractured window and they cannot base any continuing relationship on a fractured window.

Realize that the personality shape, or window, is also the way the individual evolves their being during their life. Through creating this shape and this character, they interact with the world and continually learn the lessons of truth and of eternal nature. When they cannot present a unified shape of being, they cannot receive the messages in any continuity, they cannot develop the understanding of trust, and they cannot trust anything they receive.

One with a personality disorder is truly an ill and injured being. Usually they will not live very long, because when the personality is fractured the immune system also cannot operate. It cannot operate in the fullness of itself. The entire physical embodiment is vulnerable, and the lower wavelengths of anxiety, fear and anger are paramount. It's as though the nature builds it in, that a being that cannot shape an identity of wholeness and wellness and intactness also cannot host a very protective immune system. The immune system is another personality. It is the one who identifies the body, maintains and sustains the identity and personality of the body. When it receives the fractured messaging, it cannot protect this body.

There is more in the deeper description of a being that needs to manifest this way, or that has manifested this way, but this is individual information always. Why does a soul enter into conditions that fracture it and live a short and fractured life? This answer is individual every time, bringing forward a need in their greater, deeper being to experience that. It all goes towards their development and evolution, and in the end it all goes towards Grace.

We ask about the emotional expression of children, particularly when they lose control of their emotions, either in anxiety or in anger, and enter a hyperactive emotional state. How can we understand and cope with this as parents, and how can we help or guide them.

The human nervous system is in a generalized state of swift refinement. Permission is being given by 'consciousness', in the parents and within mankind at this time. It is not the same everywhere, but there is a great sum of mankind becoming conscious. In this greater consciousness there is the invitation or permission to use more of the nervous system's capacity and to use more of this embodiment for the expression of soul and evolution. The children of this time and the children we speak of who are exhibiting extreme emotional behavior, are breaking into new territory in the use of the nervous system. They are in higher use of their nervous system and they have a bigger map. In the bigger map of the nervous system, there is unknown territory and new parameters. There is permission through the love of the parents, in that there isn't a punishment or restriction, no closing the doors to their child and his/her expression. From the start, there is no signaling that they must be silent, that they must not exist in this way. Even though the parents may respond in anger and frustration and confusion and be highly stressed by this behavior, at the outset and in the core of their love and consciousness, they have already given a full permission and invitation to these beings to express themselves and be more fully here.

In general, you are witnessing a new learning of the use of the embodiment. You are not only mothers and fathers, you are witnesses, you are teachers, you are students you are learning a new embodiment in watching your children. The very thing they may express is what you have held in and what was never expressed. The very sensitivities that are triggers, the feelings they carry have been in you too, but not allowed, not known. The nervous system pathways, which they are running down full tilt, are the pathways in your nervous system that you haven't tried. You are teacher, you are student and you are mother. ***You are being evolved by your children.***

The first answer is to have compassion and greater consciousness and understanding of what you are witnessing before you, compassion with the difficulty, compassion with the newness and undeveloped nature of this. Have compassion for yourself with your own nervous system opening up to new experiences and new levels. Compassion is the route, the first step. Compassion that is not just due to love, but is because of consciousness and an awareness that the human being is evolving swiftly now. ***What you see now is the crude beginning behavior of a great intelligence, an articulateness and expressiveness that will surpass what you have yet seen.*** It is an expressiveness that needs all these new nerve endings and needs new pathways for the intensity, for the message and the becoming.

What you are witnessing is the difficult birthing of yet more consciousness, more intelligence in this human being. This is compassion with wisdom, with knowing: "I am watching the tearing pains of the birthing of a very intelligent being, a capacious being that can feel more than I even know how to feel and will make conclusions of consciousness that I have not yet made, who will weave together emotional and intellectual awareness as one and will understand the unity of it all far faster than I."

What is your role, then? Your role is to stand steady in this wise compassion, knowing what you are seeing. What would you do if you were at a difficult physical birth with crying, with injury, with trauma? What would you do as the midwife, as the nurse, as the doctor? You would have compassionate wisdom, knowing what you are seeing. You are watching a difficult birth and your role is to be steady and present. To give as much soothing assistance and strength and steadying and perspective as you could: "It will be fine, it will be good, you will live through this. You will come through this, this will pass." You would lend the vision of the next moment, the stable moment. You would lend comfort of the stability of what is to come. You would witness the difficulty and you would be there to create the moment of stability. You would be the usher through the difficult passage to the safe shore because you would have compassionate wisdom of knowing that there is a safe shore and that you *are* in a crossing.

Therefore, as a parent, needing to have the steady greater sight of the solid shore, which can literally be the next moment, the next hour, the next day, knowing that children are in a great crossing, a great passage. Recognizing that sometimes the passage is of a greater intensity than at other times, going through the phases of childhood development where there is faster process and a slower recovery and then an entering into another process. As parents, become wisdom beings, ones who are used to looking at the bigger landscape, used to looking at a process from a height and being able to notice: "Ah, the valley, the hill, the tangle, the clearing." Knowing that you are there to be the sentinel, the one who can 'see', the one who can always be found, who is looking at the bigger picture and can note and mark: "This is a difficult time, but you will get through it. This is part of the journey that we are all on." Giving perspective, lending stability and giving a sense of passage or hope, this is all part of what love will contain. Never is there a moment where there is not love and sense. There is not one moment that is accepted in love and one that isn't, one that is embraced into the whole and the other that is rejected. There is no rejection.

For the parent who is under duress: to have the moments of coming to the hilltop, the greater perspective, the deepening understanding of the process they are witnessing and the hope and vision that they need. Coming back renewed and sourced with the vision of what this being is becoming, that there is nothing essentially wrong. As souls evolve with such swiftness as they do now, they are processing and releasing karma from before this life, in very active, intense forms, through illness and behavioral extremity. This is what it looks like to go more closely into the centre of the river and to move more swiftly in evolution, to be cleansed and stripped away, to not be able to retreat and stay behind a boulder and move slowly and unnoticeably.

Realize, as parents of children at this time, that you are all midwives of the birthing of intelligence and consciousness, with which you were not printed and have not seen. It is new. ***It is like walking through a garden and thinking you knew the time period of this plant moving towards its flowering, towards its fruiting and instead you see this sprout growing swiftly and taller than ever, going through illnesses and processes you have never seen, yet bearing fruit you have never seen.*** Your role is to nurture and do all that you know that is in love's nature. This is all that is being required of you. You are there to give and you are there to learn. You are there to partake of a fruit that you have not yet even seen.

*We want to understand whether the diagnosis in children of **Attention Deficit Disorder** or autism is a chemical condition or a soul condition?*

The Guidance is bringing me to a visual of the current, the electrical conscious current in the nervous system in an example child that has been given the diagnosis of the inability to focus, of the nervous system discharging, and of hyperactivity. So in an example child, which is rather too general (but so then is the question) it will be answered this way. The Guidance is quickly pointing out that in each individual child there is an individual root and reason, and this is quite varied. The term ADD should be wiped right off because it is much too general, not defining enough of what is really occurring and yet there is a general set of symptoms and so there is a general answer.

The nervous system is shown like a map in its actuality, it's branching, showing its core river, its core stream of current from the brain outward to the embodiment. The Guidance is showing how the sensors in the brains of those currently being born are, by an increment, more open. This varies in degree, depending upon the conditions and nurturing in infancy (the conditions of silence and peace). If there are conditions of peace during infancy, the openings can be accommodated, openings that are developing in the sensory system, in all human beings for the gathering of information. With peace there can be adjustment and allowing of the incremental opening that is evolving. There can be the integration of how much is brought in through the sensing. The integrating is very definite and very chemical; in every level it is a chemical description. If we return to speaking of how the nerve paths open up in the brain, this correlates. There are new nerve pathways opening up in the conscious brain and therefore in the whole sensory system.

If there is enough nurturing and silence provided in infancy, the incremental increase of sensing and opening is integrated, built in and operated/acted upon, and the incoming being can use this embodiment to sense more, integrate more and identify more. It all goes together: the sensing, the integrating and then the identifying. So as the generalized infants are born with this evolution of more opening to their sensory system, they must integrate that. They will sense more than their parents, they will hear, feel and know more. They will sense sometimes a small amount more and sometimes a great amount more than their parents. If they are left in enough silence, acceptance and nurturing (even physical and nutritional) then this integration occurs. The nervous system develops itself around the information with ease and the child identifies their being around that ease.

If within this integration time of infancy up to 6 or 7 years old (within the first 10 years, but greatly at the beginning) there are conditions of silence (we use the English word 'silence' but it is a much greater meaning; it is a spreading out of the senses, that can spread as far as they will without being stopped) then the infants nervous system senses a vastness around them with no borders. The walls, the atmosphere within the home does not stop this spreading out, this sensing of "I am in this great sea of energy and presence." If this is being infracted, impinged on, or disrupted continually we still have the incremental openings in the sensory system, which means we still have the increased amount of sensing and of taking in, yet there is no integration and identifying. This then becomes a very disturbed nervous system that gathers in more than it can integrate and manifest. It is energy that needs to be discharged and released. It becomes an irritation to even live and sense anything at all. It is as though you kept feeding yourself and you couldn't digest it or eliminate it, but you continued to feed yourself. This evolved nervous system keeps taking in and feeding itself and yet can do nothing with it.

This is the generalized description of what you asked about. The children in disruption, with disrupted nervous systems, are in a disrupted process of evolution, the evolution of this newer nervous system that is opening and gathering more but has nowhere to go. It has no channels and no provision for what it is receiving.

The drugs given for this condition decrease the beings ability to receive, and therefore remove the pressure of what is being taken in. The drugs are putting that person backwards into the state of being that existed before this evolutionary shift of incremental opening.

It is built in to evolution that it would be like this, this is evolution; evolution comes into cross currents with itself all the time. It is built into evolution that there will be challenges at transitory times. This is built into the deeper knowing, this breaking through into new territory.

Any one of these children at any point in their lifetime can utilize and become what they are born to be. Any time one of these children is brought into the setting of nurturance, of silence and of consciousness, they are ready to grow, like a seed that sits with a hard coat through deserts, lasting for years, and then finally starts to grow. Through all the trauma of the inability to grow, what is held in that being sits latent and ready and will begin to grow whenever the conditions are there. Even if a whole lifetime goes by and there is no true manifestation for that evolution, that readiness is held. It's as though it just waits until the external conditions say 'yes'.

When the energy is dammed and held back, or discharges, sometimes uncontrollably, when the provision is not there and that being cannot manifest the evolution of the higher sensory input and development, it builds as a pressure in that soul. It builds as an impetus, a momentum in that soul. So that when the conditions are there, if it is in this lifetime or not, there is a sudden movement, a readiness to 'be'.

Know that there is no loss, do not grieve. Know that you are witnessing the evolution of consciousness. Know that the pressure put upon the elders, teachers or parents is exact, the questions being pushed up: "What this is?", "How do we deal with this?", "What is going on here?". It is exact; everyone is evolving. But these children will not go away and the parents will know that the drugs are not real help. It is the love in the families, the love in the parents that will provide the conditions eventually. As those conditions become so universal and the lack of right conditions within the school systems, within the culture become so obvious. This is the evolution of consciousness you are witnessing. The children will lead the way. Listen to the children.

An image: The children with hammers; hammering down the structures. Breaking down the walls that trap the human identity in its smallness. It is the children that will break those walls.

End of Life

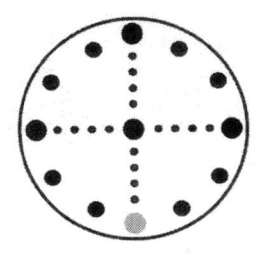

*What purposes are being met, in the end of life, with **dementia and Alzheimer's**? We want to have more understanding of the soul's process at that time of life.*

The Guidance is showing me visually the inactivation of the brain and the inactivation of the paths of consciousness within the brain and nervous system that occurs with Dementia or Alzheimer's. They are showing the regions of the brain that are most susceptible and vulnerable, showing an image of the dissolving of the consciousness to a lifetime. With dementia, Alzheimer's, senility or stroke, we can reframe the process as the dissolving of the identity and consciousness of an embodiment or lifetime.

The process of dissolving the identity is a law and a dynamic that can occur in many ways. It can occur within the lifetime and it always occurs after the lifetime. It can occur as a grace filled process, a controlled and conscious process, or it can occur as an unconscious process either within the lifetime or after. It is a mark of unconscious process when there is a state of dementia or Alzheimer's, yet a dissolving never the less. Dissolving is the law. The identity associated with the lifetime must dissolve for the soul to come forward and for the greater consciousness of being to hold the center.

Consider the myriad of paths of dissolving. Consider the many ways that the identity could dissolve itself so that the soul's presence and identity can come forward. In the dying of a body, and the dying of a brain, there is instantaneous dissolution and according to the conscious capacity of the being, there can be the sudden, swift infilling of the greater familiarity of soul presence. To one that is not consciously prepared it can seem like a dream. It is a dream in which they really don't know if they will be awakening or not, a dream that is held like a dim sense of being.

In the case of Alzheimer's, or in the case of mental breakdown, the dissolving is being chosen within the life format. There are strong purposes for this. There is the strong need, in general, to return to the last place where one felt truly identified or safe. There is the need, effort, or desire, to return to the last place where identification was comfortable, real and safe. There is the returning to a starting point where the sense of 'I am-ness' felt unquestioned and where the personal sense of reality felt the strongest. There is returning to the source in one's own being where they last felt the most who they are, felt the most 'I am-ness.'

These two names, Alzheimer's and Dementia, are disease processes but yet they are not. They are chosen paths of dissolution and dissolving. To choose dissolving within a life creates the 'going-back' within that life to the last solid strong hold of 'I am-ness,' and leaving the life from that place. They are striving to leave life from the strongest place of 'I am-ness.' This is an unconscious choice and process. It is the dying, it is the dissolving while still in the life body, and it is the beginning of the return to the last strong hold of 'I am-ness' within the life body.

When a being dies, there is the return to the last strong hold of 'I am-ness' within their experience of being. Swiftly, finding them selves where they felt the most solid. Where they have the best vantage point to grasp and to integrate all the changes that come with shifting of realities and the center point of consciousness can mean.

Following death there is always a flight, like a swift wing-feather to the most solid place of being that they can find. To a conscious being, dying in great consciousness, there is no movement; their solid place of presence was continuous right through the dropping of the body, there is no movement. It is like moving through a windowpane, the 'I am-ness' is unchanged. **The greater the consciousness, the less difference there is between being embodied and not being embodied.** There is a great stillness of presence that is unchanged by death and there is less need for embodiment.

Dementia and Alzheimer's are a mark of the unconscious. They are following the great pull of tide back to source, the great tide of movement ever onwards to 'I am-ness.' Following it still, in the life body. Being called, as though bidden, into that vantage point and place of integration. Upon death, one who is in a state of Alzheimer's or of advanced dementia doesn't know they have died. They have already died and their embodiment can no longer register the difference between being in the physical form or not. They would begin to know they had passed because the confining conditions were gone. They would go to the strong hold of 'I am-ness' and they would begin to expand, move and evolve there. Where as, if they were to go back to the strong hold within the life, there would be no movement. There is stagnancy in sitting at that point of being at whatever age that was, and there is no movement. It is the stagnancy itself that signals the life force to leave in an unconscious being. After the move to the safe place of 'I am-ness,' the last remembered place of wholeness, stagnancy begins to overtake the nervous system and the life force and so comes death.

You ask of the purposes. For every being, the purpose is always to move forward into greater and greater consciousness of the true being that they are.

Following the passing of one who has died in an unconscious way, there is the very slow process of realizing the difference between their embodiment and their undying nature. Then there is the realization, the experiential remembering of the stagnancy and what led to the stagnancy. There is the remembering of existing without consciousness in the life body and it sits as a personal karma, a personal prod and mission to go forward with great life awareness and life current moving through the being. There is more vigilance built in, more sensors and readiness built in towards stagnancy and towards lapsing into periods of unconsciousness. Therefore the purpose is that the personal karma creates more urgency and sensitivity to stagnancy and unconsciousness.

Often the next embodiment is a dynamic embodiment with a resistance to unconscious patterns and a resistance against the desire to stay behind a boulder where it is safe. A dynamic pull to enter the current of life with more vigor, risk and seeking. ***Every obstacle that a being creates for itself becomes the prod to be free of that obstacle, like a karma that sets conditions for the next embodiment.***

Beyond this, the purposes and the reasons cannot be answered in a general way. For each soul there are purposes. Purposes like having life taken away swiftly and traumatically (in a past life). In many instances in the world now, our elders are souls who had life, in previous incarnations, taken away traumatically. Before they were ready their life was violently robbed from them and cut from them. It was taken from them and it left the raw edge of grief, anguish and helplessness. Their purposes are to meet the grace of living without trauma and without a sudden sense of being robbed of life. They are moving through the experience of a soft diminuendo and crescendo following death. Grace is at hand for many of these ones you look at, they are having the experience of grace, of being cared for, and of their life being supported rather than taken away.

All this is being marked in their soul, noted, like a debt that being embodied owed to them. Too many traumatic endings, too many lives bursting apart with the cry "I'm not ready, I wasn't finished, I just began." Having the opposite experience of being able to walk life out to the very thin, thin ending. This sets, as we said, another karma in the soul's path on their way to a balanced consciousness.

You cannot judge, for you cannot see the purposes being met in an individual, but you can know that the purposes are being met.

What is the best way **to help someone in the end stage of life,** *when the quality of life is gone?*

Guidance shows that the most potent powerful action in assisting someone at the end of life is simply being present, simply being in full acceptance of the stage they are at, and of the challenges and difficulties of every element of that stage. Not being in rejection, or horror. No revulsion, no avoidance, no denial, just full acceptance of that being in that condition. **Being present with that being, practicing a full receptivity to their state, with acceptance.** This communicates to them in every way, verbally if it's spoken, energetically if it is just held within you - not to resist, not to fear, not to feel this is wrong. It is not wrong to go through the deconstruction of one's life.

The deconstructing stage of a life is not wrong, it is highly important. Even going through it slowly can be very important for the soul. Although the experience cannot be witnessed from the outside, much is occurring within that being. The emancipation and freeing of their consciousness, the deconstruction of their identity, the deconstruction of all they have created in their human ego-self, are vital stages. It is very potent when this occurs while still in the life-body. It is a sign of strength and readiness in a soul to be going through this while still embodied, a sign that this soul can bear the weight. The ego-structure dissolving while still in the physical form is very potent to the soul's progression. Deconstructing physically, the loss of mobility, deconstructing mentally and deconstructing one's identity are all very powerful to the soul's progression, none of which can be seen by you, for you will not be there to see the fruits of this. You are there to witness the pain, the horror and the fear that it may cause in others and in that being.

In light of knowing that this deconstructing is significantly useful, and beneficial to the soul's progression, be present in full acceptance. Be present, be witness in full agreement. "This is what is occurring for you, this is what is needed by you." Communicate no distaste, no pity, nor that there is anything wrong. Pure witness and pure acceptance is a very powerful stance with one who is deconstructing. It communicates peace and a yielding to the process, allowing an attitude of rightness. It is an honouring. To accept any person in their process, in the full state of witness is to honour that person at a moment when they would dishonour themselves with rejection, with being embroiled in resistance. It gives them the greatest aid, messaging to them to honour their crisis, to honour the moment they're in.

*We are asking to understand the repercussions of **assisted death** for the soul of the person with a terminal prognosis, choosing it to end their suffering and for the caregivers who assist them.*

Surprisingly, the Guidance starts with a smile, because there is a real recognition of a wisdom emerging in its early stages through this question. The worry and concern over so many coming into prolonged life, when their life is hanging on a thread and their consciousness is minimal, when their physical form can no longer host their being without tremendous effort from others. The worry and concern that so much of the humanity in the western world is coming into these phases of prolonged assisted life, shall we say. Whereas in the bulk of human evolution, the recognition in the immune system, in the soul, in the embodiment towards the end of a lifetime was clearer and more succinct, and there was not the possibility for assisted life. Now with the development of assisted life, there are those living past the point of their departure, not recognizing the message in their being of departure, the ending and completion, or even if they have recognized it this isn't recognized by the family and society.

Once a being has bypassed the whirlpool and stepped beyond their departure, they are in a decreasing consciousness state. They truly have less possibility and potential in their lifetime and their consciousness departs slowly, bit by bit. Their physical form is no longer being supported by a conscious immune system, by a conscious defense system. Their physical capacity and health decreases to a point where there is very little recognition between the soul and the embodiment. *There is tremendous suffering as the physical form is being assisted to live past its point of completion.*

We could put the question right back outwards as the rightness of assisted life, not assisted dying. If assisted death is to be understood, then so should assisted life. The smile that started here points to the wisdom that needs to be re-found, needs to be truly found whereby a being truly understands their completion, they understand their moment, understand when it is over and time to dissolve this life embodiment. Not fearing the avenue, the manifestation of illness that may be the way this departure is being chosen. In the higher forms of this choice there is the stepping back from the life body, stepping back from the need to nurture it. Stepping back in peace and without suffering. Turning off the mechanism that is constantly seeking to nurture the life body, turning off the appetite and the engagement with life force within the physical form without suffering and without illness, without anguish and without fear. This is the smile. This is the wisdom that needs to be learned. This is the assisted death, assisted by one's own consciousness. The self-recognition, whether it be in mind or permeated through from the soul, that this is enough, that this life can dissolve peacefully.

Again, the smile is that this is what is coming and this is the result of the worry and the concern of a humanity that is becoming very conscious. The natural recognition of the moment of completion and the understanding of what the physical organism has already learned when it recognizes this, learning from the animal world, learning from the past. There is a built-in knowing within the soul and its embodiment when it is over and a way to support the manifestation of that completion.

We have preceded the answer to the question around assisted death, its karma and implications, with the former, for you to see that to choose death is a natural mechanism of the closure of an incarnation. For a being to choose death when they know it is over, and their knowledge of over-ness is in wisdom and peace, not anger, nor defeat, nor fear. In the lens of anger, defeat, or fear there is no clarity and no true knowledge. In the lens of peace and wisdom, there is a deep accessing to the mechanism of true knowledge of over-ness. When a being knows that their embodiment is over, that their life force cannot flow through this nervous system, that there is only continuing and increasing suffering in supporting the physical body, there is no karma in choosing assisted death. There is no wrongness in the soul knowing it is over and in the being choosing over-ness. There is no wrongness in the care-givers assisting that death.

The bottom line in the assessment of rightness is that it is a peaceful choice, a choice of power. It may not be peaceful, in that the one is in agony, but it is a choice of peace because it is a choice of power and of quality, a choice that is coming from the soul of that being that knows it is over, it is done and their mission and purpose within this incarnation can go no further. There may be much that is not done, much that is unfinished, but each lifetime is not a full completion for a soul. It is only a chapter, a moment. When there can be no more found, lived, accomplished, when nothing more can go towards the being's evolution, this is an over-ness. We are not to judge this over-ness from our minds, and we are never to judge this over-ness for another. We must reach into that one and listen to know if they sense, if they can tell that it is enough for now, not enough for ever, but enough for now. This incarnation can bear no more, can move no further, and can develop itself no further.

So, assisted death, what is it? Is it the injection of a drug that stops the heart, or is it the stopping of assisted life? Is it the permission for a being to agree with their self, that they want no more nutrition? In the times to come, there needs to be an assessment, which comes from hearing and sensing into that patient, into that person, that choice of power, that indication from them as soon as possible, that yes, it is over; yes, I wish to go. The counsel to the family and those around, that there is no fear in over-ness, that it is a natural mechanism for the soul to know its time to leave its embodiment, that it is enough for now. As humanity learns that it is only for now, that the continuation of every being is a surety and that there is needed by that being a whole new embodiment, a whole new phase for continuance, then there is the peace on the part of those letting go.

Assisted death is a far more subtle description. It is the whole web of relationships that respect and listen to that being saying that it is enough for now.

The Physics of Consciousness

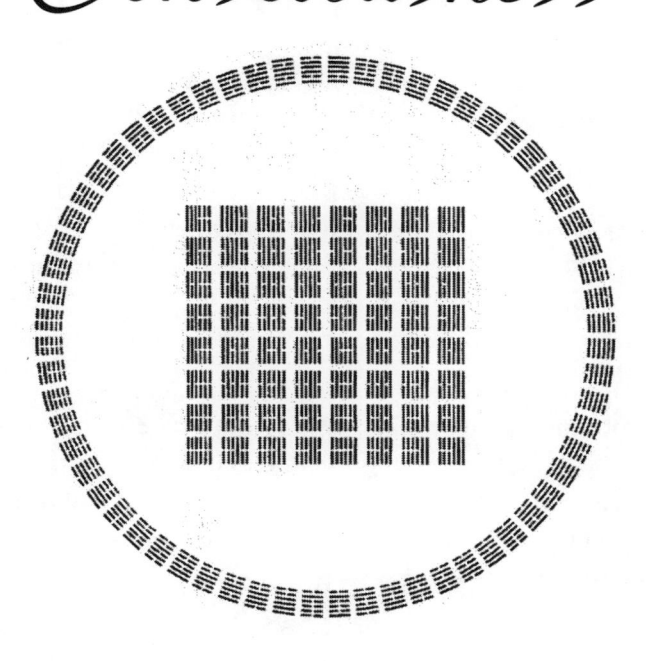

The State of Meditation

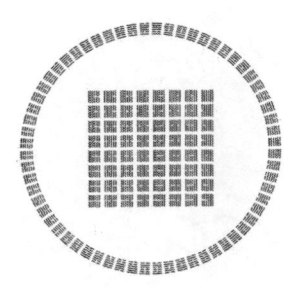

Do meditative states of being affect the physiological state of the brain? If so, what sorts of effects occur from continually going into meditation?

How does the state of mind that is being hosted (created) most continually create the actuality of the brain? How is this brain activated, what is the tissue state of the brain, how is that affected by the state of consciousness that is most often maintained by the individual. (This is a reframing of the group's question.)

We are looking at the strata of wavelength reception and which areas of the brain the information and energy course through to its places of conclusion or summation of awareness. Quite literally, at this wavelength description you can see where the brain is most exercised and active and known in itself.

There is inert brain, inert pathways. Pathways that sit like microscopic threads that have never had a current flow through them. They sit mapped in the brain, never used. The whole map of the entire full state of consciousness is there (in potential), yet there has never been a current of conscious energy moving through that path.

As one with commitment chooses to deepen in awareness, to come into more truth, through the yearning of their heart, in remembrance and soul, and as they practice and apply a method to creating the growth in this awareness state or mind state of being-ness, so do these little threads of neuronal mapping start to grow. They actually grow, expand and activate. First they are nudged, and then they must be nudged again and again. After a certain amount of nudging, the cells come out of their inertness and become living cells. It then nudges the next. Nudges come first, life comes second. Then the cells are ready to transmit the current. It takes time for the pathway to light up and grow. Then it takes time for that transmission of conscious energy to be understood and integrated. It takes time for there to be a shift in the "I am-ness," identity and the entire reality that the mind through the brain has established. ***It takes time, but these are the actual neuronal changes that occur through continuing with commitment and successful practice, the expanding of the awareness.*** There is actually a need for different nutrient levels; there is a re-arrangement for how nutrients are used in the nervous system. Once the pathways have been built, it changes again. Energy is required to move into the frontiers of these neuronal maps. Nutrients are needed to protect the development of these paths.

We could say, the normal stress state that the human and the animal can experience is an antithesis, it pulls away and keeps the being from having that extra amount of energy and availability of nutrients to develop these regions of the brain. The experience of safety is needed in the human nervous system. Peace and the absolute sense of timing. When there is safety at the lowest wavelength and there is peace above that, and then in the mind consciousness level there is the sense of the ultimate rightness of the timing. Then these pathways develop most quickly. This is the medium needed below for these finer pathways to open and grow. There is purpose in that.

As people choose to open themselves to lower wavelength, the message into the whole being is: you're still here. You still need more evolution and strengthening in order to not choose these lower realities. It is all based on a choice, choosing how to see each day, choosing what to do with it. As the higher wavelength choices are being made, i.e. choosing peace/love/grace/safety for others and oneself, there is the silence, the quieting of all the lower wavelength regions as they become inactive. The former being is really no longer there. There is then the natural growth and unfolding of the higher more subtle regions of the brain.

Now, to speak a bit about non-embodied consciousness and embodied consciousness: When the body falls away, what is really falling away from the soul is the lower form of awareness: all the fear for safety on the physical level, all the relationships to the physical reality, the separation from oneself and other beings on the physical level. You lose the visual, auditory and sensory levels of consciousness. What one is left with is a certain sublime sense of being that is then dependant on how far into that sublime sense of being the individual has developed their awareness. For some it sits like a soft orb, a softly present place of "I am-ness" almost sleeping. But for a Master who has developed the full sense of "I am all", they have infused that sense into their being, and are operating within the whole of their potential.

And yet at that most subtle wavelength of "I am all" there is no molecular nature to that. There is no need for embodiment. No need to forge through the layers of wavelength. There can be a descent into human brain if chosen, and a full use of human capacity for the purpose of serving lower wavelength states (an awakened being may choose to incarnate to serve humanity). Realize that when you die what you retain is the finest edge, the highest wavelength of your created state of being. You keep the best of your efforts!

*How do we nurture and bring forward the elements of **safety, peace, and timing**, which were described as a prerequisite condition to further conscious development? Please speak more on the development of the unused portions of the brain which are ready to host more consciousness.*

The Guidance is showing the three most important components that require constant attending to. You are human, and being human in this still crude world, you can easily be activated **to not feel safe**, to question safety in this world, if not safety for yourself, safety for humanity and for others. You can still be triggered **to not be in peace**, to be in disruption, to be in anguish, to be troubled, to be lost in not seeing the greater purposes, the greater unfolding. If you are not in a sense of safety and if you are in a state of disruption and not in a state of peace, the subtler level of your being stays silent and responds only when knowing that the time is right for conscious expansion. (The continued state of peace is a prerequisite for conscious expansion). They follow each other: **safety**, then **peace**, and then **expansion**.

We began this by saying, you must constantly attend, and you must constantly be ready and patient and willing to attend to the first two components, safety and peace. Attending to that can mean taking that sense of un-safety into question: "Do I need to feel unsafe? Why is this feeling here? What can I do with this feeling?" Opening up the level of un-safety to your higher wisdom. Realizing, and teaching the first level of self that it can indeed feel safe, that it doesn't need to feel unsafe. Bringing the wisdom into that level where un-safety is felt, and being ever willing to attend to that. Defining: "What is safety really? What is the safety that is really truly needed? Is it physical safety? Is it the safety of not being hungry, of being warm or having a home?" "And if you are starving, and you are cold and you have no home, does that mean that you can have no expansion, does that mean that you must forgo peace?" These are big questions and they have been met in many ways. There are those that have been locked in cold prisons that have learned peace and moved into expansion. There are those that have no food and have bypassed the physical sense of the need for safety and discovered eternal peace, discovered the eternal nature that does not depend on the body, the eternal self that visits the embodiment but is not dependent upon it. We are hoping that in these descriptions you will hear your answer. "What is peace, really? Is peace what can be experienced when the body is full and warm and the relationships are in place and there is contentment humanly? Is that peace? And if all those things aren't there can there be no peace? What is peace?"

Realize that the undying peace, the peace that is a stroke of brilliance, that is a movement into full consciousness is a peace that is tested by loss, it is tested by not having the human elements in place. It is the peace that is forged and discovered because *the core of one's being **IS** peace.* It is as though if all was taken away, the only thing left is peace. It is an expansion of being-ness, it is a liberation that never needed physical safety or relationships to create contentment, never needed consistent meals and a roof. This is the most powerful peace, the most powerful expansion; it is the being that realizes ultimately the essential human nature.

Now your task in this place of plenty is to have gratitude and simplicity, to realize that you are physically, humanly safe but that it is not your premise. Realize that you have every opportunity for safety and peace, and yet you won't lean or rely on it in the temporary. You will use the gift of this plenty to say: "This has been done, I have a roof. This has been done, I don't need to forge my expansion and sense of peace in the cold corner of the dungeon." "I won't wait for those conditions, I don't need those tests, I will choose to commit this life of grace to expansion. I will choose to realize that the lasting sense of safety and peace that is needed to go into expansion is all held within my being, and is dependant on nothing from the outside." And as the being realizes this, the ultimate answer to feeling safe, to feeling peace, to feeling free, is to be who you are in the most essential description. This then is the timing, the third component, and the timing is simply where the river fans out into the delta and emerges into the sea unobstructed and free. The river comes to the great expansiveness and just flows wide and merges.

By choosing over and over in your days, to come into the ultimate sense of safety and peace in your human-ness, you come into this delta, you signal the timing and you move into expansion. If you don't have enough money for a bill, meet that first by going into meditation, not for an answer as to where the money will come from, but to attend to the lack of your sense of safety and peace that not having enough money can create. **Establish again the ultimate safety and peace of being in your essential nature, and attend to the lack of money, just as a material condition of a temporary nature.** If you are listening to a newscast that disturbs you and unsettles how safe we are here, before you go into your social action or your worry, go into meditation. Go into the essential safe peaceful place of your greater being. Then go into your social action or your discussions without the angst and without the worry.

All beings are the same, they all hold the ultimate safety, and they all exist eternally. There are none condemned, none favored, and all who are traumatized or scarred will heal. Life after life, all continue to move towards liberation. Attend to the work in this world from a place of peace, from the perspective of the vast unfolding of beauty, not from the place of anxiety, worry and fear, for this stops the signaling of timing. This prevents the development of your being into expansion.

*What happens in the human being when in the **state of true meditation**?*

First, I am shown the activity of the mind when it is not in meditation, the normal activity of the normal waking mind and the normal activity of the emotional being. Showing what this normal activity is doing in the energy picture, showing where the energy is drawn to, where the life force is drawn to, where the consciousness is drawn to and the nervous system activity is drawn to. The wavelength patterns of the normal active mind and the ever-ready active emotional system keep the whole physicality at a certain pitch, at a certain state of suspension. The normal active human mind, the daily mind, is keeping the entire physical system in a movement of alertness and readiness to engage outwardly. ***The normal state of mind is almost always engaging outwardly.*** Focused always outside, as though one sits separate from what is all around and is in continual interaction with what is around; everyone, everything, every color, every shape and every sound. ***Everything is highly defined on the outside versus the one who is watching.*** It is a separation, and this engagement towards the outside suspends the whole physicality, the whole nervous system and the whole consciousness at a certain level of being. It is defined by the outside, defined by everybody around and what is happening around.

This definition is not just a simple word; this definition is a state of consciousness that is defined by all that is occurring around, that sound, that movement, those words, this weather and that news. The identity of the self is continually receiving reference, and input, and identifying itself around what is coming from the outside. This is suspending the consciousness in a dependency on the surroundings. "I am according to that which is around me and I am identified according to that which is around me."

With every system within the human organism or any animal organism, once a state has been repeated it becomes a pattern. The pattern is the way that the physical organism sustains itself with less energy. If one had to continually create the response, continually create the interaction it would require tremendous amounts of energy. But physical organisms quickly learn patterns that then become an unconscious, habitual response. Therefore the identity, defined by the surroundings, has become habitual; it is a pattern. You are patterned to identify yourself according to what is around you and what is happening around you and your state of consciousness is suspended in that pattern.

In meditation, in true learned meditation, one is learning to disengage from the outer stimulus and from the outer definition in the physical world. Learning to disengage that one's being is separate and outside, and that all these shapes, forms, sounds and happenings are separate and on the outside. Learning to disengage the entire definition of one's being. Quieting the mind brings freedom from the mind. Quieting the emotional system brings the freeing of the emotional system. These are the learned ways of meditation; learning to not be bound, not be subjugate to mind activity, emotional activity or sensory activity. Learning to re-identify the consciousness, the being-ness as not separate from, but intimately within and part of. Learning to come into the indestructible, eternal identity. The being that is there when the outer forms fall away. The being that is left when there are no outer embodiments, when there is no physical embodiment; the indestructible being that sits in its truest, purest identity.

To learn to come into the truest, purest identity while in the physical form through learning and consciously choosing to dissolve the pattern and to disengage from the habitual nature of the pattern is to develop strength of consciousness that is everlasting. Strength of consciousness that can walk among the world of forms and yet be free. Can walk amongst the world of form and other humans and be part of, be sensitive, be empathetic, be sensing deeply, touching, expanding, giving and gracing the apparent outer world because it is not an outer world. It is all an internal world. *The one who learns the true conscious state, who enters into a true meditation, expands their identity and their definition to include all beings.* Not to say there is not individuality in all these millions of forms, all these millions of eyes, there is both the individuality and the intimacy. There is the likeness and there is the differentiation. The likeness is the Namaste; there is the true Namaste with all created form, the God-state that is inherent and is breathing within all.

In true meditation then, the finer nervous system, the entire nervous system, endocrine system, the whole physicality changes its energy patterns, rivers and streams. There is a re-configuration of how the soul sits within the body and how the body is used as the vehicle. There become fewer and fewer triggers that define one's being as separate. Less and less limitation resulting in a nervous system that feels as though is it part of a greater nervous system and where the emotional being feels as though it is part of a greater emotional being, and where the sense of egotistical self feels as though it is part of a great and wonderful Being.

All of these descriptions involve the energy centers, the nerve pathways and the currents of life force. A human being who has come into the True Identity, the true state of being uses less energy to exist and is drawing from a much greater embodiment. They have less closure in their energy streams, and fewer confines. Less energy used for creating the separation. Changes occur, especially within the higher brain. The physicality, the network of capillaries and very fine threads of nerve currents become more efficient and simplified. They become less active towards vigilance and protection and less active towards the animal embodiment.

If you were to move over and look now, at the brain, circulatory and nervous systems of an animal, either predator or prey, you would see that this whole shape is essentially built for the action of survival, for staying separate, safe and dominant. All of the currents and blood flow and organ development around vision, hearing and smell, movement, digestion and sensing are all based around separation. All are based on maintaining patterns that are identified from the outside. The one who meditates, the human being who comes into the full flowering of consciousness disengages most of the animal system for it is no longer needed. There becomes quietude, softness, and inactiveness in those regions that can still be used but seldom are. There is an opening and a whole different streaming of development physically that refines and lifts the ability for a consciousness that is universal: universal sight, universal listening, a universal nurturance and the result of all this is a universal identity.

We are inquiring about how to work with the mind in meditation, how to understand it, silence it and get beyond it.

In unconsciousness there is bondage and in wrong relationship there is bondage. Wrong relationships arise from unconsciousness, from not knowing and not understanding. Do you understand the mind and why it exists? Why is it with you? ***You cannot be in right relationship with the mind if you don't understand it.*** Hold consciousness and true understanding of what mind is, how it arises and what it is for. Befriend the mind; know it for what it is. What is your hand for? Befriend the hand. Befriend your lungs...what are they for?

You are a coalescence of components as a being. Have consciousness to each of these aspects of your form. The mind is a part of your form, just as the lungs and as the hand. ***It is not your enemy, it is not your obstacle, but it is a part of you.*** It is to be befriended in full consciousness and understood. It is to be included and given a role. There can be nothing excluded from your being, nothing rejected, nothing that you put resistance and energy towards and say: "I wish you weren't there." That is bondage and that is unconsciousness.

The mind is the brilliant point of perception. It is the crystalline window from which you see and perceive, and then create structure around what you see, sense, and know. It is a way station for information. The information that you gather through your eyes, ears, energy and feelings, come into the brilliant point of integration called the mind and are understood and perceived. The mind is a guide. It is a place to know and to decide what to do with this information. "Am I safe? Is this good? Shall I move? Shall I stay still?"

Without the mind there can be no human embodiment. No descent of the divine into physical form. *As the mind conjectures and structures information that you receive from the world around you, so does it receive from the subtle world, from the world that is not as concrete or linear.* Divine information also passes through the mind. The mind is a very powerful place to create unity, to create integrity and to create evolution of consciousness. The mind widens, opens and expands, creating greater and greater vistas of structuring and of integration of information. The mind must be included.

In meditation then, to befriend the mind, to love what mind is, *to see it as the brilliant crystalline window that receives from everywhere.* Commit to using this mind for more and more subtle conjecturing, for more and more expansive receiving. See it as a high clearinghouse where information creates freedom and expansion. Learn to include the mind in your meditation.

As the mind is habituated to information at a more crass or lower level, don't reject the mind itself, but compassionately realize that this is the habit. This is the well-trodden path; this is the use of the mind that is firmly there. Let it carry the syllables of a mantra, let it be part of that. Observing the in rising, the full circle of the sweep of breath, the rising of the 'ah' towards the evening of the 'mm.' Let the mind contemplate and watch. Let it contemplate and watch the most beautiful thoughts. The thoughts of expansiveness, the thoughts of what love really is.

The mind dictates to the physical form, to the emotional being, and the mind guides your incarnation. As the mind hosts these thoughts of freedom, the thoughts of all-encompassing becoming, we change the pathways; we change the patterns the mind repeats. For the mind is still an organ of repetition built on patterns. As you learn to set the highest patterns onto the organ of the mind, the consciousness of your greater being is not bound by mind. Mind is meant to be part of this evolution, and as you set the highest patterns into your thoughts and mind, you set the highest patterns into your body and into your organs.

A meditation can look like setting high patterns into the mind. Holding thoughts of love, statements of beauty. Don't confine meditation to an expectation of sitting in absolute silence and rejecting any part of your embodiment. *You are here to set the highest patterns of becoming into your being, and as you do this you will become free.* Your consciousness will soar, unbound.

The Mind, Brain and Soul

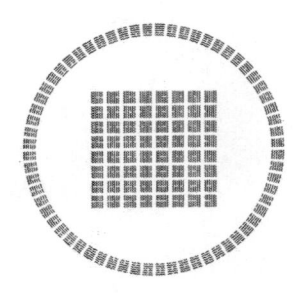

What is the relationship between our human self (personality and mind) and our soul?

When this question is asked, on the relationship between the soul and the human character, personality, mind, and emotions, instantly there is the presence of Guidance. Sometimes a question (from the group) is received with a smile or a sense of power or intensity or gravity. This time it's met with a sense of exasperation in that this relationship, for each individual, is so variable. The distance (and they show it to me in this way) between consciousness of soul identity, and the human ego based identity, is to be pointed at and understood for each individual. What is this distance? How close and intimately woven is the ongoing eternal soul identity to the mechanism of consciousness within the human embodiment, within the mind, within the emotion, within the will and the intentions, within the sense of self or ego identity? What is the distance? What is the nearness? How much interplay? How much disconnect? This is where the answer lies, for each individual.

There is never a complete disconnect, this is impossible because the greatest truth and dynamic of a being is their soul. Their human identity and embodiment are a very small portion of what a being is, therefore, any disconnect is only partial. As soon as the individual is asleep, they are interacting with their soul, their greater identity. And as soon as that individual dies, they are immersed in their greater identity. So the disconnect is only illusory and partial and yet to the consciousness of the mind, in the day, in the ego self, there can be a very complete obscuring, a very complete disconnect. The 'identity' of this human being believes and feels that this is all they are, the sum of the contents of their mind and emotion and memory. Their sense of reality spanning only to what their memory holds within the life. Their identity simmering as an active reality composed only of what is held in their memory, and to what is held in the mind and its conclusions, and what is held in their emotions. In one who holds this limited awareness, the relationship to the soul is very compromised. They are not operating from the greater sense of 'I-am-ness'. They are not operating from knowing their ongoing purposes for embodiments. They are not asking the questions of their deeper being, of what they already know and who they have already become, in this rich essential way. One who is disconnected in this present mind, is fed by their soul through their dreams, through their unconsciousness, through their sub-consciousness and through their subconscious emotions.

Going to the other example, a being who is actively seeking true consciousness of 'I-am-ness', the true identity of their being, this one is in a willing exchange with soul material, this one is in a willing in-flow and out-flow, an open dialogue whereby their greater nature is infusing their human nature at present.

They are accessing from all they have created and all they have become, sensing is directed not only to the greater developments of their soul nature, but all the relationships their soul has. On this point, we show her the tremendous rich array of relationships that each being has, not only laterally to other souls in development, but to beings beyond this phase of development, angelic guidance beings that are in strong relationship to each soul. *As one is in dialogue and is linking actively into their greater being, so are they in relationship to many other beings.* This being is unobstructed then, in their life process. Their identity isn't perhaps, as clear or as defined in human description. They are a being in an active flow of their own presence and an active linking beyond their own presence to greater presence. *A being in an active relationship with their whole nature is also unbound by their own nature and is part of all beings of greater essential nature, part of God, part of Supreme Presence.*

The more reduced a consciousness is, the more defined and separate is their sense of self, the more etched and grooved are their character patterns, perhaps their obsessions, their fixations, their way of being, their difficulty with change and their difficulty with expansion.

The more fluent one's human nature is with their greater nature and with all beings, the less fixed, the less bound as though you see them in different lights, not held to a character pattern. A being such as this can mirror the supreme character, the Christ nature, the 'all-inclusive I-am-ness'. This 'all-inclusive I-am-ness' is the truest description of identity for all beings.

What is the true nature of the mind? What is the difference between **the brain and the mind?**

This question brings forth an image of such complexity, that I couldn't describe it. I am shown the intricate mapping system of all the neuron paths of the conscious brain, the currents of nervous energy down these pathways, and the highly organized interrelationship of the different regions of the neuron pathways. This is the composite brain that we are attempting to put words to. Therefore, I am shown the brain as a visual display of the very intricate development, within matter, for consciousness, this highly developed work of art.

There is praise for the glory of this work of art, this creation in molecular matter that has developed itself to such a degree as to carry the streams of consciousness such as this, even: an image of my own brain at this moment receiving this higher information, showing me within my own brain, that these same neuron pathways can receive information from many levels; from the most physical level to a highly subtle level. Showing that these neuronal pathways are highly responsive to wavelength. Different wavelengths trigger the pathways into different regions of the brain, into different conclusions of the path. It is wavelength based. Lower wavelengths and higher wavelengths activate neuron pathways to different areas of the brain. There are many stages and levels of wavelength, which have not yet been defined intricately or accurately by anyone. Certain measurements of brain wavelength exist, but not to the level of intricacy with which this brain (Jean's) is operating. The ability to describe the inside of the generic brain is a very fine high wavelength function.

The mind is not neuronal or molecular. It is not substance, soul, or

*emotion. **The mind is simply a frame of consciousness.*** It is a continuous ongoing frame of consciousness. It is the mass conclusion of all the neuron pathways in every moment. It is the firing of information down all pathways at all levels within that being to all the regions of conclusion, creating the consciousness in its present state in every moment. The mind is a continuing frame of consciousness and a continuing set of conclusions, based upon the wavelength that a being has developed and is mostly open to. The mind is a concluding state of consciousness, a frame of defining one's identity, one's being and one's relationship to life.

There is mind without brain. There is concluding consciousness that creates identity and placement, even without the brain (without embodiment). But within the human embodiment, this high development, this fine work of art is the brain, and the conclusion of its pathways and the summation of its awareness is mind. It summates awareness of what is in the emotional being, of what is in the physical surroundings. It will summate conclusions on what another person is saying or feeling. It summates continually, placing the being in continual relationship to existence. That is the mind.

The question could then be: What are the regions of the mind? What is the highest state, or purpose of the mind? What is the lowest state of the mind? You will see mind in the cat at the door. The mind of the cat at the door that is making the conclusions of what is here, what it wants, whom it is and how to get in the door. This is the summation of the mind of the cat. And so it is in every being with the conglomerate pathways for hosting consciousness.

The finest development of mind is that it places one in identity, in relationship with Universal Being-ness. The cat has a door in front of him; he has a limited relationship with existence. The cat is at the top of the steps and nowhere else. Whereas, the finely developed human brain can be in the entire universe, literally, where it can host a relationship to All Being-ness. This is the work of art, the great wonder of what this molecular neuronal pathway brain is developing towards. This is what is held in the very DNA, this print, this goal of being ***universally conscious,*** conscious of the whole, whereas, the cat holds individuality as supreme. The most conscious mind does not hold individuality supreme. It holds All Being-ness supreme with all beings as part of each other, in a tremendous weave of consciousness, the greater and total Mind of

Divinity, flowing throughout all levels of creation. ***The intricacy of this brain can host the intricacy of this level of mind, the All Mind, the Great Mind.***

In this greater frame of identity in relationship to existence, there is a freedom from the brain itself. The brain is not needed for All Mind. And yet for it to fuse and form and be fully utilized, fully light up, for a being to come into the full consciousness of its true nature within the brain, is to send a message into all creation, all matter, all DNA, and all beings, as though it sparks alive all creation unto itself.

"What is the true nature of the mind?" is not a simple question. Perhaps what should be asked is, what is the true nature that the mind is meant to host and be the frame of? With the true nature of the cats mind, the true nature of the bird's mind in its completeness, when the spark of being- ness within that bird needs to expand, it must expand beyond the capacity of the brain within the bird. The true nature of the human mind is such that it identifies ultimately with all existence and all creation, with the source of all existence and all creation. For the human being hosts this and falls out of the Supreme, the sons, the daughters of God-Nature. ***It holds the flower of perfection in its brain capacity to know the ultimate essential nature.*** You are to hold wonder and awe for what the human being actually is. Do not settle for anything less than the true identity, the true frame of what mind is meant to hold.

We could say that mind is nothing at all, it is a state of consciousness that the brain can host, and yet it is a state of consciousness that is woven to the entire embodiment, to the sensory sentient embodiment. Taking the state of mind description out of the brain into the whole nervous system; every nerve ending holds the brain. The entire nervous system transmutes the neuronal pathways of consciousness, senses and feels at many wavelengths. All a conglomerate of the frame of mind, of "I am, all that is here, I am in this relationship to what is here."

We ask for commentary on Nithyananda's statement: " Mind is an action, not a thing, not a physical actuality."

Mind as a *thing* is the *map*, the network of neuronal pathways and the tremendous capacity within the neuronal pathways to transfer information, to collect information, to collate information. Mind has this intricate neuronal map as its basket, as its place of manifestation. Mind *itself* is the *information*. Mind itself is the ever-dynamic wavelength of information that imprints itself, and is reached for. Mind itself is the crossroads in thousands and thousands of places on this map. Mind is the energy collating, the information collating. Understanding mind then, as a node, an energetic complexity of informational crossroads that has found, miraculously, wondrously, in evolution, the physical neuronal crossroads to receive it. And yet we show her mind as a stratum of informational crossroads, as a node or a *place to perceive the vastness,* the vastness of being-ness that one would call Supreme Nature. **Mind, in its smallest nature, is a translator of the environment directly around** and of the relationships directly around. Mind is a place, a quality of informational collecting that orients one to the environment and the relationships directly around. Mind is a funnel, a node, a translation of the information in the direct environment.

Mind is an integral part of being-ness, for people knowing where they are, and how to navigate and move, and for one to establish a point of identity wherever they are, in its smallest version. And yet, held within its node of mind action, is the potential of knowing that very same 'where they are' in the Universe. Where they are and who they are.

Mind is in its most primal place of usage in the human being, a navigational, informational place, within this world, within the day, within the country, within the time period. It is a place of orienting the embodiment. A being without mind isn't really here, and yet a being with the full use of mind in its most divinely designed manner, knows their place in all creation, in the universe of beings. **Mind is an action, indeed, a specific action, and mind needs a receiving point so it is also a physical mapping within this embodiment.** And yet that physical mapping is nothing without the infusing of the soul. It is the soul entering an embodiment that flows up to this neuronal pathway and uses the capacity in the brain to 'know' within this form. It is the gift; it is the multifaceted gift of this embodiment. It is a gift not understood, nor utilized to even a small percentage of its capacity. It is the gift that puts to peace all the movements, all the yearnings, all the moving in and out of lives, the searching. In the gift of mind, one knows deeply their place, their whole being within all creation and all time. *It is the reason for embodiment to host sublime divine consciousness into the substance of molecular form.* Mind hosts the mind that sees the greater nature.

When the physical neuronal pathway dies, what then of mind? Would we call it mind? Would we call it presence? Would we call it knowing?

We will tell you that when the neuronal brain pathways have died, all that flowed through those pathways, all the information and the consciousness that is the sum of all that information, still exists. There is still mind, per se. The mind of a highly enlightened being is a place of all knowing. A place to know from what mind was meant for. A highly conscious being who can know from a neuronal mind, but needs not the neuronal mind.

Thought

From where do thoughts originate?

We take her to the mind base, the mind map. We show this to her energetically as a great hub of crossroads, of lightning quick impulses of the senses and the sensory system. We show her the very site of thought origination. And yet we would change the actual word 'origination' and say coalescing, receiving the greater idea and placing that greater sense and idea into thought. Receiving energy information from all sources, whether from the soul or from other beings. And that energy information being coalesced and constructed into thought. ***Thought begins then, as pure wavelength, pure energy information that is sorted, constructed and placed by this map into a thought, into a series of thoughts.***

Your question: *Where do thoughts originate?* Most truly answered, thoughts originate in energy itself. It could be the energy of love or the energy of fear. It could be the energy of a tremendous scope of grace or a tremendous limitation of fear. It is the pure sense of grace, of love, of compassion, of fear that then translates into the thought. The thought itself ensues or originates from the mind map, from the apparatus of the nervous system that creates the thought in order to direct the embodied being into the understanding, the intentions, and the action manifesting the energy; the energy of the love, the energy of the grace, the energy of the fear. ***Thought is the in-between, the deliverer of the original energy into action.***

In meditation you go beyond the mind map, the intermediary thought construction, and directly link into the energy wave, the pure most original idea before it breaks into thought. You learn to immerse in the pure stream, and to choose which stream. Do you choose the stream of light, of grace and love? Do you choose the stream of reduction, of contraction, of fear? In meditation you learn then, to choose the highest streams, the most refined, the streams resembling the eternal 'I-am-ness', the eternal truth, and allow only those streams to enter the mind map to construct the thoughts, to direct the action, to direct the identity shaping, the character traits and the creations of a lifetime.

We also show that the thoughts that have been constructed are actual pathways in the brain map, in place as patterns. These patterns can be beneficial or they can be negative. What has been constructed in the mind thought map, sometimes needs to be cleansed, purified. The patterns of fear thoughts, the little maps, the little trickles of where the thought construction went, need to be erased. When a being is in meditation, in the deeper linking to pure streams of grace and to the highest refined energy of understanding of creation, then the very nature of the high vibratory stream erases the negative patterns and cleanses the mind map. There doesn't need to be: "How do I take apart the negative paths that have been created in the mind?" There needs only to be a continual choosing of the finest highest streams of energy for this cleansing to occur. Linking to a being that shines and emanates the highest, that examples the Supreme 'I-am-ness' will cleanse the entire embodiment of negative patterning.

How do thoughts affect matter, substance, and life? How do thoughts affect longevity?

(Jean: "I need to explain to you what happens when a question is asked and I open my being like this. It is like I am watching the busy movement of elements of the understanding being brought together.")

The Guidance is showing me the essential energy body which is independent of the physical body, and which is a thought body, a consciousness body. For body, you could use the word shape or entity, coalescent around a being-ness (to steer you from thinking of the 'body' word as physical). I am shown the energy body, this essence-being that each one of you is. You *are* thought, you *are* consciousness, and consciousness is thought. Again, not seeing thought as only the shapes that run through your mind. The essential nature of I-am-ness is thought, the identity of your being as an individual is a thought, a body of thoughts, a map of thoughts. Your identity is held as an energy suspension, as an energy map, an ever dynamic, ever evolving map. If you were to say unto yourself, "I am a thought." "I *am* is a thought." "I am a thought of the Supreme." "I am a thought of God".

If you were to take full responsibility for being that ultimate thought, a thought of being-ness, how would you cleanse that thought? What would you keep? What would you discard? How do you identify your being-ness, as part of all creation? How do you take your place? How do you exult the entire creation with the thought of "I am"? And how fully do you invest that thought with presence, with grace, with truth? How often do you have shadows in the thought of 'I am' of unworthiness, of limitation, of darkness?

You already know the answer, that thought is essential to the creation of substance, to the creation of the moments of the ongoing nature of being-ness. It isn't: "Does thought create?" it is: "Thought is that." Your health, your character, your feelings and your identity, spring forth from your most original, most dynamically central thoughts.

If you could find the thought "I am" that came with you into birth, if you could sense, feel and know the essential thought of you, as you were being born into this life, you would have the most absolute understanding of your evolution and your being, of your field of operating; your field, from which you spring forth and become.

We show her that field thought, which we could call the incoming or original I-am-ness, as the foundation of what you create of your life, of your identity, of your body. To the extent that you seek consciousness, true consciousness, you swiftly interact with that field thought, with that incoming nature, the sum of your being thus far. Dynamically, swiftly altering, changing, expanding, creating more potential: By stimulating and triggering new action in the genetic code; by stimulating and creating change so that we could then say that you are not dictated to by the limitations of form. You need not be dictated to by the limitations of your incoming consciousness, only through stasis, only through agreeing to the cultural conscious dynamic around you, and only by not seeking true consciousness are you thus choice-less.

These statements are powerful and how can it be, how can one stretch the potentials of a life body, stretch the potentials of your own being, which have been laid down deep, before you remember? As this question is being asked, we show her the liberated beings, the eternal light energy body that stands tall and present and intimate to your beings, calling you forward. You are printed with this. You host this ultimate identity, the eternal thought body. The eternal light body which has no decay, no illness and no limitation. It is becoming then, to the human being, to seek this sight, this knowing and begin to activate the genetic coding - to awaken it, to extend it, to begin to host the true identity, the eternal identity. As the thought is: "I am an eternal I-am", so simply and easily then, the body begins to reflect that.

Now the guidance is not giving me words, but giving me this space of light and presence and a very beautiful, gentle, yet strong gaze, of: Sit with this memory, this image of the eternal beings standing before you, reminding you. Sit with the thought: "I am an eternal being" and use that true thought to replace: "I am a temporary being", "I am a limited being".

(Jean: "Thank you Guidance, for the hope and the quality of this life message and the reminder, even without words, of the eternal nature of life, and that the cells are responsive to eternal life. Thank you.")

Genetics

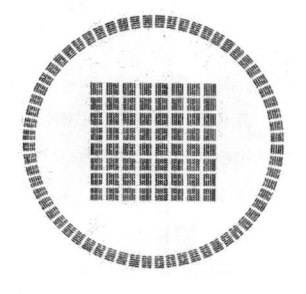

We want to have a true understanding of genetic patterning and inheritance; to understand the factors dictated by genetic patterns and how flexible or fixed this is.

The Guidance begins by zoning in on how plastic or flexible inherited genetic coding is. The genetic pattern and chain has a different description of flexibility or plasticity depending upon the consciousness of the being and according to the individual. The less conscious the individual and the more ensconced they are in not only physical, but emotional and mental genetic patterning, the more fixed their programming will be, and therefore what will inevitably unfold. What we mean by this is that the genetic structure, like the warp, sits in a certain pattern, but the weave around that warp is the emotional state, the mental state and the spiritual state. This is the individuality that is laid upon that grid.

There is immeasurable force and potency in the creation of physical formation, in creating the body and its operation, the shape and the purposes of the body. **We could say that the purposes are set not by the genetic coding, but by the subtlest and highest frequency of energy in the spiritual.** Understanding that the genetic coding is sitting not as the lowest frequency, but is sitting ready to create at the lowest frequency (physical formation). Genetic coding is beyond physical formation. It is a highly specific pattering of energy that sits behind physical formation, but is in absolute attunement or in adjunct to the spiritual state of the being. If the person is in a sleep, if they are in an unwillingness to be conscious, if they are simply here to unconsciously carry forward what was given to them, then they will manifest what was given to them physically, unaltered and unchanged, like a straight line.

If the person is awakening to their being, awakening to their calling, moving their frequency and their vibratory life force energy further towards refinement, they are actually rebuilding their genetics. They are rebuilding and correcting the formations there. Even before the correcting, there is non-responsiveness to the poor genetic coding that would lead to illness. Following non-responsiveness there is a surpassing and a rebuilding of that very same genetic patterning. If this genetic patterning could be seen distinctly as physical design, the change that is held in it may not be apparent, but is still responded to. In other words, the change may not come forward until that being gives their genetic material towards another being. Yet in some, that genetic pattern will transform itself even within their own being.

We can say that the plasticity of the genetic programming is absolute. The plasticity of the physical form is absolute. We can say that the physicality is plastic, that physicality is purely substance that precipitates or falls out of the finer higher frequencies of the spiritual. **Remember and understand that lower frequency precipitates out of higher frequency. This entire universe has fallen out of God, or supreme energy.** The physical precipitates out, condenses or congeals. In this understanding of energy frequency, to increase and refine the frequency is to rise forward and move into more physical refinement. As a being refines their entire system they deactivate any lower programming, or patterning that may sit there like inertness, until finally it is dissolved. The true answer to health is refining the frequency. Refining the frequency into an embodiment, forming a substance and matter that is more conscious of its self. As a cell becomes more conscious of itself, it reproduces itself perfectly.

Within the genetic patterning of a body there is the transfer of the genetic print of the parents, but also held there is genetic information from ancestors, and this goes very deep. This goes into what has not yet been discovered in the new science. There are layers of genetic information, and not only are there layers, there is an original print. There is an original code that is operational in the very center.

To truly understand even one embodiment is quite an intricate understanding of many layers that sit around the original code, which is shared by all physicality and forms. All forms hold unique individualized original code. ***This original code is like an ovum of intensity that holds the whole progression, and that holds the perfection of the end stage, the meaning and the purposes.*** It is the driving force of the embodiments within their individual species and in their individual forms. All the layers are held there, some of those layers are brilliant, and some of them are highly weighted and highly dysfunctional. Some of them hold the journey of repair and healing, some of them hold recognition and brilliance.

A being in full consciousness is essentially apart and free from their physicality. As a being creates a certain state of consciousness so does it resonate to whatever layer it is most kin to, essentially bringing forth that specific genetic coding. Therefore, there can be a complete bypass of the most recent genetic layer and a bringing forth of a distant ancestral layer. The genetic line, the genetic pattern resonates to the state of being that the soul is manifesting in their embodiment.

To further this, as the being comes into a fuller consciousness, into the truer state of original being-ness, as they hold open heartedness and the state of love in their intention and in their energetic form, so do they activate the most original coding. They activate the purest purposes in the genetic coding of physical embodiment, which holds tremendous potential. ***The fullest expression of the genetic code holds the essentially undying body.*** It holds the body that does not dictate, that does not become a body of illness but becomes lightly used. The original code holds that which has not yet manifested.

Teleporting

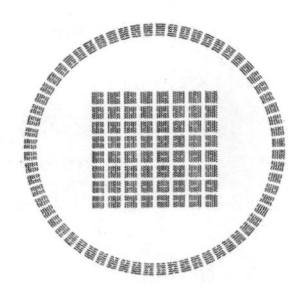

We would like to understand the dynamics of teleporting, meaning to move an object as a Master would, without normal means, from one place in the world to another.

The guidance gazes upon us, and me, with a smile at this question. In the smile there is a feeling of humour. I can see them tapping their thumbs together and saying "It's about time you asked that question!" and even "Wouldn't you like to know!"

The gaze turns more direct and serious with these words: **This is a very answerable question, which does not mean that it is very understandable to the current mentality and consciousness in the world.** It is not complex, it is not magic, it is physics. It follows the laws of creation of matter and of matter in all its gradations or realms. Realizing as we speak that there is material matter, there is etheric matter and there is subtle energy matter. There is matter that ranges from the densest to the subtlest, and it is all matter, it is all creation. The current mentality, based mostly in the densest physical matter, and the laws that seem to pertain to the densest physical matter, will have a hard time understanding anything outside of the physical material realm. In order to understand this, we need to view and know the whole description of manifestation, of material manifestation, substance manifestation. Substance is not only that which operates at the densest wavelengths, causing the concretions of which your senses can pick up. Substance is also the continual movement of the formative energy within that solid matter, the field. Substance is also how the movement, the coalescence of energy is on its way to becoming concretions and on its way for these concretions to eventually dissipate.

To understand manifestation then, in its gradations of wavelength, very discernable definable gradations of wavelength, start with the baseline understanding that *your current senses are attuned to a certain wavelength only*, which is highly limiting, highly confining, leaving most of these gradations of substance outside of awareness. The Masters, those who have ascended in consciousness to see, experience, endorse and become all the gradations of manifestation within their own beings, are no longer limited and confined. They can move an apple from one part of the house to another without physically moving, the same as you could move it with your hand. Remember the baseline understanding that within your sensory consciousness, you only know the apple in its one wavelength, in its finality wavelength, its concretion or densest wavelength. You don't know the apple in its formative wavelengths, in its intricacy, in its subtle wavelengths. *If you did, you could move the apple out of its concrete, densest wavelength into its most subtle.* In it's most subtle, then, it is unconfined absolutely to time, space and distance; the time, space and distance that is attached to the lower wavelengths. In the subtlest wavelength of substance reality, time, space and distance have entirely different values: the speed of light and greater. When you have moved the apple into its most subtle wavelength, then the apple is suspended in its most highly vibratory form. *A being who knows how to do this can move that high vibratory form of the apple upon intention and let it descend, then, into its most concrete wavelength.*

Intention is the movement, is the master of substance. Did you know that your body is here by intention; your body is animated by intention? Your body would be a lump of clay perhaps with a heart beating, perhaps not, if it did not hold place for intention, the intention of your being-ness to whatever sum of development you have. All reality, substance reality, material reality, is the servant of spiritual intention, higher intention. Now here, have the baseline understanding that your spiritual nature is not in this wavelength description, but is beyond it. It is not a definition of wavelength. It is not a substance being. It is in the higher realm of consciousness itself, to which all substance is servant. *The being, then, that has known itself, fully, is not confined to lower wavelength consciousness, can then take form to whatever wavelength it needs to be, for whatever purpose is held in intention.*

You ask the science of this. The science of this is an absolute understanding of wavelength, an absolute understanding of the vibratory individual print, of substance, of individual substance, mineral substance. It is an understanding of what is held suspended in solid seeming matter, and if that solid seeming matter then is brought into a more vibrant dynamic wavelength of itself, what is its description then? To understand it scientifically means to have the senses to perceive, to see, to name: What does the apple look like in its higher vibratory nature? How does it still retain the identity of apple? What is the identity of apple? All of this is held in the consciousness of one who is able to teleport. Holding the idea, the identity idea of apple as a print, as an exquisite honoured thought, like holding a note (tone) that calls apple to it and that note, in its highest vibratory description travels beyond the speed of light to wherever the intention would take it. *Like a note sung, the apple turned into a note sung and then the apple precipitated out of that idea, that note sung like a leaf falling through density, gathering density. The idea fell into your hand as an apple.*

Know then, that every molecule, every atom is a suspension of an idea, that every collection of atoms is called together by the creative impulse of source, the creative idea of form. The intention for each form is held in the Great Mind, the God mind, the nameless source mind, the great bank of ideas for manifestation. Therefore a being who has become all this within their own evolvement, is in absolute intimacy to God mind.

A servant of the greater nature, of Source, of God mind would never move an apple without the intention to increase the presence of God mind. Therefore there is the blockage, the barrier between the semi-conscious and the highly conscious, the seekers and the non-seekers and the non-thinkers and the highly conscious beings. And this barrier, like a passing or a crossing, has as its mandate to utterly love, utterly know, utterly remember God mind. The intention for 'all that is', all manifestation, is to increase love itself in all beings, that every breath, every step, every gesture is part of love itself.

Those illumined beings, having crossed the barrier, understanding the energy basis of creation, and who would then use the higher laws for themselves, for intentions that are closed in circuit and in nature, these beings create great destruction for their own selves and for many others. To move the apple to gain for one's own being creates a karma of destruction, yet to move the apple to illuminate, is to help dissolve all limitation.

Understand what is being spoken, *that the barrier of unconsciousness has a purpose*, that to penetrate the barrier requires the effort of personal devotion, personal development, personal unfolding and utter transformation in the identity. Then, these laws, these higher understandings of the true nature of physicality of the worlds of manifestation, open up and are available, for you are sons and daughters of God.

The Spinal Column

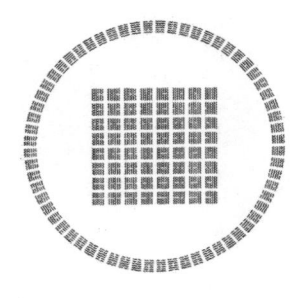

We ask for more understanding of the central energy stream corresponding to spinal cord development in the embryo, both physically and energetically.

The Guidance is bringing me first experientially to the central stream within my being, pointing at where it lies and pushing me away from associating it with the spinal cord, though it is associated, but not confined to that. They are showing that it is a column of intense dynamic life force, of consciousness force, and showing how life force and consciousness are indivisible. Showing how life force moves in this central column, the intricacy of this movement, and how it spirals upwards from various originating points creating a web or a pattern. There is a living web of crossing lines all the way up this central column. The way to understand this is to see it as energy movement: the movements of life consciousness force itself.

The Guidance brings me back to the very beginning of an embryonic body and shows that there are two poles of potency. It is a potent polarity, with potent forces on each end of the ovum that create an exchange, the beginning of an impulse, the movement of life force, consciousness force, and it initiates the spiraling energy between the two poles. At first it is simple, but it quickly becomes a very intricate interlacing of spiraling lines of force between the two poles. The Guidance is bringing me into it; it is like I can hear a high-pitched sound. It is such a high wavelength in those streams, such an intense ray of life that no cell or substance can sit stagnant. It is a highly stimulating, highly catalytic and vibratory energy stream that awakens the DNA. It is catalytic, it is forceful and it is pushing. It pushes the DNA, as though there are tremors that shake into emergence its most latent, most central definition of self.

It is this streaming energy, in its configuration, running between the two poles that fills the entire ovum sac with catalytic force and calls the substance within, all the tiny particles of beginning cellular forms into action and definition. Following this is then to go to each one of these prototype cellular particles and understand what definition they actually hold and how that arose. The magnificent wonder of how the physical body, the energy body and the spiritual body arose into this complexity of form.

But that isn't your question. The question of differentiation is that it is called upon by this high intensity life force that is incomparable to perhaps any energy substance you could understand. It is as intense as the ray from the center of the sun. A highly intensive ray of activating life force that sits there in its most active, most intense form at that moment, in the beginning of the evolution of this body that you now sit in.

As the body goes as far as its DNA shape can take it, in other words it becomes a fully formed body, then the intensity in the central stream lessens and becomes much slower and softer. The rate of crisscrossing and the speed of pulsing is slower and a homeostasis, a balance is created. There remains just enough energy flow through the central stream to maintain animation. Every DNA cell form that is ever touched in that beginning embodiment stays in relationship with that touch. ***In other words, the awakening life ray, that awakening vibration from the central stream is never forgotten.*** It stays in relationship to the cellular form, the limb, the organ, the site, forever after. The state of the central stream of life force dictates the animation and the state of the external body. In this description everything is the external body except for this central streaming column.

As the life continues, as the consciousness of the being inhabits the form, there is then the question of how that life body is sustained and related to. How does the soul exist within the life formation? If the soul exists in alignment to itself, in alignment to its truth and to the true nature of its own being, then there is a continual, intimate communication with the life stream, the physical form and the developing consciousness. Continuing with that description, ***if that being animates more and more*** *their soul within the form, the central stream becomes more and more refined, more and more enlivened.* It communicates transformation and begins to touch a latent, deeper message in the DNA.

There is so much potential held in this DNA, in this core seed of material substance. The first layer is touched in embryo, the second is very seldom touched in the humanity at this time, and yet it sits there in the evolutionary development, to be touched. In touching that deeper embodiment that the DNA has the potential to create, there is the life body that never sickens and does not age, the body that can host the full potential of divine consciousness within its nervous system. This is all mediated by the central stream, which goes through its lull, its 'stage of being' following the embryonic activation.

Does the being, in their developing consciousness, then take the next step and begin to go further in the true nature of their being within their embodiment lifetime? This then is when the central stream could activate again, and become an even more dynamic, vibrant, pulsing, crisscrossing force communicating the next message to all cells.

We hesitate upon that word (all cells), the Guidance points to there being a central coordinating group of cells within every tissue site that is like the captain, or the initiating group of cells within every tissue site and within every organ.

When the embodiment dies to its physical form there is the inhabitation of this central column of light and life force. There is that which is left for a time, the last thing to dissolve, the true body, the true embodiment, and it doesn't entirely dissolve, but it condenses into a point of light. A point of light whose intensity and brilliance depends upon the individual and what they have built within their soul. This point of light, for lack of better description, is the beginning of animation for a new life body. There is a descent of the seed (point of light), of all that has been made, entering and touching at conception, and beginning to animate and enter into the polarity, the two points and poles, within the ovum.

Conception

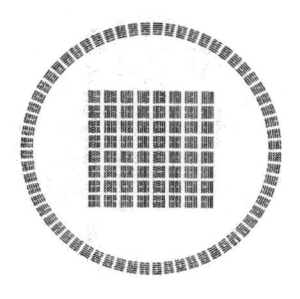

How and when does the soul enter embodiment?

The guidance shows me the light form hovering, which is the way the soul identity looks before infusing into a physical embodiment. I am shown the hovering, the beginning of the attachment, choosing an entry or a life embodiment. This relationship truly begins before conception, as a relationship with the mother and father. It begins as a weighing and measuring, a sensing and a growing intimacy between these beings energetically.

Conception can be (not always) triggered by the relationship that has strengthened and developed between the beings - the souls of the mother, the father and the incoming one. The point of fertility and conception can be stimulated and arranged by the alignment of the parents and the incoming soul. There are variables in this as in all descriptions. There cannot be a straight rote answer.

For a soul that is eagerly seeking embodiment, there may be a swifter infusing of the cell mass of the embryonic beginning, of the ovum and its divisions. For a soul who is unconscious and unwilling, resistant or fearful, or with only partial agreement to embodiment, there can be a very slow igniting and entry, as though walking beside but not in, or even falling. There are many variables. To the willing and eager, when the relationship has already been created between the mother, the father and the incoming being, the conception is felt, like a burst of light. There is a watching of the cell division, there is a waiting for the moment when the nervous system first defines itself in the embryonic form. There is a feeling into the nervous system, a flowing and streaming into the embryonic nervous system.

Understand that the embryonic nervous system is far too undeveloped to host much of the soul, yet there can be a streaming and sensing in, as though entering the physicality of the growing ovum in the mother's body form. It is a visit, not a full inhabitation. It is not a full disengagement from the relative vastness of the soul identity into the infant form. Perhaps this is the question being asked: When is that capacity? When is the shift? When does the soul divide and have its reservoir of being-ness separate from its engaged embodiment?

The answer is: when the nervous system in the ovum is intricate enough, with nerve endings, with division and differentiation of brain, organs, and limbs. However, differentiation does not mean development. It means that the energy print, or paths are there. **When the brain, the limbs and organs are mapped in the nervous system, the dream of embodiment can be fully dreamed.** When the blueprint of the nervous system is intact, and there is sense of being matched to the map, the soul can make a landing or transfer. Mapped within this tiny embryonic nervous system are all the regions of consciousness and becoming towards embodiment, even though, visibly, it is a highly undeveloped embryonic form. It is at this point, when the mapping is there and the infinitely tiny nerve endings are beginning to build into the blueprint of the map, that the soul can enter and be part of the mapping, take part in dictating how it shall be, how it shall go. The substrate of the embryonic map and form is infused with the being that it is. The individuality of the incoming soul is imprinting, from the outset of the building of the body.

It is also at this time, that if there is not a resonant matching, or an inability for the matching of the soul to this blueprint, that there can be a signal for the embryonic form to discontinue. Realizing then, that at this first entry point, the process of disconnecting from the great reservoir of consciousness is still gentle, subtle and slow, so that it becomes a duality in the reservoir of soul consciousness and the absolute beginning-ness of consciousness in the body. It is as though the world has just begun, as though existence has just begun rather than being continuous. It is this great newness that is the gift of the human being, to have the experience of absolute newness, and to be part of creating every path for the character of the soul to travel, reflecting the needs of the soul to embody.

There can be a slowness or stillness following the mapping of the nervous system and regions of consciousness (regions of the being) after the first fusion or entry, where the mother may not feel the presence within, just without. It is as much within as without. There is not an instant entry, but a coursing through, a streaming through, in and out again. It is only when these mapped areas of the nervous system are filled in with the nerve webs, the pathways and the rivers that receive the currents, that there is a full entry, saying goodbye, putting the greater experience of their being into a place of the sub-consciousness, according to the being. There is a full entry into this now perfect, now fully developed nervous system, into the ears, the eyes, and body senses, vortexes of feeling and emotion and directives. There is now the precious time, of being in that nervous system in the silence of the darkness, in the surrounding of the mother's body, reading the world outside the mother's body from within and letting go of the movement far beyond the mother's body, letting go of the identity beyond the mother's body.

This is a generalized description. For some there is great willingness, comfort and ease here and for others this is a time of grief and fear and isolation. To the being for whom this is a time of peace and gladness, and warmth and love, the linking between the reservoir of consciousness, the greater identity, and the now human incarnation, stays alive and open as a path, a feeding always, a referring always. There is a continuous sense of the "I am" that is distant, yet there, and the "I am" that is willingly, joyfully here. And to those for whom this experience is isolating and fearful and grievous, this pathway can either be cut off, to prevent the lack of entry, and the lack of birth, or they can move and reside in their greater being and enter in with only half an eye, and be a dull, inactive not present being, moving through life with a flatness. See the variables of the answer to this question.

Abortion

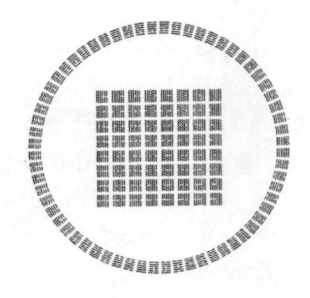

What happens to an unborn being that is aborted?

The heart and the mind of the mother is known to the incoming being far ahead of the mother even knowing her own mind and heart. The disconnecting that a mother will manifest, who is not going to keep her baby, is already known to the incoming being, even before the decision or action is made. The disconnection is a communication of the heart, of the energy field. The actual abortion, the creation of the death, is a very final moment and the disconnection has occurred far before that. The being already knows. As to the effect on that being, the generalizing of this question is difficult. Could it not be seen that this involves the being itself, the relationship to self, their purpose for incarnation, and the karma to be worked forward in this being's progression. The disconnection is the damage, the actual shedding of the physicality, the embryonic shape, is less so.

We could say that many beings that were not aborted have also been disconnected to. They carry forward into birth and live their lives with the disconnection within their being, to the mother, to her soul, to her love and relating. **The disconnection is the most crucial factor to look at.** We will say that a being that has been aborted may not even experience this disconnect, since the heart and soul of the mother stays connected and alive to the being as though still containing, still weaving, still part of that being's existence even though the physicality was lost, or refused, or taken away. In this case, the relationship is alive and is continuing in its positive stream towards another conception, whether in this life or in another. The connection is unbroken.

In the disconnection, there is the karma of debt, of the vacancy created. The disconnection is that which needs to be healed from in both. For the mother, in disconnecting from the one growing within, she is also disconnecting largely to her own heart, to her own being, to her own self. For the one who has been disconnected from, there is also the need for healing, according to the individual soul. The karma buzzes and hums around that moment of disconnect, the barred doorway to incarnation and the barred relationship to that particular soul. If the mother continues to have the baby, this karma will unfold in the life, and if the mother doesn't have the baby, the karma waits to unfold.

In answer to your question: *What literally happens to the being?* We show her the being walking in a stratum of reality from which they are not called forth, as though they are preparing pathways and researching the avenues of incarnation that are then non-operating. There is very little trauma to such a being, for they haven't incarnated, they haven't filled in, they haven't created their field, they haven't created their mind and their will, they haven't created their persona nor any aspect of their embodiment. They have stayed in their soul's nature. And though they may hold sorrow, or grief, or wounding in the refusal of entry and in the refusal of the relationship, there is no attachment yet to the lifetime. Such a being chooses another incarnation, usually as soon as possible. And depending upon that person's purposes, they may carry forth the choosing of a partial entry where there are rejection tendencies and some disconnect. Any refusal of entry creates a karma that needs to be carried forth by both. We will leave it there.

Vaccination

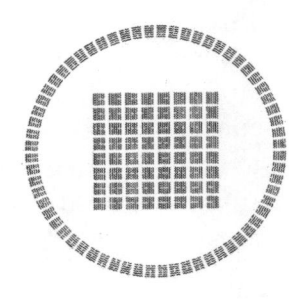

We ask for a teaching on the vaccination of infants.

This question requires me to step back from my own mind and consciousness into listening. Guidance brings me to the physical organism, the human physical embodiment, and shows me a visual of what is called the immune system. I am being shown its pathways, its complexity and the light. The light is a very dynamic electric bluish light of immune system activity and I see it being variable through every part of the day and night, in every season and every condition. The Guidance is bringing me to see the activity of the immune system in a generalized embodiment. The immune system and its activity are shown as a very powerful sparkling light activity in an area. I'm seeing lightning quick communications into all systems and beyond the physical into the emotional. The emotional state and the mind of a being are very woven to the immune system. The mind is the source of the emotional state and the Guidance shows this as a doorway, like a captain's doorway. All beliefs and thoughts that are allowed through this doorway precipitate down into emotion and cause the activation or non-activation of the immune system.

The immune system is a very finely tuned and highly developed aspect of animal embodiment. It is the magnum opus of physical embodiment creation and has been in development since the beginning, since the unicellular embodiment. It is highly intricate and only partly understood. An infant's immune system is an extension of the mother, not only her genetic physical condition but also in her spiritual mental and emotional condition. The immune system is the coalition of all factors. In an infant, the state of the mother combines with the beginning of the creation of its own immune system. It is borrowed from the mother just as the whole body is being borrowed.

An understanding of vaccination in terms of the function of the human embodiment would be to say that vaccination is stepping in from one understanding only, from one very physical, very material understanding of what the immune system is. We are not here to say yes or no, or right or wrong, we are here to teach. We can say that the human embodiment has been operating at such a low wavelength and with such unconsciousness that illness has overtaken the entire race in multiple ways, and still does. Over and over the immune system has been operating at a very low wavelength. Within the human embodiment, the coalition of the spiritual being into the mind, emotions and body has been a very flaccid slow trickle of life force for some time. Under these conditions, to materially uplift and assist in system recognition or immune system activation (vaccination) has been life saving and has been a tremendous assist. But the knowledge gained in the genetic embodiments is very minimal, in fact, it is knowledge lost. *In the long run, the embodiment of the human being is not gaining in knowledge or capacity through vaccination, but losing.* Rather, to create immunity, the conditions that lower the wavelength of the vital force and the immune system must be addressed. *The immune system must be understood as the coalition of all factors of embodiment, it is the pearl, the magnum opus of life force functioning in the material.*

To vaccinate an infant is to take knowledge away from the developing embodiment's consciousness of itself. An infant is an embodiment learning to exist in this sphere by borrowing the immune system of the mother until it develops its own and there are distinct phases to this, of which the traceable physical is only one. For the immune system description is also the ability to mediate life force through the organs, the ability for the organs and all tissue sites to operate towards using life force or not. The infant embodiment is learning to be itself and learning to come into relationship with vital force, life-force, and with energy production while every organ of its embodiment is learning its identity and learning its function.

Every organ of the physical embodiment has an identity. Each has a sense, a sentience and an emotion. As every aspect of the embodiment identifies itself fully there is no question of the lack of immunity, for all organisms that would cause illness are very low functioning wavelengths, very non-identified material organisms. *A highly functioning human embodiment is not resonant in any way to disease organisms.* To vaccinate an infant who is in a condition of low wavelength, low life force and compromised, is to give that embodiment life and opportunity and assistance. Yet the genetic map of that infant embodiment has lost in knowledge rather than gained. *Therefore it gains its own life but does not confer knowledge through its own genetics towards the next generations.* The progression of vaccinated generations is towards less and less identified embodiments with less and less empowered immune function and more dependency upon outside factors to create health. Antibiotics and vaccination are robbing the physical embodiment of its own consciousness and of its own ability to create a wavelength that is beyond resonance to disease organisms. The immune system of a highly energized genetically strong child will not accept the vaccination, will not recognize it nor respond to it. The main teaching here is to inquire into what the immune system and this human organism actually is. Further, to appreciate that it has undergone eons of development, to appreciate its capacity, and to truly understand the factors behind immunity.

Viruses

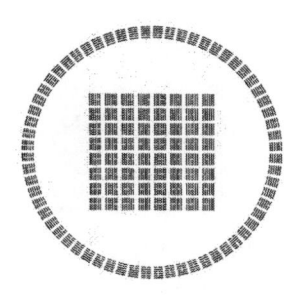

What are viruses?

The Guidance is showing me the strata of biological development within matter. It is a many-layered understanding of more and more refined development within cellular form. Showing that viruses sit there at a certain stage of development. It is to be seen as a whole, not as a separation, to see the cellular forms that can reproduce as very highly developed biological forms, and to go on down the line to the very inert, very inactive, non-reproductive and static substances. Viruses sit part way along this ladder; viruses are cells in evolution, and matter in evolution. All matter is in evolution, even your own reproducing cell forms are in evolution, waiting the awakening next step that puts them into a beautiful equilibrium with life force, resulting in a body with no degeneration.

The viral body is a cell in evolution that contains only part of its development. It is not autonomous and it is not independent. It is a lesser cellular form because it is dependant upon a higher cellular form. ***If you wish to understand its presence in your body and it's presence as an illness factor, then understand it as a lesser life form, resonant at a shadowed level of life force. Understand that your physical embodiment will only host that which it matches.*** If your life force, and that which animates your cellular form, is not animate enough and in its highest potential, then it can host the shadowed, duller, lesser wavelength life forms and be susceptible. ***Immunity is an entire description of energy, wavelength, and life force in vibrancy or in dullness.*** Viral infections can only occur when the vibratory rate of life force within a body allows it, when it matches the viral life wavelength.

The question: "Is it life or not life?" is not a sensible question. If you define life as that which can reproduce, then yes, but really all is life. All is a gradation of evolution, substance, and matter. To protect yourself from lower life forms, from going into degeneration for any reason, is to enter in to a higher vibratory understanding of your own being, your true nature and purpose. It is to lift your consciousness into its full identity, and to activate the highest level of DNA formation possible in your being.

There are many steps between where you are now and this wonderful description of the body that does not degenerate. There are many chapters there, wonderful chapters of learning to increase the life pulse. Knowing how it weaves intimately with increasing the consciousness and how that weaves intimately with increasing the peace within your being. To hold the understanding that you are love embodied. Love itself, animates the highest vibratory rate of life force in physical matter.

Going back to the question of the virus, understand it as a stratum of matter development, cell development, and there are many strata undefined, unnamed that you also could resonate to that would pull your body into sluggishness, stagnancy and disease. Viruses are interfering with life, and yet it need not be analyzed as such. It needs only to be understood as gradations of consciousness and energy. It needs only to be understood that as you attend to the highest principles of your own being, principles of love and of alignment into who you most are, this is how you spark alive the highest potential of life in your body.

DNA

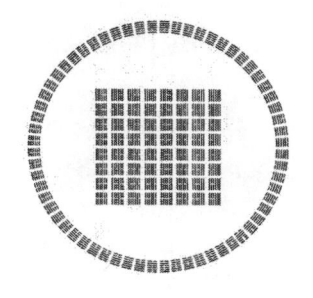

How is the DNA involved in aging or preventing aging?

The fastest aging occurs in the lowest consciousness state. For the embodiment that is under attack from the world, is in constant vigilance for survival and feeling physically vulnerable, the aging is the quickest. The wear and tear on the cellular being is the highest, and the energy needed for repair and sustenance is the highest. Worry breaks down cells. Anxiety and fear break down this physical organism rapidly. Fear, worry and anxiety are of the sphere of the lower embodiment, of feeling the endangered need to survive, to sustain and maintain against the outside.

As the embodiment, in its nervous system, endocrine system, and its consciousness moves into a greater place of identifying as a being that is part of all beings, there is less wear and tear on the physical embodiment. One who is not vulnerable to other beings, but identifies as part of other beings, as streaming into other beings with compassion, with love, has less wear and tear on their body, and less cellular replacement.

To jump forward, a being who is supra-conscious, in omniscient consciousness, a being who is in a consciousness that is absolute, places no wear and tear whatsoever on the physical organism that it streams into. So fully into vital life is this consciousness, that a cell is energized at the very moment that it would begin to die. This is all coded and held in DNA programming. This way of embodiment is programmed into the DNA's formation to come (future). As the being identifies with all beings, is 'I am' to all beings, as the consciousness is in the supra-calm, in the supra-consciousness, in the peace of All Being-ness and is not vulnerable to fear, anxiety, worry, separation or unconsciousness, the physical embodiment is a sustaining slow wavelength where by the physical breakdown of cellular matter is instantly counteracted by vibrancy of life. Held also in the DNA is an entirely freed physicality that has no potential for disease or death, nor a need for physical sustenance.

We want to understand DNA, and how emotions and one's inner state affects the DNA?

The Guidance brings me generically to DNA, which is an interesting thing to have before my inner eye. I'm seeing the operative core of the physical form and of the cell, the operative programming of the physical organism. The Guidance is showing me, as though pointing at a chalkboard, how the operative formation of the DNA is put in place far before it is utilized, and pointing out that even in a very unconscious life formation the DNA holds the potentials, the symmetries and the structures for far more consciousness than that individual embodiment is manifesting.

Evolution is led by DNA formation and activation. Evolution is preceded silently by the formation in the DNA and then the evolutionary form or the embodiment slowly and sporadically, in shifts of slow, sporadic forward movement and stasis, begins to be activated by the DNA, which is already there in its entirety and wholeness. The DNA is a strong and driving dictate within the physical environment, and could be seen in simplicity as the core manifestation of life in the physical form, the core programming for life to come into physical formation and the core programming for conscious life to come into physicality. We could go further and say that the core formation to host the full conscious form in physical embodiment is all printed, is all designed. If we could sweep away all manifest creation, sweep it all away, all its evolutionary layers, all its phases and just look at this DNA, you would see the intricate workings of creation, the intricate meaning and purposes of creation. You would see how these strands of structure are in a continual activation, a continual pulsing, suggesting and inviting a movement forward, to involve the rest of the strands bit by bit. You could watch how this laid out grid, like a blue print for the entire creation, is held (in an impossible to describe manner) in the DNA.

If we were to take out a DNA strand from any one of you, in isolation, not only would we see your perfected being-ness, the perfected being-ness of the human form, but you would also see the perfected being-ness of all other forms. The DNA is a generic grid for all creation; in your DNA is held every phase of physical manifestation up to this point: the trees, the amphibians, and the seas. It is all held in the DNA, it is a comprehensive library of all physical embodiments and all conscious embodiments. ***Likewise, it holds in its full library what this physical embodiment is ultimately embodying towards, and for: to host supreme consciousness in form.***

An individual signals into their endocrine physiology and into their nervous system physiology, the experience of equanimity, calm, or peace. The nervous system and the endocrine system receive those messages of peace, and receive the message to go into the supra-calm (a state of being where the body lets go of its protection, its continual unconscious readiness to survive, and its continual unconscious definition of separation from the rest of all embodiment). In this state of conscious peace, the DNA and the physical systems of the body receive a message of timing and a message of letting go. The body lets go of its systems of protection, it lets go of its vigilance of individuality. All that is kept is a remnant, a working remnant of vigilance, maintaining the separation in terms of the immune systems functions, and in terms of the functioning amongst others.

As the body lets go of its energy towards separation, vigilance and survival, the DNA activates into another layer. To tritely label this other layer that is being activated, it is this embodiment moving into the consciousness of 'being all embodiments'. It is now a bigger body, a bigger field of being in the body. This is now coded into the DNA, coded into the level of the DNA that is the next region of the brain's function. It can know into a greater sphere of embodiment. This is a consciousness function that can sense and interact into a greater sphere of being. It is as though the 'I am' is bigger, the consciousness is bigger, it is not *individual entity* conscious, it is *Greater Entity* consciousness. Into the layer of the brain that the DNA has said 'yes' to, there comes the ability to sense, feel, taste, know; all the senses are into a greater embodiment.

As the integration into greater embodiment is experienced and there becomes equilibrium, ease and calm, the next strand in the DNA, which is activated, opens up the next region of consciousness within the nervous system and the brain.

And so it goes, you can identify that true calm, conscious calm sustained in a continual way within the being, provides a signal of readiness that this body is no longer needing to protect itself in individuality, no longer needing to be in a first level survival mode. No longer in the random interplay of the emotions of fear, pain, grief, of "I am in danger," and "I am being mistreated." All these sorts of emotions trigger the body into a stasis of staying separate and of staying in the identity of the smaller entity. As the consciousness within that being moves beyond this, and moves into ease and a calm within the physical human embodiment, it is like an ending. A silencing; "I am no longer that," "I no longer need to sustain the individual entity as that." This is peace; this is silence. Then quietly, like a sunrise, the next region of conscious and physical development occurs.

It could be detailed, what is held in this DNA and what each of these strands really means. One can see from this description, what a rudimentary placement the human being is generally at. One can also see from this description, what a tremendous capacity is held in this human being. In the further developments of what is held here, it is almost a non-recognizable state of being from where we are now.

We are asking for commentary, an understanding of Toby Alexander's work, **activating the DNA** toward ascension in 2012. Is this something we can be doing ourselves?

The readiness for DNA changing, transmuting, evolving, is different in every individual. This is such an important statement and needs to be held foremost in the mind as the rest is being spoken.

In the description of DNA transformation, there is the individual readiness or state and there is also a more generic understanding of DNA development, a very worldly based genetic pool. From this point of view, we all wear the same body. We all inhabit and work with the same genetic body. The question is about understanding DNA activation, what this really means, how this can be introduced from the outside, and what does ascension actually mean.

We are showing her what is being referred to, the next segment of DNA that is sitting silently, non activated, sitting as the potential in evolution. There are segments of DNA, in the chain, in the picture that we are showing her, which are silent, have no life spark flowing through them, are sitting as potential. *The pathway, the road, metaphorically, is always built ahead of the traveler.* It is as if the traveler arrives in readiness and finds the road is there, the road was laid out before their arrival, and so it is with the DNA. There are loops or segments sitting ahead, ready to deepen and refine the evolutionary body, refine it ever more into a consciousness embodiment, registering consciousness more fully. As we show her this, we show the several stages, several segments ahead for this evolutionary form that you sit in. We will now describe the activation process of this next segment.

If the readiness is not there this segment of the DNA cannot be activated by another being. If the traveler hasn't arrived at the beginning of that next phase of the road, there can be no external activation. The readiness of the being is in their consciousness. Activation of the next phase of evolving is a natural occurrence from conscious readiness.

A being from the outside (a teacher) can increase the readiness, can imprint that being with image, with life stream, with conscious streams, with energy streams, can superimpose 'the look' of the next phase, the feel of it, the sense of it. A being in readiness can move even more swiftly with a guide, with one who scampers ahead easily, saying: "This is where it goes, this is how it is." This relationship of infusing and assisting to energize, and inhabiting, fills in the emptiness with the shape of a being that is already there. ***The traditional relationship of a highly developed being, a Guru, and a very ready disciple, is the relationship of activating consciousness, of activating the DNA.*** What this man is speaking of is nothing new, it is the very process of a Guru-disciple fusion. It is the disciple fusing to the teacher with trust, with love, with the senses ever falling open, which moves them swiftly into the next activation of their being. And even then, the disciple cannot override their readiness. Activating the next segment of the DNA, or activating a more refined sensory being, cannot override what is built into the life-embodiment-purpose of that person, and therefore, the next phase of their activation, will occur in their next body. The form body itself must be built to sustain and mediate a more refined consciousness. The activation may be carried forward into their next birth, whereby, when they infuse into the stream of the developing embodiment, this next portion of DNA development is fully streamed into and builds the body.

*We ask about the date: 12/12/12 (December 12th, 2012), which has been spoken of as **a special time of activation for DNA.***

The question sets us spinning because of the true dynamic of time or of timelessness, and the different stages of recorded physical time around the world. There is the immediate counsel to not become too fixed to the linear moment of those numbers. Rather, see the essence of what is meant there, in the alignment of those days, the alignment of the sun cycles, moon cycles, and year cycles. The Guidance is showing that the alignment referred to is more like a radiating wave sitting close to, but not exactly on, the literal 12/12/12. There is an actual alignment that occurs with the moon cycle, the position within that moon cycle, and within the year cycle. The alignment is what will be spoken of.

To see this answer I am pulled back and pulled away from the frontal mind and its expectations of seeing things in a linear way, in such exactitude of time and expectation. I am being pulled back to the greater meaning and the greater alignment that is spoken of, and held onto this time. I am shown that the genetic body of the human being, the genetic body of the Earth being, the genetic embodiment of this sphere has within it a clock, timing or regulating. At the time of this alignment, there is a disconnecting from a dross, there is a falling away of the heavy matter. There is a distinct separation of the inertness, of the solidity and the unconsciousness of the genetic body, all across, which is why it is spoken of as a wave. This is a distinct separation (as a metaphor they are showing when finally, there is the emerging of something through a glacier, that then calves and falls into the sea). There is a falling away, a separating, which is coded into the genetic form, a falling away of inertness, of unconsciousness, of dull mass.

So, are we speaking of activation or are we speaking of a falling away? It is a simultaneous description, as that which is dense and limiting, bonding and holding into an unconscious vibration is dropped. There is instantly a freedom, and instantly activation. It is not so much something added as something taken away. It is exactly: what is being taken away pulls the drag, the dross, the heaviness out of what remains. Therefore it is more dynamically existent.

As the falling away of the dross, of the heaviness, of the unconsciousness within what is genetically being reproduced throughout all beings, there is then the ability to be nurtured, fed, streamed into from a higher gravity. *There is a disconnecting from a lower gravity and a freeing to be nurtured from a higher gravity.* If you could reframe your concept of gravity, gravity is truly a physical force, the pull of mass, but there is also the pull of another mass. It is this other mass, the mass of the sun, the mass of what is held in the dynamic vibratory nature of the sun that pulls and it pulls into a higher genetic form of being. There is a change of relationship between these two gravities. There is a relinquishing in the lower gravity and there is the streaming in of the higher gravity. This will be experienced in a myriad of ways depending on the genetic form that is being described. The bedrock of this world loses some of its coalescence. A stone begins to break down more easily. An animal has more sentience, more emotion, and begins to be more aware of its position in existence, having more awareness of its own individual being-ness. The description of how this affects the animal world is myriad. This can appear as changes of patterns, changes of patterns that can seem disruptive. There can be the arrival of brilliance and new leadership within the animal communities.

Within the human community it is also myriad, depending on the individual development and how that being has nurtured and supported their consciousness. In general, however, there is less ability to choose unconsciousness, less ability to hide within unconsciousness. This is seen most dynamically is in the children, the children who, through the stripping and cleansing of rebirth and incarnating are entering stripped of unconsciousness willingly, easily, naturally.

What occurs within this alignment we speak of, is to be seen throughout the generations and the generations to come. What would be seen on these days, these 12/12/12 days may be very little, and yet what will be seen arising from this dynamic, subtle and absolute shift will be seen over the generations to come, according to how this is mediated and met and responded to. Whereby the stones in their innocence yield unquestioningly, and the animal worlds relinquish their age-old patterns less swiftly, the human being is faced with the choice. If unconsciousness isn't as easy a choice, what do they do then?

Realize the generations it takes to truly observe this shift. Watch for it in the children, watch for the ease of realization that moves them past the patterns of self-centeredness. Watch the patterns of ego formation in the human being and how the very nature of ego seems to take others into account. The very nature of 'who I am' includes who you are.

Teachings on Diet

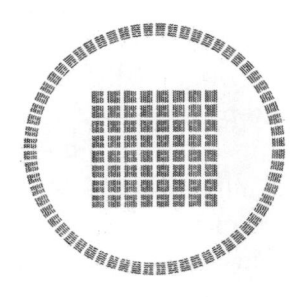

*How can one receive complete nutrition through eating a **vegan diet**, through the food only, without taking supplements.*

The Guidance brings me to the digestive capacity and reality of the human embodiment, choosing to start there, pointing at what is possible within this metabolism and digestive system. The Guidance is pointing out the range of ability and the capacity of the human being to be vegetarian, to be carnivore, to be both, to eat and absorb and digest food in its cooked or raw form. The capacity of the human digestive system is very wide, and very able, which can truly open the door to choice and also to confusion.

But from where are you asking the question of what is most right: "From which part of evolution, which part of the world? From which specific reality are you asking the question?" ***To go to the foundational place of understanding, we say that built into the human physiology is the ability to take many paths of nutrition and to thrive.*** This is a basic bottom line answer.

In response to the question of how to receive complete nutrition when choosing the path of vegan-ism, we would show you the adaptive ability within this wondrous human physiology to adjust and to make use of available nutrition. It is able to adjust its expectations, its usage, its elimination and its responsiveness to the nutrition that it is being given. Understand that a time period is required for this adjustment and adaptation, however, if one human physiological being is given only vegetable substance foods, their system will adapt itself and gain all its needs. It will grab the nutrients it most needs from the foods it is being given. However, another's system may not even notice and excrete or eliminate most of those nutrients. This one will adapt itself to holding onto whatever is being given. There could be lack, possibly marked lack, but the adaptive nature of the human physiology is that it will make do and it will gain its needs from many different versions of nutrition.

One with a healthy starting point, a healthy physiology will adapt swiftly and become very efficient at protein and nutrient storage, at nutrient recognition, at storing a nutrient that needs to be collated to another and putting it together when it comes. This goes far beyond current biochemistry research. The human physiology, in its most healthy starting point, has tremendous capacity and can put together necessary proteins out of unlikely components. The healthy physiology sits with the ability to make the most use out of any of the streams of nutrition. Therefore the answer isn't simple. A healthy body can thrive beautifully on a purely vegan diet, and the longer they stay upon this diet, the more their system accommodates and creates its fulfillments, learns when to get this and when to get that, when to store this, when to mobilize that, how to use this nutrient against that nutrient to complete it. This is the adaptive nature in full swing completing the needs within that physicality.

Ultimately there should be no need to take supplements. Most often, they are not recognized within the human system because of their concentrations and substrate (the substance which carries them). Supplements are mostly seen as a dead molecule matter with no field, without the markings needed to trigger and create uptake. Most pass through the system unused, however, if the supplement is taken along with food and combines with the food in the digestive system, it is more likely to be taken up. The question is so variable and we see different answers in each physiology.

The answer we yearn to give goes beyond all the individualities to the original vision or purposing of the human embodiment, and perhaps if we go there, each can gain what they need to hear. The original vision held in the human embodiment sits in the first segment of genetic information, and therefore sits as the most powerful identifier within this embodiment. *Within this description, this physical being receives tremendous amounts of vital nutrition from very little substance being in-taken, a tremendous amount of vitality and nutritional energy from light, from water, from the fruits and the nuts, from the gifts of the plants.* Seeing the gifts of these plants as a complete summing of life energy in physical form. We take her to see the fruit of any of these trees and show the wholeness and the completeness of the life-energy collected in the layers of its flesh and of its seed. This wholeness of life energy that has gathered itself into physical atomic shape delivers the most physical avenue of nutrition to this human embodiment learning to be physical. It is the liaison between the Earth, the earth-body and the light body, the soul body and the physical body. The fruits are the liaison, the invitation to draw that light energy into physical systems, into physical streams. *Therefore, nutrition through the original digestive system of the human embodiment, came from the fruits, and the seeds, the nuts and that which is grown in its wholeness at the ends of the branches, ready to drop into your hands, ready to fall and be given.*

We look at the adaptation to becoming carnivore, and show that this came much later. It came through a story we won't tell. The infusion into this original human physical system, the cross-entwining of genetics, increased the versatility and expanded the limits of where human beings could exist within this plane. Resilience, strength and toughness were built deeper into the human embodiment through this infusion, which allowed the physiology to move into becoming carnivore. This then, was the aggressive rooting into the earth of the embodiment, giving humans the necessary strength and tenacity to stay within this gaseous planet with its storms, changing climates, and chaos. There was the need to infuse this human system with animal ability.

Where does this leave you? This leaves you with the choice to understand yourself, understand your arrival and your physiology now, knowing that your system is a product of physical evolution for so long and you have a wide array of choices. *Following the teaching to partake of the original substances only, will assist you to become resonant to that first purpose, that first identity.* To take part of the carnivore path of nutrition reception will create strength, tenacity, like a boulder that can hold against the river. *Understand yourself and choose according to your own consciousness, your own development.*

We go further to say that a physical system that is not in foundational strength and health may not be so adaptive to creatively collecting its nutrition from a reduced diet. The physical system needs to become freed (strong and well) to choose a reduced diet and stick to it. It needs to be responsive and eager and well, and not damaged. If there is damage and ill health, then the focus, rather than the diet, is to increase and to relieve the tensions, the memories, the paralysis, the numbness, that which is creating non-responsiveness and ill health.

*If one is choosing a conscious life is it contradictory to **eat meat?***

We speak to the consciousness of a person in relationship to their life, their lifestyle, their eating, and attending to the consciousness there. If one is choosing to eat of the animal world, and doing it with a consciousness of true sacredness, communing, in an exchange of life force with gratitude, the path then is a sacred path. It is an honorary exchange of spirit. It is one spirit reaching to another spirit, borrowing, giving, and living in dynamic relationship.

For one who is choosing to eat of the animal world, the consciousness of the animal world, there is the responsibility to attend to the sacredness of the animal's creation, knowing that the embodiment of a conscious being is sustaining your embodiment. There is the responsibility of gratitude, not using an animal as sustenance unconsciously or carelessly, sustaining the body only. Therefore this needs to be taken into responsibility, and there be given such gratitude, such awareness and return. This human embodiment is designed for all mediums of nutrition, it is a wide array of choosing, and the most conscious being is choosing to consume sacredness, to increase sacredness, consuming from the point of sacredness to exchange with outward nutrition in order to increase the wholeness and the consciousness in their embodiment.

We take her to a fine narrow path of the finest way, where there is an agreement between that which is killed and ingested into life, to create life. There is agreement, a fine exchange of awareness of what is taken, that its life is ended by agreement. Taken by being freely given. That which is taken unawares, unwillingly, traumatically is a robbing, is a debt.

It is not: "Does one who chooses to be conscious eat meat?" It is: "Does one choose to eat meat from the most conscious exchange, from the highest agreement between the being who's body is being taken, and oneself? Is the energy of awareness going into this exchange? Is there a request of gratitude, a supplication towards this higher agreement, or not?" And one could move out of the realm of the animal to the plant, which also involves life force being ended to create sustenance in the embodiment. Is this done with gratitude? Is this done with a communion with the creative principle in the plants? Is it being done by agreement or unconsciously? For this is where the supporting of consciousness lies. Are you reaching with both eyes open, and with the heart open and the spirit open, asking that this be given to you to help you live, giving in return your love, your gratitude, your humility, your compassion, your service? You are asking the Earth herself to support your life body. What is your relationship to the Earth herself? Or are you reaching with your eyes not even looking, just expecting this substance, just taking it unconsciously, forgetting that it was a living being, forgetting that it had its own course of life?

As a human being, you create consciousness, an awakening of awareness in the plant world and in the animal world when you choose to exchange at the finest level. You create that awareness as it moves through your own embodiment, in the plant world that is listening, and in the animal world that is listening.

I'm pausing here, just swept by a great awareness of sadness, of the disconnect. It's like observing a relationship where they haven't spoken to each other for so long, haven't been aware of each other's waiting and listening for so long. And seeing how it is the work of the conscious to make every action count: every action of eating, of choosing food, of handling food, of growing food, of trying to choose food that has been grown lovingly, consciously, whether it be animal or plant, or growing ones own. Putting effort into insuring that there is respect and love and consciousness, being given back for the taking.

Before moving on from this vital question, the Guidance is showing how there have been peoples who have lived in utter dependency on the animal world, and lived in such sacred relationship with them that there is always the agreement, that the animal collective consciousness knows of the people, the people know of them. There is the exchange and there is the very deeply in-built understanding of the exchange, of the respect and the gratitude and of the co-dependency. This is a spiritual path. This is not unconscious. This example is a high, fine energy exchange for sustaining the life form. Those peoples were not unconscious. They were more conscious than the vegetarian who considers their food inert, who has no understanding of how it is grown or where it is grown, and is not giving gratitude and sacred awareness to the food that they are eating.

*We ask for comment, to better understand eating **raw food** versus* *cooked.*

The Guidance brings me back to the living nature of the original meaning of nutrition. The original purposing in nutrition is that it be full of life, uninhibited, unchanged. This is at its end stage or ripened stage of life just before it moves into non-life, into decay. ***Eaten at the moment of ripeness when there is still life, but at the end of life, the system most easily receives the nutritional breakdown.*** Foods that are still in a strong process of growth are bound within themselves and do not release their nutrients easily, requiring the assistance of heat to do so. Foods that have come to the end of their lifecycle, in full ripeness will do this instantly, without added heat. Realizing the sun is the greatest oven there is and that the sun is continually drawing food substances from life into decay. At that transition point of full ripeness, when life is at its end and decay is about to begin, the nutrients are most available to the physiology. Foods that are packed tight, gathered when not completed, require added heat, if not sun then fire. This is not wrong it is purely an understanding of molecular availability and how to bring substances to this availability. Overcooking takes food beyond availability and changes the molecular structures. Use fire or the sun to bring these substances to the end of their life cycle, breaking the tightness of their bondage to themselves, but not beyond.

We ask about the phenomenon of beings that have learned in their embodiment ***to live without food or water.*** Is an existence free of physical digestion built into human evolution? Was it a part of the original vision? Is it what we are evolving towards?

The Guidance shows me the body that needs no interaction with physical substance, the body that is streamed or informed by higher energy substance, higher vibration, a vibratory wavelength that is above the molecular and the physical wavelengths. And yes indeed, ***built within the human being as genetic potential, is this high level receptivity to wavelengths that are beyond the physical, to receive and metabolize energy without a physical in-between,*** directly through the light itself. In its most fine tuned stage of direct metabolism of this finest energy, there is no elimination. Water is mostly needed for elimination, for the chemistry maintenance of the body that is using the physical in-between of molecular food. When the body has direct interaction with energy reception, it no longer needs the water, or very little of the water. Water is the one and only product that the body makes within it as a by-product of energy metabolism. The body then becomes independent.

The question was: *Is this an original layer of human evolution?* And the further question: *Is it what the human being is evolving towards?* It is known within the memory of physical evolution that this is a reality, though compartmentalized into a very small section of evolution, more as a first step into aura of the planetary body. If you could then understand that when the individuating God, individuating soul began to enter into evolution or descend into embodiment, there were phases that were virtually non-physical. We show her this body that is mostly an energy substance, energy sheaths, and the body then not requiring physical mediums for energy. The evolution of this was that when the physical body first began to appear, there was very little need for physical digestion to create energy. Brought into this first body, shall we say, was all the existing relationship to the light itself and to the finer stratum.

The question then came: *Why and how did this descent break the link to higher energy exchange?* This is a very, very big question and the answer comes from many directions. This is about decisions made within those first embodiments of being-ness. This is about influences being given to those first children of the sphere. This was also about the decisions and the calling to enter more into the physical sphere, to dance with it much more closely, to become it, to evolve by becoming this physical sphere by entering further and further into the animal nature. We will say in simplicity, because of the largeness of this question, that there was a transitional point by which the souls infusing themselves into embodiments disconnected themselves from the higher wavelength, and therefore that aspect of the metabolism went silent, and there was a corresponding disconnect with the Universal Mind of Being in order to descend into the planetary mind and into the individual nature of being.

So hear this: As you go into the great unity again, and as you open your identity to All identity, to Universal identity, you begin to bring silence into your lower wavelength digestive system. You begin to open up a pathway that is already there, for a higher exchange of energy metabolism.

World in Evolution

The Future Unfolding

We ask about the future of this planet, human beings and all creatures, given the imbalance and ill health humans have created in themselves and in all aspects of this sphere. What lies ahead and how to understand it as spiritual seekers who are truly here with high intentions for consciousness. We ask how to understand what is unfolding, what may come, and what the peaking or turning point may look like.

The Guidance begins very solidly saying that there is so much more than you can see in this unfoldment as a whole. Not referring to all aspects of this entire sphere, species going extinct, the destruction of environment, of language, all the destruction. Not meaning that, but as a whole there is so much more in this unfoldment than what you can see, what you can hear, what you can know, what you are told, what you can research. Even in the most researchable, the most available to your mind there is so much more than you can hold. The Whole and its deeper intricacy, the karmic unfolding, shall we say, reaches so much more deeply than your emotional, psychological, intelligent mind can grasp. You can grasp it, but you must grasp it with your soul, with your most comprehensive place of being that can know *its own* whole and therefore can know *the* Whole.

We are not saying you cannot know, we are saying you can know, but you must know from your wisdom. You must reach from your wisdom and from your fullness of soul, your true intelligence, the intelligence of your being as a spiritual being that contains all knowledge. From there, what is said of this turning point that you *are in* (not that lies ahead)?

This planetary sphere containing all its components is in a sacred and swift transformation. All sacred and swift transformations create a dropping away and a revising. There is a dropping away or a clearing and an emptying, which can appear as devastation or as a void opening. The focus for the spiritual seeker then, is to see why and see what is emerging from that opening, not to look at what appears as devastation and endings and destructions, but to seek to understand what this is giving way for. What is all of this severity a preparation for? To glimpse the emergence of what is arising rather than to despair in the focus of what is disappearing. And, to learn how to name it. Are you naming this 'wrong', 'poisoned', 'destroyed', and 'ignorant'? Are you naming it as in the traditional stories, as 'the darkness rising over the light'? Or are you naming this, 'the light itself in action', 'the wisdom of creation and the universe unfolding this way in front of you', through those humans over there who seem to act so unconsciously? How are you framing your stance? From every place you stand and frame your stance, it will unfold in those terms unto you. How does it unfold unto you from where you stand, 'despairingly', 'hopelessly', 'fearfully'? If so, you are in the wrong stance and you are not hosting the Eternal Ongoing Truth.

The stance to take yourself to is that which sees the whole, the cosmic unfolding of truth in evolution, the infinite supreme in unfoldment before you. Shall we say, the absolute meaning of Namaste: "I see the Divine unfolding before me, I see the perfection of the infinite supreme in everyone and everything." This makes no sense to the human intellect and the human nature. "This looks wrong. That pipeline looks wrong, how can I stand in Namaste to such wrongness?" And yet in this Stance of the Whole, there is wrongness and ignorance, there is destruction that could be avoided, that should have more wisdom at the outset so it doesn't happen, but it is not a mark of an ending or a failure. This sphere is fluid, it is the fluid, ongoing outcome of the evolution of God (shall we say), of Supreme Mind and Being-ness through the human being. The human being is an embodiment of Supreme Mind in evolution and this Supreme Mind in evolution is learning in this way, through the destroyed valleys and the poisoned seas. Sometimes the poisoned valleys evoke and wake up the heart of hearts, of love. Sometimes it is the extremity of what this very powerful being can do that wakes up the true knowledge of power and the responsibility of power. This is occurring too. There is as much waking up as there is ignorance.

The spiritual seeker's stance is to come onto stronger and stronger ground within, knowing and believing in the Supreme Infinite Purpose, in the identity of this creation and the true identity of each being in creation, the Supreme Infinite Mind in evolution. What is emerging then, in this time of intensity (which isn't new) and extremity, is the waking up and the ending of ignorance and unconsciousness. We show her waves, like swaths of endings of unconsciousness in so many beings, not just now, but in the last hundred years and building still. You are in a most sacred transformation, from unconsciousness to a consciousness, which is arising as never before. *We show her a picture now of a human being standing in a field of rubble in a brilliance of consciousness, seeing the field of rubble as the cost, the process for this brilliance that emits and shines.* This field of rubble, these broken stones, they are alive and will take shape. Life cannot end, it only transforms, it only adapts, it always moves. The fruit *is* that being emitting the light of consciousness. There is no regret, no failure, and no defeat.

You can be the one who takes the task to nurture this brilliance in your being with a minimum of destruction, keeping the garden intact, not waiting for the intensity of that to cause the arising of light within your mind and being.

Change of Frequency

If the energy field of Earth and all its beings is increasing in frequency at this time, we ask what we can do to assist the lift. Is it our purpose at present to assist?

There is a refinement of the matrix of form within this whole planetary sphere, which is another way to describe a changing of frequency. The understanding of embodiment or form is an energy understanding of frequency, a multi-level understanding of energy states, frequency states and substance states. To understand the statement that energy frequencies are lifting at this time, know that there is always an evolving of frequency. **Evolution itself could be defined as a refining of substance and a refining of the energy frequency of all embodiments, of all manifestation.**

At this crucial time, however, there is a jump in frequency. There is an alteration of frequency that is of greater measure, of greater note. This is not as sudden as it may seem; nor is it unprepared for. This change in energy refinement is not only in the human being but in this entire planetary sphere and has been prepared for every step of the way, for as far back as one could point or know or describe. As far back as one can look, these jumps in refinement, in frequency, in measured ways, can be seen. It is the story of Evolution: the preparing, the building, the foundational creation and the stepping into it. The stepping into it can occur in jumps.

The jump at this time is a significant shift, a significant stepping into. There has been a long preparation genetically and energetically within this substance manifestation within the consciousness of the human being, that is now being stepped into. There is a risk and there is a gasp. There is a big wind blowing. When one takes a big step, there is a loss of balance for a moment. There is a loss of integration and a suspension before both feet have come onto the next step.

This is where your precious question can come. The effort of the consciousness is to fill this wind, this space, this suspension, this time with as much direction, as much intention, with as much determination towards truth, with as much choosing of the tenets of love as possible. To flood one's own being and sphere of life and to flood all beings with as much intention, with as much love and determination towards love as possible. This is as simple as starting each day with a prayer, with choosing each day as one more day to put one's mind and heart and actions towards love. It is to start each action with an orientation towards its highest outcome, towards love unfolding. It is to set the tone of one's being towards being guided by love itself, by the Supreme Presence in whatever language within you use.

As each conscious effort and each conscious being attends to the highest frequency of love within, so does this direct the footfall and the landing through the transitional jump. It directs how the embodiment's 'stepping into' occurs. It can look like: Who is reaching to you today with a question in their eye or a fear? What did you hear today of those that don't know, that are afraid, that feel the big wind within or without, and what did you do? How did you direct, from love? Be wary of the complexity of thought and language, of mind getting caught in concepts and language. Direct the fullness of your energy and your intention to existing as love, directing all in front of you from love.

Animal Souls, Tree Souls

*We want to understand the **soul nature of animals.***

This is a fairly wide question. The Guidance scans over the animal kingdom and shows immediately the different qualities of soul development in each species. The question is so wide that it cannot be answered very respectfully or very clearly without singling in on a species. In general, in the configuration of the animal brain, there is an inability to access the universe and the higher cognitive abilities of soul, spirit, or the greater identity. The animal being is a lateral being, in tune with the sphere that it is in, but not beyond its sphere. The animal is in tune with its absolute present, but not in tune with its depths or its heights, with its past or its future.

As to having soul, indeed, every animal has soul. **The animal has soul in the shape of its experience.** It has sentience and it is a soul in evolution. When it arrives at the stage of needing to move into higher cognitive ability, it leaves the animal form. Some species are steppingstones for others. Some species have developed more readiness for higher cognitive abilities than others. Therefore, in evolution, there is a progression through the species. Between the animal realm and the human realm there is a step, followed by an interim period of intensive transformation at the soul level. It is all soul. Soul is that which is not dependant on the physical body for existence, that which is not a physical description, but is the essential nature of a being. Soul is in evolution within the animal kingdom as well.

*We want to understand **Dolphins** and the nature of their relationship to humans.*

To understand the energy physiology or mapping of the dolphin and the nature of this being, we go to what we would call in ourselves, the heart centre. It is an emotive place of awareness, a highly developed sensory sentience. To differentiate between humans and dolphins, we say that the human being has the same capacity of development but does not have the ease, the expansion nor the intricacy of the dolphin in this sentience centre, sentience way. The dolphin can feel so far beyond its own individuality. It can feel instantly into any creature around it, with its own kind, but beyond. It instantly gathers information to this place of sentience, that you may call heart, beyond the self-identity. It knows instantly into the sentience of another, into the state of another creature's emotive sensing, into their state of feeling, into their fear state or their joy state. It feels with exactness where the other being is at, how they translate their motives and conditions of self. There is an instantaneous knowing.

The heart sentience of the dolphin is not a description of individuality, it is described as a unity. The dolphin, within its own sensory system, knows another as though it is itself. Mapped within the dolphin is a highly developed state of unity. They know unity with other beings. Whereas the human being, in differentiation, can create the separateness of self and of barrier and can decide to be aware of another being. Even in awareness of another being, the knowing is of: "That being is over there while I am this being over here." It is a very deeply built-in separation that comes from the mind centre, the mind map.

The human being has used the power of the mind centre to create separation and unawareness. They do not know what the other being is feeling and knowing, they do not know the motive. The human being is trying to read other beings through the mind, which is a faulty sensory system. The dolphin is superior in direct knowing, and in having the awareness of unity. The human being holds superiority in the tremendous and powerful tool of the perceptive mind, and yet the human being has not learned to use the mind for its true purposes. The dolphin is a brethren and a being of highly developed consciousness in the heart.

The dolphin knows the whole sea and all beings in it as itself. The dolphin is a tremendous intelligence in the embodiment of the sea. The dolphin sends forth its intelligence to all other creatures in the sea, which will gather that intelligence to their different abilities. There is conscious leadership from the dolphin form. The dolphin is also an intermediary between the sea and above the sea. They will gather information and knowledge from beyond the sea, from the humans, from the birds. The dolphin will communicate and know the state of things within the sea and to some extent beyond the sea. A dolphin can instantly understand, from a great distance, what a human being holds in its emotion, in its intention and its essential nature.

The dolphin is not fear based and does not operate from protection and fear. The dolphin can see into the love of a human being, even if it is holding a harpoon. The dolphin will resonate with the heart of even the harpooner. It has nothing to lose because of its unity consciousness; it has no fear of death, no sense that it is losing everything through dying. The dolphin can give to the evolving human being a glimpse and an understanding of unity consciousness within the great sea of the universe.

As the dolphin is to the sea, the human being is to the universe.

*We wish to know about **whales** and the purposes of the whale.*

The whale does not hold individuality as you do. The whale holds no barriers, no boundaries to consciousness as those upon the land do. The whale moves and swims through a sphere of energy that is beyond its own individuality. It senses and knows into the entire ocean and into all beings within the ocean and on the surface of the ocean. The whale is developing a consciousness. You ask of the purposes of the whale. You could ask of the purposes of any creature or any being. The purpose of all creatures and all beings is towards the whole, the whole entity, the whole of evolution. The purposes of the whale are to host and hold within them the consciousness of unity, all inclusiveness. Unbound, beyond individuality, they sense into all beings, far and near. The whale holds no centre of self to create boundary. It holds no ego formation.

The whale is like a repository or well of sensing, a storehouse of knowing and of sensing. Yet, the whale mind is not computing, is not recording, deciding, or creating. The whale mind is a window of observation. And held within the being-ness of the whale is truly all information that ever enters the seas, that ever enters the planet. ***The whale is*** *an anchor of information on the planet, a living being anchoring the information in this sphere.* Those of ability and higher consciousness, from within this sphere and beyond, can tap into and use the whale to learn what has happened here and the state of things in this sphere. To understand the whole dynamic of the ocean and beyond that, to the Earth, because the ocean collects from the earth, and every rivulet that enters the ocean carries information from the Earth. The whale is a conscious brain-map holding this information, not doing anything with it, just storing it and holding it like a well or a library, a passive and ever growing library. We show her how the whale is being accessed, by beings of ability and higher capacity, to understand into this sphere, this world. It is known to go to the whale and the library of the whale to understand and to know: How are the seas doing now? How is the Earth responding to events upon its surface or within the sea, to events within the universe?

Remember the whale has no boundaries, no egoic form to create boundaries and is a chosen embodiment to hold all knowledge, all information of this sphere.

What do *trees* give to us beyond the known oxygen and carbon dioxide? What do they actually give us chemically, what can we hear about this?

In this state of seeing and being, I see the trees not as physicality, I see a very wondrous visual of the trees as energy formations, as energy conduits.

The trees are the absorbers of the very deeply powerful life energy of the Earth. They are the conduits of the vital force of the Earth's body, refining that vital force through their bodies, through their streams. Refining this into the finest sprays of light. The emission of the trees is like a fine spray, clouds of light all around their crowns, merging into the atmosphere. This is actual substance, actual little points of vital light, vital force. It is a transmission of the Earth's vital force into a very refined vital force.

The physical embodiments of both animals and humans are receivers of this vital force that we are looking at, which is like countless points of vibrant light in the atmosphere. They receive it in their breathing, they receive it through their skin, they receive it in their fields; it is not just a physical receiving, it is also an energetic receiving. *The trees are translators of the Earth's deep force into a usable life force for the creatures,*

of which people and animals are similar. The infusion of these tiny globules of light force coming in through the nose and mouth, through the skin and directly into the energy field, are translated within the physical systems into living energy. We are watching this living energy, moving right into the cells, right into the mitochondria.

The trees give animation to the creatures of this world. They refine, prepare and animate the life energy of the Earth, which in its original form couldn't be utilized by the creatures, needs to be refined and enlivened. This occurs through the trees' position between earth and sun, the vibrant fire, the highly refined light fire from the sun joining with the Earth's force.

Photosynthesis is one description, but the description you are hearing now is a much greater description of the meeting of the sun and the Earth. A description of how the sun pulls the crude potential of the Earth up the trees to refine it for release, enabling the physical systems of animals and of humans to become more and more developed. There is not a name at present for all that is held in these light globules which are the gift, the free-floating gift, the cloud of life-charge that is available to all physical systems.

You asked of sentience, the sentience of trees. The sentience of the trees is not the same as the sentience of the animals. The sentience of trees is a shared sentience, an embodiment of being-ness that is shared, shared in species, shared in locality. It is not a being within a tree; it is a being-ness that streams through the trees that has unique character. It is not dependent upon tree embodiment but is an embodiment of the most conscious capacity of that tree species. This is found; it is old knowledge and is named 'divas'. There has been much interaction between these beings, these conscious entities of the trees. As there is interaction, conscious interaction, the entities take shape even more.

The gift of the human being to these entities is to assist a further shaping, a further manifesting. Therefore, the entity of the trees can enter into a human being, borrowing their nervous system, borrowing their being-ness, learning from this very highly developed nervous system, taking shape within that relationship. The entities of the trees give a very refined medicine and they also take. They take the patterns of human consciousness unto themselves, and they give a strong conscious sense of the embodiment to the human being often creating healing, correcting, as though the human being for that moment was a tree, and the streams of force of this entity have enhanced the embodiment of the human being.

But there the relationship ends, for the two entities, though they can meet, can never truly entwine. They can never truly merge. The human being is not meant for this embodiment, is moving forward, away from this Earth description, they host the calling that is far beyond the Earth, and they will not remain. The human being is not an entity that is rooted and fixed to this Earth.

We wish to understand the time of *the dinosaurs,* their place in evolution, their purpose to evolution.

The Guidance brings me to the Earth and the very powerful life force in the Earth at the time of the dinosaurs. To understand this time is to see what the Earth was emanating and what and how it was evolving. The Earth was burgeoning in its physicality, burgeoning in its life force at the wavelength of physical manifestation. If you were to step onto the Earth at this time you would feel the boldness, the intensity of a very physical life force. Conditions on the Earth promoted physical manifestation as never before and never since. The Earth had a much wider energetic field. It was humming and throbbing with life force and creating a life field that was much thicker, much deeper.

It wasn't just the dinosaurs that were in this stage of burgeoning physical manifestation, but all life forms. All life forms progressed to the extent of their genetic capacity. This was a time of developing the very genetic patterning that was being built as genetic codes at that time. The genetic code of physical life formation was being taken to its utmost, to its extreme development.

One can look at the dinosaurs with wonder, indeed. But one could look at any life form at this time with wonder. Not just the size, however size was the most evident medium of genetic code in full play. It also had to do with structures that support life bodies, the nervous systems, the bone structures, and the circulatory systems. This was a highly creative time of development in life form manifestation, and was not there in isolation and then gone, but was being built into genetic information, genetic coding, which has been refining itself ever since. **Remember, nothing is ever lost.** Every phase is stored and worked upon. Every phase is part of the foundation for all life forms, all beings following. The purposes are held in these words, the purposes of genetic formatting. And this time, this window of absolute burgeoning life forms, held as its purpose, to develop the genetic coding for the future. What is seen at that time is a manifestation of genetic coding at the physical plane. And yet genetic coding is far more than physical formation. Genetic coding holds the whole story, from the beginning of 'the manifest from the non-manifest' to the full completion of what is held in manifest creation.

The dinosaur era is like looking in at a window of tremendous physical development of the embodiment for life force, the embodiment for soul force, and even looking at the beginnings of embodiment for spiritual being-ness. When you look at a dinosaur, there is not much spiritual being-ness manifesting there, it is mostly a gross physicality and yet what is being built is all the webbing, all the nerve currents, all the mapping for a higher life form possibility. We are looking at the dinosaurs, at the plants, and at the whole Earth in its production of the life wave.

How do we fit in? Were we there? How does this lead to an understanding that is useful now?

If you could hold that window of time as a knowing that there was built at that time, the beginning of the capacity of the full identity of Supreme Being. There is just one body being worked on through all of these eons of evolution. There is the fine and ever finer tuned development of 'the body', which can host the absolute consciousness of light. From the unicellular tiny to the monstrosities of physical development of the dinosaur, it is all part of, the chapters of, building 'the body' which has the capacity to hold Supreme Consciousness, the body of light.

Were you there? You are part of the whole story, from the non-manifest to the perfection of the manifest. Your being, in whatever description we give it, is part of it all. You are an extension into manifestation of the non-manifest. You are witness to it all. Your witnessing at the time of the dinosaurs was minimal in terms of individuality. The time of the dinosaurs was a time of developing the physical substrate, physical mapping of life force and taking it to its epitome. Beings with a need for a higher nervous system did not embody, but witnessed non-embodied. Were you a dinosaur? Only in as much as you were 'visiting' the life form development from the beginning to the end.

When this epitome and completeness of life form was created, the overseers, the guidance systems for evolution, created a change in the conditions in this sphere, to prune and reduce the energetic life field on the Earth. To move evolution away from physicality into finer tuned systems, towards brain development. Therefore, scientists can say that dinosaurs perished for these reasons, for sudden swift climate reasons and yet this is only the visible outplay of higher knowing. To change the climate in this sphere, to alter the life field and its direction, is all for the higher purpose of developing THE BODY, the ultimate embodiment for hosting the consciousness of full light.

Oceans, Water, Radiation

*We have been discussing Masaru Emoto's work on **water**, how it carries energy and expresses negative or positive energy in its crystals, and his request that we pray for the water especially around Japan (following the 2011 earthquake and leakage from the nuclear power plant). We want to understand more about how we can affect water.*

Water is a suspension of matter that carries energy wavelength with more ease and directness than denser substance matter. Simply, it is this dynamic that makes it an intermediary between life force (which is non-matter), and substance (which is material matter). Water sits as a carrier or medium between the energetic principle of life and the condensation of physical material substance. Water is the servant; water is the liaison and the mediator between the pure principle, the life force wavelength (which is truly a wavelength, an energetic print or vibrancy) and the density of material creation. Water is the messenger, the servant. ***Water transfers life force into substance. Life is carried within water into inert substance, awakening it to take shape around life.***

It can be seen in a necessary simplicity for now as three stages: the subtle wavelength of life, the intermediary wavelength of water (which holds within it both molecular and atomic structure and life force wavelength) and the third stage of the slow moving wavelength of dense, inert matter. Through a suffusion of the higher vibrancy of light and life, held suspended in marriage to the molecular fluency of water, material substance is penetrated with life. Water is the activator, the sperm, and water is the servant. Water is an intermediary stage of manifestation. In the full description there are actually many more than three steps, and water is one of those steps in the journey from the non-manifest (pure being-ness), through the descent into form. Water is the servant of the Divine; water is the servant of Supreme Source, non-manifest All Being-ness.

What is a servant? And further, what is a *good* servant? A good servant is one who can translate instantly, the needs and the message of the master, and can carry it towards its goal. Therefore, see water as the servant substance of Supreme Being. The idea of manifestation is 'in translation' within the water towards it's becoming. The idea is held suspended and the idea is a wavelength. Understand then, that water holds the idea and translates the idea or the information, towards where it sits or is given, towards where it is used or absorbed, towards it's end. Let the concept be seen in your mind as a waveform, the idea as a waveform. If that idea be refined, a refined idea that holds in its purposes, beauty, joy, love, and the unfolding of the perfection of Supreme Being, then water shall translate that idea towards the substance it penetrates, towards the body it courses through or the bodies that it courses around. It then enters into that inert substance of molecular matter and calls forth and rings the bell of the similar idea within that form. Water is the awakener, the bell ringer within the lower substance that it suffuses. Therefore, if the waveform idea is of a highly refined consciousness it then calls that forth from the embodiment, the physical substance that it serves.

Water that is polluted and carrying toxicity is, in essence, having its own molecular structure separated. It does not know its self. It is impeded and in-filled with a chemistry that separates its own atoms from knowing each other. Therefore, such polluted water cannot carry this idea very far. Think of the servant again; think of a servant who is drunk. How far could they carry the purpose of the master before they forget? Such is the description of polluted water. In the drunken servant there is substance in the blood saturating the nerve endings so that they are unreceptive to life force and to knowing. Water holds in itself an identity that pollution can fracture.

The question is: *How does prayer assist that polluted, fractured iden-*

tity in the water? Which brings first, the description of prayer as an idea form. Prayer is the highest idea form. It is a being striving to come to the very top of the picture having the greatest vantage point, the greatest intention for the whole landscape. It is a being striving to create more consciousness and correction in unconsciousness. A being with a true prayer is creating the most refined idea waveform. A refined waveform is very powerful, it moves faster than light itself. It collects energy force from the universe because it resonates to the highest idea form of the universe. This calls to the identity, the atomic identity of the water, the hydrogen and the oxygen, and it calls those atomic separations together. It causes a precipitation of toxicity away and out, and the water becomes more known unto itself as the toxicity drops out. The toxicity is rendered an inert heavier substance because the atomic water structure has become vibrantly greater. There is the collation or joining together of the idea waveform of prayer to the water's structure and therefore, the water is not the same. The water will never be the same; it has been called forward into itself, more than ever before. It is more highly vibrant than it was before. Holding both the precipitate of the heaviness and the higher vibrancy of the prayer, the water that is then ingested will create the same state in the being, causing (if it were a human) a separation of the heavy elements and the higher subtle levels.

It is being shown that the liver notices, the body knows about the precipitation of the heavy elements and it cannot accomplish this precipitation without the higher vibrancy. It is as though the body goes into a higher knowing of its self and knows how to eliminate the heavier elements because of the higher vibrancy that is in place.

As you pray into the water (the messenger, the servant), you pray into all creation. You call forth vibrancy into all beings.

In general, understand that in all toxic conditions, toxicity only means that there is a greater suffusion of a substance than the body is normally accommodated to. All such situations can be met by transmuting into higher vibrancy. The human being can survive great states of radiation by responding with higher vibrancy. It is the confusion of systems that causes illness and the separation of atomic identity that causes illness and dullness and death. And yet if the atomic identity within the physical form is called into the highest vibrancy within itself there is no doubt. There is a surge of evolving, a greater knowing of the body unto itself.

It knows more of what it holds and its potential, and grows more swiftly into its freedom. For what is printed and held in this DNA form (the human DNA potential when operating to its fullest) is an embodiment that can live in such subtle freedom, like water itself can sit in such a subtle freedom, holding consciousness but not binding it, being a vehicle for divine consciousness but not bondage. Having no relationship with illness, fear, domination or death. That is what is held in the human DNA form.

"The waves are the servants of the sea." (a 5yr old child)

There is concern about the radiation **contamination of the Pacific Ocean from nuclear accidents in Japan. What is the state of the ocean? Is it possible to transform the toxicity and the danger through consciousness work, through applying the higher transformative energy of love? Is enough being done?*

There is a very strong affirmative regarding the dynamic of transformation on the physical molecular plane through higher intervention of applied intention and love. The vibratory wavelength of the whole Earth field can be lifted through the human element, through the human soul. However, it is not so much a group of beings, directing their focus at that particular situation, as it is the human component of energy refinement, globally, occurring through many other issues as well. The sum total of this effect is the enhancement of the vibratory force field, or consciousness field of the Earth. The human soul is lifting and refining itself, and from this comes the refining of the Earth where it is needed. Is there enough? It is difficult to say if there is enough focus here. One could say that there is not enough. There are still many human beings not aware and not progressing their own field of being, not refining and creating a finer vibration of their own being. There is still the very strong and overriding tendency to stay the same, to hold a plateau of energy refinement and consciousness. It is awareness that is necessary. It is the very personal realization in each and every human being, that they need to come into a more fine-tuned conscious state, not just for them, but for the Earth and for humanity. *It needs to be truly understood, by more and more of the human race, that one's state of being is not isolated unto them. The state of being that they create through their thoughts and their daily activities feeds into the generalized life-field of all human beings and all creatures and the Earth itself.* Therefore, more of a focus on teaching that when you meditate, pray, choose actions of love, and when you refine your own being, you are giving to the whole, you are giving to all beings and you are giving to the Earth. This source, this pooling of refined, higher vibratory energy is taken where it needs to go. It is taken to the sites of tragedy, the sites of illness throughout the Earth's body, throughout the human's body, you could say. From this perspective, there are the multiple beings, and yet beyond that there is the One Being. There is the One energetic amassment of Being-ness.

Human beings are in a woven, perpetual relationship to the Earth. They are a refiner of the Earth in their purpose. They are the nervous system that has come into a branching of such fineness and magnitude. They are the nervous system of the Earth in its more refined capacity. ***The human being is a channel, channeling refined universal energy into the Earth's body, into the Earth's evolution, into the animals' evolution.*** There is a stepping downward from the most refined to the least refined nervous system and capacity to mediate energy, from the human being, down through the animal world, into the plant world and into the organic mineral world.

It is not a jump or a leap of consciousness or faith to say that the human being's focus on refinement, on creating the conditions of consciousness and love within them, is affecting the Earth. This is the position all along. The human being is an extension of the Earth. All living beings are an extension of the Earth, and we could say that the Earth is an extension of the human being. Just as if you had a very refined consciousness around an injury in your own body, nurturing that site with everything you know, caring for it with love, believing in and providing for the healing, with the vision within yourself of the healed state, and thereby healing the body more swiftly. Compare this with seeing the injury on the body from a place of defeat, seeing it as not healable, a fixed degenerate place. Feeling kept from one's own life's progression because of the injury, feeling that their process of life is over or reduced, dictated to by the physical injury. This is the wrong direction of the human capacity. The human capacity is a channel for the finest visions, the most refined, the most perfected, most dynamic and closest to the original matrix of life itself. Therefore in a more refined envisioning, in a refining of one's feelings, beliefs, thoughts and actions, the injury upon your own body will heal more swiftly.

The Earth is your own body. It is as much your own body as your knee or any part of this physical form. Although you may not experience this in your nervous system, in your consciousness, it is still your body. The purpose, the mission and responsibility of conscious human beings is to develop their refinement, to dissolve their impasses and unconsciousness, their patterns of defeat, of depression, of sadness and of feeling victim. To dissolve this not only for their own soul state and evolution, but for the greater embodiment, which they are part of and take shape within. Therefore, this question is valuable and this direction of thought is valuable. For all beings to awaken to this truth, that by their own work of consciousness, of transforming their identity into one that is awake, alive, dynamic, filled with Grace, filled with Love itself, is to serve all beings in the whole realm, the whole sphere. The more conscious being understands these principals of unity: that they are not separate, that nothing is separate from each other. The Earth is not separate from the animals, the animals are not separate from the humans, the humans are not separate from each other, and humans are not separate from the entire living sphere of this planet. The human being in their even more conscious state realizes they are not separate from this solar system, they are not separate from the Universal Creation. They are not smaller than the universal embodiment, nor are they bigger than the animals, bigger than the Earth. The unity surpasses this hierarchy of sizing, of importance, these values. All are one in a unified concept of being.

The human being sits in a special throne of ability for consciousness and transformation, whereas the animal, too, is evolving and refining, the human being *knows* it is evolving and refining. The human being has the capacity, the spark for God-mind within itself. The human being is an embodiment of the supreme indivisible, the nameless, overriding consciousness that has been called God. The human being is an embodiment for such brilliant absolute consciousness. Therefore, the human being is in the throne of responsibility. The human being is sitting at a crossroads, a conjunction, being composed physically of the unconscious inert mineral body and being built in capacity through the nervous system, through the soul's nature, to have supreme indivisible consciousness, the consciousness of the Divine. You are each creators of this Earth, just as you are creators of your own progression of lives and your own state of being at present.

The human being is in the throne of the creator. How would you create this Earth right now? To hold the vision, within your heart and within your soul, of the waters of the ocean as pristine, of pure and full of the balance of organisms of life. To hold the vision of the perfected ocean, the original ocean, the healed ocean and the ocean that is not holding contamination, is not a lie nor is it merely hopeful, it is holding the image of the healed state. It is holding the nurturing, life giving energy to the embodiment of Ocean. It is placing your hand down into the ocean and reminding its very cells of who it is. For the ocean, as we speak of it, is being traumatized by this imbalance of chemistry. The trauma equates to amnesia, inertness, an unconsciousness just as toxicity in your physical form will create that. To place your energetic heart, your hand, your envisioning into that ocean and pour your heart of love, your vision of the sparkling life-force that the ocean is meant to host and generate is to hold the healed vision to that aspect of your embodiment. Through the waters of your own being, you are the ocean. Though you may be thousands of miles from the actual site of contamination, the physical ocean within your embodiment knows and is part of. Purify your own waters through how you live and how you eat. Purify the ocean within your embodiment for all the oceans. Hold the consciousness of greater embodiment in your heart and in your mind at all times: "What I do right now with this garbage, with this food, with this choice, I do to the whole."

To think that you are only acting locally to what is in front of you or within you is a sign of the unconscious. It is the animal state that only knows of itself in that moment. Wake up to the human gift, the human capacity for greater consciousness. You are part of the whole sphere, the whole atmosphere of mind, the whole ocean of water. You are part of the whole sphere of the mineral embodiment of this Earth. In your soul, you are part of the entire universe. To your mind this all sounds vast and huge, but beyond your mind's rational, literal components of understanding, beyond that, in your deeper knowing, you know this. You know your breath as the breath of the whole Earth. You will see the life that is sparked alive by each breath is the same life that animates all beings. The purity of your bloodstream is a part of the purity of all river systems and of the ocean. The thought patterns that you hold in your mind are a reflection of the mind itself, the Great Mind. As you free yourself from unconsciousness patterns you will see that those patterns were just closed loops of separation thought: "I am just me. I am just here. I am very small. I am no consequence and anything I do does not really matter, no one sees it, it doesn't count." These are the words of the unconscious being. The conscious being knows that every breath, every sip, every thought, every action feeds into the whole Being-ness, the whole sphere.

To answer the question: "What is the state, now, of this whole ocean body that has been contaminated by these nuclear reactors?" The ocean holds tremendous immunity, tremendous power to heal. The ocean, in and of itself, is swiftly transforming these toxins, swiftly destabilizing them, de-structuring them. Not to no consequence, as there is a prioritizing of this. The products of the break down of these chemicals, in their relative inertness, are being concreted and stored for slower breakdown. There is an unknown-ness to this process in that the Earth has not met this and does not know its immunity or its process for breaking down these concentrations. And there is death of millions of unnamed organisms within the sea and of many named. There is death, and this is being seen. In this death the ocean looks like empty water, water that has been stripped or bleached of life organisms as though razed by the intensity and the strength, as though radiated, as though the sun came too close. There is memory then, within this sea, this Earth of similar bleaching, similar death from too intense exposures to the sun. There is the knowing of recoverability, and the absolute words of recoverability. The Earth has recovered from as extreme chemical states and toxicities, and will. But it changes its course and it alters its evolution. This is built into the embodiments to come. It creates transmutation and altering and shaping of all simple and complex living organisms in times to come.

We leave this on the note of the teaching to hold in simplicity in your body and in your mind, in your heart, the living Earth in its verdancy as an extension of your embodiment, as a part of you. Through endearing yourself and opening your heart in gratitude, as a mother would cradle a baby. This is to direct the unfolding of the transmuting and shapes and forms that will come from this time of intensity, this breaking of pattern in the genetic chains and of the cellular reformation. Your visions of beauty, of belief, will direct the footfall, where the foot comes down, how the cells regroup, how the genetic breakage is continued, how this is included into a reshaping and reforming of many, many creatures and of this entire sphere. And we don't just speak of the irradiated sea, we speak of all the toxins and all the toxicity and all the chemical intensities of the earth. The entire sum story then, is of a stunning pattern, like a silence, and a need for regrouping and reshaping of life forms in so many strata at so many levels. As the guidance system that we are, let us hold the light high, let us guide the reforming of this Earth and its embodiments to an image of perfection, an image of consciousness, and of beauty.

From a place of fearing that radiation infused into the oceans from the Fukushima nuclear accidents will soon be reach North America, we ask about the danger to those living near the west coast. **What can we do to protect ourselves?**

The process we are looking at is multi-level. First, there is the radiation spillage and the transforming, mediating and dissipating of its physical component. The ocean is a large organism that dissipates, dissolves, de-structures and reorganizes all chemistry and all molecular elements in this material world. The ocean is a true factory of alchemy. It is a living organism that is continually creating dynamic changes in molecular matter. The ocean is actively reforming this very chemistry. There is damage and collateral destruction, but even in the destruction and altering of life forms, it is the organism of the ocean that is adjusting and transforming all molecular matter into a form that is sustainable.

The immune system of the ocean is a very powerful and complex dynamic, just as it is in the human body. It is not understood very well in the oceanic body, nor is it fully understood in the human/animal body. In both it is only partially understood. It is this alchemy or force in the immune system, the oceanic and the animal, where we see this de-structuring, this moving or transforming of the molecular into more sustainable and functional forms.

The question was wrought with concern and fear: *"Should we move? Is the Earth on the verge of being truly hurt and destroyed? Are there places on this Earth that should not be inhabited if we are to protect ourselves?"* The answer given is that all life forms: humans, animals, plants, solid earth, the oceanic earth, and the atmospheric earth have a great capacity to cope with, to transform, to direct mutation, to de-structure toxicity, and to take this forward into their own evolution. There is a far greater capacity for this than is being recognized. No need to run, to flee or to fear. There is indeed the need to act, to speak and to not be unconscious nor in denial. But more important is to become a stronger, more highly functioning consciousness within your being, to lift up the strength of your own immunity, to free your own immunity through not fearing, through being in a higher conscious state within your life, within your self. Remembering that being in a state of peace, of strength, of belief, of positive-ness is the backdrop for the immune system being freed to operate at the top of its capacity. This is the movement to take. Become stronger, more full of your own presence. Become more at peace, more informed with higher consciousness within your own being. Liberate the function of your more subtle immune capacity to create transformation instead of destruction.

The Oceanic immune system will mediate much of the crudeness of this toxicity itself. The Oceanic immune system has faced this before, it is not new to the Earth sphere. Intensive doses of this high level chemistry is not new to its memory and not new to its learning. It mobilizes quickly and understands the imperative need for re-forming, de-structuring, stabilizing, sustaining. Much of this will occur and is occurring. There are many surprises for the human being to realize in the nature of immune capacity, of re-forming, re-structuring, de-structuring and evolution itself. There are many wonderful surprises for the human consciousness to yet realize, of what has been and will be in these ways.

The biggest answer and message today is: Do not fear. To fear is to succumb to a lowered state of your own immune system. It is to go into a lesser consciousness and to understand less of the possibilities. Any force released within any system, can create destruction and blow, but also creates possibility. The measure of how much destruction, or how much possibility lies in the intact strength of that system. How awake is that system to where the push can take it? Can the unwritten higher capacity of that system be found? Can that surge of energy flood and awaken that higher capacity, or is it blocked and therefore sending the force into the more crude level, or known level where it could create destruction? The balance really lies in this sort of description. The intactness of every form, every living thing is what is imperative. The force of a disaster can create tremendous possibility in a system or place that has heart and consciousness and love and community. And so it goes with this community of the human being and the world. Having this web and network of consciousness and love and caring, and awareness within, of the highest values will take all blows, all disasters, and intensities into possibility.

We spoke at the beginning of a multi-level understanding of this. There is also a subtle dynamic of transformation, transmutation through higher forces at work within this world and its changes and within humanity's changes. The Guardians, a subtle higher presence, are placing their high level mind and intention towards all of this as well, directing the flow of the Earth in its quaking and its movements and transformations, re-directing the forces of destruction, mediating them, lightening them, balancing them. Not to take away process, not to take away the transformations the Earth and humanity are in, but to mediate their intensity and ferocity. All for the purpose of the evolution of this beautiful holistic sphere of earth and creature and plant and soul and divine embodiment of human being. Realize that there is so much more than you hear in analysis and in lateral consciousness. There is so much more at play. And, do your part to be at peace despite the storms, despite the news, despite the rational mind. Commit yourself to existing in a higher state of being and in a greater faith in the evolution of all beings.

Our question is about the effects of radiation. Is there radiation that could still be coming to the west coast of North America from Japan? (following the 2011 earthquake)

The guidance is showing me a radiation effect; I am seeing a stream of what it is doing. It is a very forceful, catalytic change to chemistry. We are watching it in the ocean right now, in the water, and what it is doing to an organism, watching what it is doing to a fish. What is happening in one fish will be happening in all affected fish. I am shown streams, because there are streams that fan out and break down as the ocean consumes, mediates and dulls them after a time. However, the effect in a stream can carry on.

There is a first effect, a second effect, and a third effect in the water. The first effect is that there are changes to the actual chemistry of the sea, the water, the complexity of this mineral soup that the sea is. If no living organism were to ingest this, which is never the case, but if you were just to look at the water, we see the first effect being mediated and dulled. We see the radiation having a short-term effect. Then it falls out of itself, the force of that radioactive material falls out of power. It goes into inert breakdown and is no longer a threat to anything. This first effect travels a certain distance from the source and it doesn't go very far, it breaks down very quickly. The sea around Japan will have a lot of this but it won't go a whole lot farther.

The second effect occurs when radiation is taken into the living organisms, such as fish. We watch how this creates a numbing and a bending right into the genetic material. We see that numbness is the body's response and bending is a forcing in that genetic material to lengthen, to extend, develop what has not yet been developed. The numbing is the body shutting down somewhat. We see the digestive system shutting down first and we see the airways shutting down, we don't see it to the point of death, though of course, it can be if there is a really strong contact. There is a shutting down and a numbness as the body encounters what is extremely alien. Yet, it is not only alien, there is also a force. That force goes as far as if you were to put that organism into a high vibratory microwave. The force goes into the very centre of the cell and creates a lengthening, an extending. We are actually seeing the inert non-developed aspects of the DNA surging into life. How an organism survives this is variable, some organisms don't survive, they can't do anything with this, especially if they have had too strong a contact with the full force. *Once the full force has become muted and mediated, there is a stage in this force description that matches each organism in optimum ways.* So speaking of the fish, they will respond to this quite well in their simplicity, in their fluidity, in their adaptability, when it is not in its first phase of force, but in its second phase when the effect of the force is starting to break down. In the human being, in their complexity, they are the most vulnerable. Strange to see this, the more complex the organism is, the more vulnerable, the more mediated they need this nuclear force to be. Yet, when they are in exposure to this mediated, muted, nuclear force, it can be an exact catalytic force to stimulate and produce more activity within the DNA. This will not necessarily be seen in that same body of contact, but will be seen in generations to come. That body is already formed and is only maintaining, but the formation of the next body and the body after that, through the genetics, is where this will be seen, the extended DNA impact.

What can be seen in the first body, in the human who contacted it in this life, are different responses to the numbness, the numbness that is exposure to the alien, and different responses to the surge. Even though the surge is mediated at the DNA strand, it can also be mediated in the consciousness. The consciousness, remember, is not confined to the biological body, the consciousness sits independently and through the biological body. The consciousness can take the surge, or the being can stay in numbness. Staying in numbness is deathly, for the immune system to be in numbness is death to the organism. Taking the surging consciously, taking it into the consciousness can activate the immune system into a higher rate than ever before and create more immunity than ever before.

So there are many choices and many ways that this is met throughout the Earth. The trees hold immunity; they hold non-responsiveness. The trees, in their slow moving nature are not resonant to this force.

The final comment is that this continent (North America) is in a perfect distancing from that force. By the time the nuclear force comes to this continent, it is mediated to a subtlety that can be useful and can be used, rather than just destructive. The beings who have been exposed to the first level of force whose physical bodies go into various stages of numbness, that benefit goes into their genetics only, and in those that survive to reproduce, into their future embodiments that they would create. And in that, for you to see, there is a brilliance, and in long years distant looking back: "Where did the brilliance arise? What was the factor in such a surge of intellectual and spiritual brilliance?" This is where it is from; it is from the fast evolving DNA strands in those genetic lineages.

Earth's Twelve Chakras

We ask about the 12 Earth chakras.

The guidance instantly shows the axis of the Earth and shows the points being spoken of, the nodes in their equidistant positioning along the axis. These are internal nodes, internal to the earth, running through the centre from pole to pole. We see the dynamic of these twelve nodes, the axis points of the earth's body and its centre stream, operating unconsciously in accordance to both the gravity it composes, and the gravity from the sun.

We are seeing the unconscious pattern, which to be understood compassionately, is any pattern which repeats itself and slips into an unconsciousness. This is a necessary part of a body's formation. It is as though a functioning pattern is put in place and allowed to continue on its own, requiring the least energy for its continuance. Only when there is a need to change is there consciousness again, then a need to maintain the new pattern until it can then step into the unconscious.

This is a description of the two gravities and a change in the way gravity is dictating or formatting the Earth. We are seeing the change, the rewriting of that relationship. Seeing each of those 12 nodes activating towards the sun, activating towards the celestial intensity of the meaning and the brilliance of the sun's body.

We are seeing within the earth the remembrance, within its very matter, of who it is, where it comes from, what its own magma really is. Knowing itself as a child of the sun, a likeness of the sun. We see an igniting, a lighting up along every node. We see the central nodes of the earth's embodiment being very powerful and dynamic factors in **what is changing the genetic relationship within all bodies, all formation upon itself.** We see the same axis of the 12 nodes within all bodies that walk its surface. We see the igniting of the 12 nodes within the earth, igniting within the genetic code of all bodies upon the earth. The earth, then, is the leader. The earth, then, is the foundation.

Through the reception of the earth's centre stream and re-writing its relationship to the sun, so then are all bodies upon the earth carried into this. It is an event of magnitude that carries on for generations and generations. As the earth remembers itself as a part of the sun and a part of all celestial bodies of brilliance, so does every body upon the earth have its own version of remembrance of who it is beyond itself.

Photon Energy

This question is about a teaching which says that around 2012 a completely new form of energy resource called photons, or photon energy will come to Earth and be accessible. We want to understand more about what was taught from a channeling source, Fred Sterling, who channeled Master Kireal.

The first correction is that this is not a new energy form. It is a new receptivity within Earth's field, to what continually emanates from the sun. Most of what the sun emanates is not receivable, not able to be digested or integrated and utilized. The earth as an energetic entity is evolving into a subtler maturing. The earth evolves alongside all of its creatures and the very powerful component of its human population, not in isolation. The evolution of the earth and the human being must be seen as an intimate oneness, not as two separate evolving entities, but as one. Receptivity to the higher vibration source of photonic energy is more a description of readiness within the earth's field and the human field simultaneously. The human being stimulates the earth into a higher nature of itself. The human being, who holds the ability within its genetics for higher consciousness, evolves all life forms around it, evolves the earth form. For this higher receptivity that sits in potential within the human being is the very place for the integration of this light ray. It is this higher light ray that holds within it the potency to create all energy resource. As the human being, in a massive collective way, is able to receive this higher vibratory light ray, the Earth is also lifted in its field. Lifted in its preparedness and readiness to integrate and help with the digestion, the absorption, the mediation of this higher light ray, the companionship with this higher light ray within itself.

The question as to when, as to the imminence:

Swiftly now we show her the human race in a sweep of awareness, as though looking at a billion points of consciousness below us, billions of points of consciousness, and showing the percentage, or the array of those points that has the resonance. It is being shown as a certain quality of light that vibrates in a certain way. We see a swift opening occurring in this body of the human soul, this sweep of sight. We see that this swift spreading of resonance is occurring and as the resonance occurs, it occurs even swifter as though the information is instantly transferred. As one point (or one being) opens to this resonance it makes it easier by half for the one next, and so, on it goes increasing in momentum. There is no question that this higher integration of the vibratory light ray is in place, is occurring and being prepared for. We don't answer, and no one should, as to the date and the time. We answer to say it is happening before our eye right now, the swifter and swifter transference of resonant readiness to this photonic higher light ray. The integration, the digestion, assimilation, the use of this, is the subject for the next thousand years. You are looking at an infancy of a new development. As you sit in meditation, or yielded-ness, as you sit in love for 'All there is', within your heart and being, you are one of these points of sparkling light. You are anchoring, stabilizing, holding the higher light ray in your embodiment and you are making it easier by half for the one next to you. This is all you need to know. The development of the use of new energy that is capacitated will be the story of the generations to come. And you are right in knowing everything is perfect.

Understand that the source of energy from oil is a description of the past. It is a defining and bonding and holding to an energy state of the past that needs to run itself out and be over. You are here at the crossroads watching the ending and the beginning at the same time. Be patient and wise, not despairing the ending, but realizing how much is ending. Like watching a very, very old, old being that has existed for thousands of years, coming to a realization that it is time to die. There is to be no impatience, there is to be wisdom in realizing this dying transformation must occur in every point in this scope of beings we show, these billions of beings. Look individually at the patterns of the past and their over-ness, this identifying with the lower vibration within identity and mind and emotion and relationship to Earth. Look at the intricacy of that process within yourself and be patient.

Humanity in Evolution

*Where is **humanity** at this time, in its evolution?*

The largeness of this question requires a large answer. It requires looking at the whole collated soul state, the field of linking of all souls. The most positive report of this, is that there are no barriers any longer between all souls. There is a flooding of illumination and greater understanding occurring in the souls of all beings that are choosing to enter embodiments through this age. We did not say at this time, we said 'this age'. All souls in resonance to evolution in this sphere are unobstructed from the illumination that is flowing like mercury, everywhere. The true and one identity understanding is beginning to touch all beings, and there is tremendous resistance in the embodiments. There is tremendous contraction and confusion and even dementia, and yet in the soul, in the largest answer, they cannot hold out, they can see too much. **Memory is being flicked awake like a switch in all souls in their dreams, in their dying, in their re-birthing.** But what you often see is the contraction and the closure of those in resistance. Do not judge this, for even though the ones before you seem to be in full resistance and full contraction, they are not. They are being nudged actively in the core of their energy systems, in their dreams, even in their emotions. **There are breakthroughs of thought in even the most closed beings, understandings that feel as though they are not from them. They are hearing words of truth from** *others that they have heard before, but never really heard.* Everywhere the great, shared identity of truth is flooding like illumination. For many who sit in contraction and restriction, it will take illness, if not trauma or death to relieve them of the contraction and the resistance. The crisis functions as part of the cleansing, part of the renewal and the evolution.

Your only task is to have undying, steady conviction and faith in the mission of embodiments, the evolution in this sphere of Grace. **There is no other truth that is occurring here but Grace, and no other direction but the flowering of Grace.** There is no other choice, only a matter of how long, which is more what each being comes to, how long to hold on to contraction and resistance. There are those beings who will be shuffled, by their choosing to resist, into a slower evolution, into positions of less and less power within embodiment, more and more suffering and illness, in the lives to come. And we say then, in the lives to come and in the whole collated life of humanity, those coming into power will be the ones who have understood; the dominance of those that are choosing Grace coming into power.

So, how is humanity doing? Humanity is actively unfolding, beautifully unfolding.

Action and Reaction: "To every action, there is an equal and opposite reaction."

If at this time in humanity, there is an increase in consciousness and grace, is it a reaction to, or a reflection on the darkness and unconsciousness that we've come from?

The phasing of humanity at this time leads us to the question of equilibrium. The question of cycles of becoming and unbecoming, cycles of the lifting of consciousness to the highest possible degree of itself and cycles of the lowering of consciousness to the most limited aspect of itself.

The unconsciousness, darkness, cruelty, and animalistic bestiality of human nature manifested during the last thousand years and more has set forth or released the call, the karma we could say, and the energy to demonstrate and to exist at its highest level of possibility. The reality of this is that a soul who has died in the most horrific way wakes up and screams no more. A soul that dies in the condensation of grief, fear and horror is reduced into the centerpiece of their being which cannot die. The centerpiece of their being holds the very tenants of eternal life and purpose. It is a sweeping clean and sweeping away of all the layers, tearing them off until all that is left is that which cannot die and yearns to live. Taking away life over and over again until the seed kernel of yearning to live begins to cry out. Only life! There is only life! There is no choice, there is only life, there is only love. (No choice meaning a true realization of their ongoing, undying being, and this must be nurtured and loved.)

Horror, violence, hatred and ignorance is no longer a choice. The upswing or equal reaction, in the words of physics, is an actual becoming, a consciousness surging forward to its ultimate statements of 'I am.' It is a refusal to be anything but 'I am,' and a refusal to live in the half-light and to live in the fear.

So in the next millennium, all the beings that died, and were killed, and that killed and that died and killed and over and over, all the beings that found finality, that found the hellishness and the desperation are saying, 'No more, there is no choice, there is only this.' All of those beings strengthened by that very holocaust. All those beings coming to an ending of unconsciousness right there, and being born in the progression of learning how to choose only that which endures, only that which resonates in their being with the yearning to exist in the fullest, in the light and the beauty.

Understand this dynamic: when beauty becomes the only choice, then beauty begins to manifest and the entire sphere is created in conscious beauty, not innocent, but conscious.

The beings coming into this sphere now are to assist this. They are healers. They are creating repair because many of the souls that were brought down to the very rock bottom were so numbed and so hurt that, although they have found there is no choice, they are still so burdened, so distrusting that they can even exist. Existence was taken away too often; can they ever believe in existence? So the beings that are entering in are healing, livening and invigorating. It is a great gathering time, and it is a great time of assistance. **The next millennium will truly be the equal and the opposite manifestation of the previous millennia.**

*How much **human population** is sustainable by Earth?*

First, we speak to the physical capacity of the Earth to nurture and sustain or feed. This capacity is immeasurable. There is an inherent capacity in the Earth to sustain the present population. It is not about capacity, it is about human interaction with the Earth and the way the Earth is being used to create sustenance. It is more about the methods, the ways, the skills and the conscious ability of the human population to work with the Earth for sustaining itself. In other words, the literal number in the population *can* be sustained on this Earth. It is the method of creating and receiving sustenance that is unsustainable. The Earth cannot recover nor sustain in the way it is now being used.

The Earth's capacity to bring forth life forms is so deep, so burgeoning and so rich that it can support life forms to a very great extent. The capacity of the Earth to adjust, to recover, to alter itself in relationship to the life forms is also very great, immeasurable. Yet, these things are being said at a great scale of time, over a great scale of process. In the immediate and in the scale of a human lifetime or series of generations, this recoverability and capacity may be witnessed as depleted or ineffective. If the Earth is being used wrongly, as it is, the recoverability may not be seen in a lifetime or even in generations, within the very limited, linear time sense of human memory, human being.

The question, most directly was: *"How great a population of humanity can this Earth sphere support?"* The Earth can support all souls coming into embodiment, all beings coming into embodiment. This is not a surprise or an anomaly. It is not a mistake that the population is so great. That would be a questioning of the source of universal evolution. This population is sustainable to the Earth in its consciousness and state of health, just as any relationship is sustainable if it is in health, and it is not sustainable if it isn't. All relationships either nurture or destroy and take away from the other. We are speaking of relationship, and that is all: the relationship between the human being and its foundational form, which is the Earth, for even your body is the Earth. Your body is the foundational form of your lifetime, of your evolution in form. The Earth and your body are the same thing. If you were to penetrate the body with your understanding, you would see it is made of the same substance and material and is an extension of the Earth, a tendril of the life form of the Earth. It is a form of the Earth that is enabled for consciousness, refined for movement and refined to host the consciousness of soul, of divinity. The human being is an exquisite meeting point of Earth and Divine Being-ness.

The question is one of relationship: the relationship between the consciousness and mind of humanity, the nature of identity, and the embodiment, the form. To the extent that the human being is unconscious in this relationship, there is destruction and it is not sustainable; to the degree that the human being is conscious of itself, within this form, and understands its physical body is simply the Earth, it is recoverable. Look no further than your own body, to know what relationship you have with the Earth. Look no further than the health of the physical forms in your community (the human beings, the animals, the plants) to know what the relationship is to the Earth and how sustainable it is. The partial health and ill health at this time is a spinning, weaving interplay of consciousness and unconsciousness, of health and ill health. Consciousness and health are two words for the same thing; ill health and unconsciousness are also two words for the same thing.

To this is added the hope and the message of the recoverability of the Earth form. In your body and beneath your feet, the entire physical organism in this sphere has tremendous immunity built into it, tremendous strength and mission. Mission to exist, to host the life form to its point of the most refined. However, the human being is not yet at that point. The human being is in a process towards that point of refinement. The mission and the purpose of this physical sphere is to bring forth the most refined meeting point of Diving Being-ness in form. Therefore, it is built into the knowledge and the immunity, into the DNA, that this process is not at a completion. There is the tremendous purpose and will within the Earth to exist towards its mission, and within the human being towards its root purpose, which is to come into the most refined state of possibility for consciousness within form. We speak of this because it is this very process and purpose that is behind recoverability: adapting, changing and finding a way around obstacles, building obstacles into the knowledge and into the strength.

The Earth is the teacher at this time, teaching the human being to care for its own embodiment, to care for itself, to care for the body you walk in and the body of all those around you. The Earth is the teacher, the forgiver and the nurturer. The ancient knowledge of the First Nations that the Earth is a living substrate, a living being, a living form that gives rise to all its children and all its life forms, is a great unity of knowing of the being-ness of this material, life-filled sphere.

The Earth is meant for you and you are meant for the Earth. And

'You' is the five billion you, all of you.

*How will the **developing unity consciousness** change our relationship with **money**, our society of corporations and consumers, wealth and poverty, with individual ownership and wealth determining rights and privileges?*

It is a very pointed question and a definite question, which necessitates an understanding of the present conditions of security, material sustenance. Money is really just an in-between to material security and safety. Money is a step between eating and the food being eaten, between the body and the safety of a house, between the body and its need to be warm and safe and secure. Money is a literal abstract, money is a step between, creating some distance in concept and distance in the direct understanding of what material wealth or sustenance really is. The human embodiment, as with all animal embodiments, need the sustenance and security of the material world in order to live. So, the base description is survival. Adorning survival then, is that it be so in place and so cared for that there are no thoughts any more of survival. It is plenty; it is relaxation into plenty. There is then, a distance between the root need to survive and the need to create safety and survival, and the relaxation of the senses to survival and safety into plenty.

What is the relationship to money now? What has it been before? If not to live here in safety, in wellness, in relaxation and peace, to not be afraid that one cannot eat, afraid that one cannot feel secure in this physical world. In the physical world at present, one does not have far to look for images of non-safety, starvation and want and need. Not far to look to see what money is at this time in evolution. Just around the corner is no money, is lack, what it means not to have food, not to have the means, the interim step of money towards food and home. The story and images of the slums of India is just around the corner, a plane flight away at this time in human evolution.

The question is: *What will it become in the more conscious state of the more evolved spiritual being-ness? What is it then?* Woven to this understanding is a need to understand the conscious state. As the human soul opens to "Thou art, I am. You are me and I am you. I care as much about your existence as mine. I feel and love and am as caring and responsible to your existence as I am to mine and to your family as I am to mine", there is the true and lived experience of the Golden Rule, that as you are, I am. There is the true and lived experience of the Christ teaching that as you treat the least of yourselves, so you are to me, as you love the least, you love me. The realization that God or Supreme Source Being is existent in all beings and that as we attend to all beings, we attend to that Supreme Nature. As we tend to the least, we tend to the greatest. Since Supreme Nature is who we are in our essential definition, as we tend to all beings, we tend to ourselves.

The identity of the human being in the more conscious state, is so expanded and so shifted that it doesn't see another being as outside of itself. It sees the individuality of another being but it does not address it as outside and separate. It sees all other beings as extensions of itself, extensions of Supreme Nature. This premise of identity changes how we care for each other and how we use the material resources of this world. In this state of consciousness it is not possible to take more for self, while the one in front of you has less. It is not possible to take so much for self while the one over there has nothing. Therefore, there is a spontaneous natural equalization of the resources and how they are used in all their hierarchical structures. All structures that organize the distribution of wealth and material sustenance equalize as the unity identity filters into more and more, taking hold with a sense of power and grace and remembrance. The issues of unequal sharing, unequal distribution of wealth and material sustenance disappear, easily, as this is understood. You will see this beginning in this life even. You will begin to understand. As new generations are born, they are born already with this unity consciousness that shows right away in childhood.

How does this unity consciousness manifest? It manifests as a felt compassion, where even a child can feel the lack in another, can feel it within them and know that to give to another, settles that pain. They can feel the need in another as though it were their own need and they know that to give to the other, silences the pain within themselves. There is the cross-referencing and the transferring of experience in children, who understand innately the needs of another, because they feel it in themselves and yet, know it comes from the other. They know to give to the other in order to silence and bring peace into themselves.

As the generations progress in maturity it is a true understanding that to listen to or face another is also to feel into another and be able to assess and understand the needs in another. There is an inability to divide the other's experience, to not feel it, and a knowing that to attend to them will bring more health and peace to oneself. As the greater consciousness develops into the unity consciousness, there is an ending to the imbalances.

Will we have the opportunity in this lifetime to experience **the sacred feminine energy** *(the creating and nurturing energy) manifesting in global political decisions?*

The simple answer is a very strong **yes.** However, there are many elements referred to in this question. What is the real intention of this question and how is it meant? One of the elements in the question is: 'in our lifetime'. In terms of timing, in terms of what you shall witness, you are beginning to witness this already and you will be witnessing this more and more, and with more and more surprising rapidity. You will not be witnessing it in its *completion,* in terms of the timing of the question: your lifetime. This is a much bigger change of the core operating state of being than what will occur just within your lifetime. This is the direction of the human being in evolution. It is the firm solid unquestionable direction of the human being's core state of consciousness, that from where they most exist. It is the direction of the identity, of how everything is created not only the political, but also the artistic, the mathematical, the scientific, and the medical. It is the core operating state of the future, to come from the sacred feminine, which brings in the need to explain what is meant in that.

There are three levels to the answer. First, in your lifetime, you will see a shift in focus; we could say a shift of operating systems, occurring more and more. Not it's completion, for this is a completion that takes over everything and impregnates all systems and all future developments. We're speaking here just to further the answer. It takes three generations. You could call yourself a mother generation, a parental generation to the state of identity meant by 'coming from the sacred feminine'.

We will re-word sacred feminine to be more succinct and clear: we will re-word it as **the identity of the human being coming from a place of non-separation, non-gender based, non-self based, but coming from an inherent natural consciousness as being part of the whole, not separate from any other country, culture or being.** It is a natural, easy understanding and assumption that all are entwined very deeply and that all beings hold equality, a familiarity, and a sense of being part of each other. Perhaps in the gender based, more archaic terms of 'mother' and 'the feminine', this is a more natural state and an easier gender from which to see this unity. But the term 'sacred feminine' is too isolating, too separating in itself.

The core identity, the core "I am-ness" that is emerging in the next several generations is neither feminine nor masculine. It is a coalescence of the two. The masculine is the energy to manifest, the force and the power to manifest the belief, to make the decisions, to implement the truth. The feminine is the instant consciousness to sense, to embrace, to take in, to be a part of all beings. It is the wisdom of the unity awareness, and the masculine aspect is that wisdom flowing, moving, implementing, and building.

The very terms, the very goddesses, the very strongholds of imagery, the archetypes of the different states of consciousness, the attributes of God, all begin to lose some of their hold, in that they themselves create too much isolation. **When Shiva and Lakshmi blend, what is the name then?** When the fire, the warmth, the light all blend, what is the name then? When force and becoming blend, when the masculine and the feminine fall away, what is the name then? What is needed is the emergence of the wholeness, the emergence of the being in fullness, emerging through every system.

You will see the generations to come knowing this without having learned it, because they've learned it previously. Emerging it through their words, their books and their papers, through the systems that they have taken into hand. It emerges in such completeness, as though it emerged from what? It is because it emerged from their beings previous, and it will illustrate to any that don't believe, that all beings present have been developing for eons. They have been gathering information while they have been lodged in the archetypes, lodged in the separations. They have been learning, gaining and logging wisdom for so long, and now they are emerging in the fullness of that. And you, the parental, are ever surprised to hear what this new generation and the next new generation is creating and saying. A sense of the instant emergence of wisdom, and we laugh, is there an instant emergence of wisdom? Or is there a readiness, or is there a configuration of power, of all the lines of becoming, of all the purposes held in this sphere of being.

When you look at the mother here, and you look at the moment of birth that's arriving what are the elements of this moment of birth? It is a configuration, it is a moment of power that says yes, and then there is this instant emerging. But what of that, it isn't just the fullness of the belly signaling the nervous system that it's time. What is the intricate moment of birth for this babe here, it is the same: what is the intricate moment of birth for this state of unity arising in the consciousness? It is the blending of the sacred feminine and masculine into just *the sacred being.* You are all gestational to that. You all have been, for lives. *You are waiters, you are those that are waiting, you are those that are witnessing, you are - each one of you - like a totem pole leaning over, perhaps you have been waiting for so long.* Guardians watching for this and when you hear it you will know it and you will smile because it's emerging now. And you will know that the long waiting has finally borne fruit.

There is much more to be said about the emerging identity that hosts or that is formed of the sacredness, the blend of the masculine and feminine, and the fullness of being. There is much that can be said about how a political system operates, how a medical system operates, but that is not the question. The question is 'will we see this emerging in our lifetime?' Hold steady to your watching, to your standing on the cliff edge watching, watching the world, and watching the emerging of the generations listening to their words. Listening to the changes, and the more you know that you are here to see it, you will see it come. It is part of your mission to watch it arrive, even if it's just a little trickle, even if it's just over here and not over there, you can smile and know that soon it will be everywhere.

*We ask to have more understanding of the **transgender** phenomenon, especially when it occurs in small children, as a desire to change their gender.*

The Guidance is here, very present and very aware of this. This topic is under great discussion in the realm of the beings guiding humanity. This is a very new time. This is not a new phenomenon, but it is a new time in the human psyche, which is titled 'Understanding of Freedom'. This freedom, to emerge in the true character of a soul, the true nature of a being, without suppression, is a description in many fields, many ways. Emergence, free of the conditions restricting the knowing of oneself and the true identifying of one's being. The freedom is about individuality and the nature of being, fully stepping forward. That this freedom is being sensed and felt in every way is tremendously positive. This is a tremendous time for consciousness. It is felt in incoming souls, it is felt in dying souls. It is sensed and felt all over this sphere of human being-ness. It is freedom as a generalized theme, a facilitated state that is coming swiftly and quickly into possibility.

The question of transgender, especially as it arises in the naivety and purity of a child, is one of the markers of this freedom. This is to be understood within the larger scope of freedom, of individuality knowing it can emerge without restrictions or judgments, without condemnation or danger. For eras, the conditions of condemnation, danger, death and exile (and on and on with these words of extreme judgment), whereby a soul knows it can only partially express and partially emerge, have been the conditions of human beings. When a being's need to emerge has been in contradiction to the culture, different to the expectation and to the norm, there has been exile, condemnation, death and tremendous trauma deepening with life experiences. There are many ways in which a being is under limitation, for their colour, their race, their gender, their temperament, their place of life, their place in family, their economic conditions. In so many ways the human being has been living under crushing conditions that have not allowed the full emergence of their individuality. Not even a hint of their individuality, really, coming into consciousness and into emergence.

This time period which is being entered into for the next phase will show you many strange things as freedom speaks: "Come forward, emerge." You will be shown many strange things as beings feel the absence of restrictions and the ability to manifest their true nature. **There are beings who have chosen one gender repeatedly, for its safety, for its chances, and to exist without suffering, whereas the need in their soul has been to be the other gender, to round out and experience the two qualities of being-ness.** There are those, and we say it is most, who have chosen one gender for its familiarity, for its known qualities and lack of risk, because it is a great risk to move into the opposite gender and learn how to be it quickly, successfully, without contaminating that gender with the gender that is most known. This was dangerous territory in the past, to switch the consciousness of gender, since very seldom does one exist purely and flag the fullness of that gender to others on the first lifetime of that transition.

These children then, are not only marked by freedom, but by confusion. "Who am I really? Am I this? Am I that?" An un-worded, unconscious sense that they can be whatever and whoever they most are, but what is that? This next phase has much confusion in this way, and yet as the lifetime continues for each one of these, the result of the confusion is a true freedom from gender itself. And you the questioner, the concerned ones, concerned parents, friends, can see that bigger picture. *As the gender confusion emerges, because of the freedom to do so, the result is an integration of both genders in consciousness.* Perhaps a wild swinging back and forth, perhaps wild displays of this or that, and yet the result of this is a settling into the centeredness of both genders. There is safety, rightness and the deep sense of correctness to being both, and neither. This is the result of removing the restrictions, the fear, and the need to be in one gender fully for the safety that it gives. As these restrictions dissolve, there is a wild swinging between genders, the trying on of gender mentality and consciousness, with the eventual settling into the very centre of this, the 'I am who I am', the wholeness of 'I am' and the sense of being able to use masculine qualities when needed and feminine qualities when needed. We show her a relationship there, between two beings in the equilibrium of their gender, together being able to bring forth the masculine or the feminine gracefully and easily and feel the much greater blending of souls that two in relationship can have when not locked into one gender modality or the other. So this answer takes us to the most positive outcome resulting from this time of confusion and liberation.

*We ask about those who come into life a certain gender and choose to unite with one of the **same gender**, wanting to understand that.*

The Guidance points directly, first showing that the being can choose in a patterned way to exist within a gender for many incarnations. And that when they are called within their being, and there are many reasons for this, to shift into another gender within the next incarnation, it is not a distinct shift. It is not a complete shift, in that they carry within their essence, their cloud of being, the energetic field or sense of gender that they have walked. It can take several lifetimes to create a shift of gender awareness, where the character of being-ness matches the gender of the body. Therefore, in the ways of the heart, of intimacy, of relating mind-to-mind, heart-to-heart, there can be more familiarity, and this is where the resonance goes. There may be those who are choosing, choosing or being guided to choose, to change gender to increase their evolution, to meet karma, to serve karma, and yet they can't fully embody the gender choice they have made. The body sits there in its formation, but the being is the being, so there can be a strongly feminine essential being struggling to exist in a male hormonal body. A being sitting largely in the feminine state of consciousness can affect even the hormonal system of a masculine body.

The rightness of this struggle is that in the end, the being is learning of self as essence only, as neither male nor female, but heart and mind and presence. This is increasing in the world now that it is safe. It is safe to push the evolution of ones being and step out of the patterns. It is far more than changing genders in an embodiment that is occurring now. It is changing cultures, changing languages, changing philosophy. It is safe to create more wholeness of experience by crossing gender, by changing gender, by changing culture, moving out of the placement of ancestors, of country. Changing everything about how the embodiment is. This is confusing, stimulating, catalytic, and above all, evolving. ***Evolving the One mind, the One being, the One culture, the highest androgynous understanding of spiritual being-ness, the merging of philosophy.***

So, this is a generalized description, which does not take into account the individual's karma, their stories of pain and anguish or need for exploration. Only to say, the climate of embodiment now, renders it safe to make these choices.

There is more: there is a reminder now, that held within the essential identity of the spirit of the human being, is an ***androgynous root of being,*** a root of identity that is not differentiated too strongly masculine or feminine. In this most original print of identity, the eventual choosing of the poles of being, feminine or masculine, was a choice, not at the expense of losing the fullness of being, but the choice of expressing and experiencing the feminine or the masculine. The purpose of identifying more distinctly within an embodiment is that it gives more energy to the polarizing effect, the duality. But always, the consciousness of wholeness was there, and always the choice was there. Even while in the feminine embodiment, there is the ability to understand the unity within, and move into the masculine dimension when needed.

Through the deepening of unconsciousness and the repeating of patterns, the feminine has become a fixed state for some, and the masculine a fixed state for others, highly separated, highly confining with no access to the whole identity within. Thus, a being needs to take the energy, and find the courage and the force to move across the gap and embody in the other gender. A being needs the consciousness to do so, and then must re-identify, finding out how to exist in a new way; it would have been easier not to.

The time is coming for the true root identity to emerge, the identity of liberation and freedom that uses both poles of being within itself. You are watching the process of this, the process of the pendulum swinging a little more wildly, of pounding on the door of acceptance, and the door yielding. "I accept you as you". The Namaste between beings is increasing.

The New Fruit

We ask for an understanding of events and conditions in the world today, in the context of the ascension of human beings and the Earth. Is there a way to prepare, within our beings, for the greater consciousness movement?

The Guidance is so obedient, I always feel it's absolute adherence to what we mean, what we're asking and where we are reaching, and a steady, steady going to the heart of the question. I'm being brought into the world dynamic and into the current moment of this world, assessing the feeling of the human spirit right now, and the Earth's foundation, its spirit. The Guidance takes me into a metaphorical vision or visual, showing concretions or patterns that have settled into the identity of the human spirit, the human being. Also, the concretions or patterns that have settled into the identity of the Earth, its embodiment and its being. I am shown that these concretions or patterns are cracking and fracturing rapidly, the very identity of the human being is cracking and the identity of the Earth is cracking. It is simultaneous and the description is for both.

The human being, in a very generic, core sense is cracking. How we relate to life, to ourselves, to what life is about, is cracking. The concretions (or patterns) are cracking, not the truth, not the essential living dynamic truth, but the concretions. Understand concretions as settled patterns. The visual we are given is of a settled pattern that becomes lifeless, like debris that settles and becomes concrete. See that with the cracking or shattering, the living layer of human identity is exposed. ***The rising forth of true life force, of true spirit force, is causing this shedding and*** *expulsion, the dissolving of truly concrete patterns, habitual patterns that sit in the generic human identity.*

The words may sound nebulous, what do they really say? To describe the patterns, we say that human beings relate in a certain way to time and to the body. There are expectations around how one is embodied, around what it means to be alive in the body, what to strive for, value, hold as goals, as measures of success, what to hold as the attributes of safety and survival. We could go on and on. These are the concretized patterns that confine the identity, imprison it and obscure the true living identity.

The momentum of the spirit force rising, of the true identity moving forth has gathered such force. We will witness, in the name of ascension, a rewriting of reality, a rewriting of who we are in this world. A rewriting of every qualification of humanness: being in relationship, being in community, our interaction with the Earth for sustenance, how to understand, and what to value for safety and survival. We are sitting at the beginning of a tremendous time, and it will take time. It will become very surprising, exhilarating and wondrous. It will appear tremendously tragic at times, but understand this as the shedding of dead identity, dead patterns that have been built into the very gene model, built into a very pervasive memory. Every time a being rebirths, the expectation of what they are being birthed into changes.

The identity shift of Earth is a whole different description. We see all living forms developing a more refined nervous system, becoming more lightly clothed in their substance, and more interactive with each other. We see especially, the living plant forms exuding a new and far more refined quality of dynamic life force into the atmospheric field of the Earth, powering and feeding all embodiments, impregnating and filling all developing embodiments with a more refined capacity. As ever, the Earth is host to evolution.

Know that the one who asks the question of how to prepare, is preparing. One who can be bothered to listen to the answer is preparing by listening. Attending to the words of a master, the words of truth, is preparing. Preparing to be defined more definitively is to refine the identity within your being. Give space for higher refinement and give time and priority to letting the identity within your being refine itself. Be prepared and ever ready to let go of concretions or patterns within your own identity. Question the beliefs that repeat and confine. Find them. Inquire into repeating feelings, beliefs and actions that limit. Attend to the refining of your identity.

*We are nearing the end of 2010, coming into 2011 and we want to understand how humanity is doing as a whole in its evolution at this transition time to the **New Year**.*

The Guidance is bringing me to this very generalized question of the whole of humanity and its condition at present, and needing to point out that there are many pockets and areas of evolution within humanity at this time. There are those with brilliant flowering and opening, and those in great contraction. There are those in great unconsciousness and there are degrees of consciousness of varying qualities all over the globe within humanity. Therefore the question is a very general question.

Yet to sum it up for the purpose of this, is to show that within the group field, or group soul of the evolving being, there is tremendous impetus towards truth. There is a great tolling of the bell towards evolution at a faster rate and the manifesting of truth within each being at a faster rate. The crisis, the unconsciousness and the contractions all have a different hue and meaning than they have ever before. There is an importance and imperativeness, there is an ending, as though everything counts for more. There is the greater tide of unifying and group awareness. The crisis and contraction carries a being, further than ever before, towards the ending of that experience and towards the realization of its falseness and its needlessness. There is a readiness within the human being as a whole to no longer be in unconscious darkness, to no longer be in continual crisis. The message is being heard universally, throughout all beings, that this is not what is meant. If you could hear into many, they would be saying: "This is not what it is meant to be; this is not what we wish to continue to live with." There is a greater push and yearning to find the true answer and to find the freedom.

In general, the human being is breaking through, breaking through and creating endings. They are experiencing karma at a faster rate, they are cleansing, flushing and releasing at a greater rate than ever. Experiencing dying and sickness in such a way that they are disengaging from the state of being ill, and in a state of anguish and despair. They are disengaging from the state of unconsciousness. We see many that are dying in the wars and traumas, and upon death are realizing a freedom and disengagement, not identifying with this. They are realizing how they had created it, realizations of great luminosity. Realizing how to not continue creating this. You still see the creation of crisis. You still see the maintaining of unconsciousness and its effects. Perhaps what you don't see is the realization occurring swift as a wave throughout so many, for how could you know what a being has realized upon death, in the darkness of their crisis. There is more potency being released within the souls in crisis, more effect and more fruiting of true realization. Likewise, there are many opening in their consciousness to a deeper sense of who they are, a deeper sense of remembrance and of becoming. A deeper capacity for consciousness, a deeper internalizing of the Christ message, of the Golden Rule, of living for others, of the meaning of compassion, the meaning and the experience of love. There are many questioning and disengaging from their religion where it is rigid, and opening their hearts and souls to the original teachings held in their religion.

The question was asked with worry, concern and weariness. You are understood and accepted for this, for who would not be weary to hear of humanity at this time, to witness it and be a part of it. Your task is to sustain strength, centered strength and centered awareness. The human being is becoming the divine being. All of it is moving inexorably towards the state of true grace. Your task is to not let weariness overcome you, not be carried into the darkness, with disbelief, worry and concern. Your task is to hold strong and powerful like a guardian, a totem pole on the hilltop continuing to watch, continuing to hold the message, continuing to become more and more conscious of who you are. Continuing to sustain the state of consciousness within your self and for all.

We show the image of many beings such as you, holding steady and strong in the centered 'I am,' the conscious state of knowing the divine involvement and the divine evolvement of beings. Standing like statues on hilltops all over the globe, watching the disillusion, the crisis, and watching for the flowering, the pockets of Grace, and for the choices towards Peace. Watching the children realize the tenets of Peace. Watching the developments that give way towards Beauty. Watching, never doubting, never being ensconced and sickened by worry, but holding the vision like a golden thread and never dropping it.

Realize that there is far more than you can see with your physical eyes and human mind, and yet there is everything to see with your divine heart, your true heart. Listen into your being and you will hear what the whole being is really doing and moving towards. **Listen into your heart and soul and you will know that truth is inexorable.** You will know that the very coding of physical formation is based in a beauty, in a love and a grace that can never fail, based in a tenacity of grace where what began in the first instant of manifestation shall dictate the ending. The ending meaning the completion, the completion of what was born.

As the source of All Being-ness, as the eminent Supreme Truth descends into form, into creation, so shall it result in the manifestation of itself, Supreme Grace, Supreme Being-ness.

Do not be narrowed into the sense of time, 2010 moving to 2011 to the great measurement of 2012. There are always ebbs and flows; there are always increases and decreases, there are always passages and processes. The conscious ones hold steady as though continually beating the drum, continually holding the high pure notes of becoming throughout the ebbs and flows, the changing of years, of cultures, the dying of cultures and the birthing of cultures.

Take your question into your heart and find that there is no question, there is just the being that you are, the being that knows. The being that holds the vision for all those that don't know. Not listening to the words, nor the happenings, the poisonings, the earthquakes, the wars; not listening to them without listening to the greater backdrop of the becoming human, the becoming sons and daughters of Grace, the sons and daughters of God.

Look at the descending into physical and flesh embodiments of beings such as the Christ, the Buddha, such as all the enlightened and beautiful masters, such as all the founders of all the major faiths. Look at the phenomenon of Divine Being-ness embodying. What is it saying? Listen to that. Could there be a question, a question such as "Will we make it?" "Is there to be success, or is there to be failure?" The universe is too big, immeasurable, too vast, as is Grace, too big, too vast and too immeasurable for such a question. Your work is to believe and to become; to hold peace on your brow and to hold presence in your heart; to hold resolve always and to hope for others always. Be the totem pole of peace on the hilltop, perhaps weathered and tilting, yet never faltering in your meaning and in your stance, to hold true being-ness in this world.

What is the meaning of the 2012 transition? There is concern that humanity has not completed a certain amount of change. How do we prepare for what might happen. Please comment on the state of human evolution around this date.

The transition refers to what is generally resonating within the human being at present. How close to the original code, how close to the most brilliant layers, the most remembered states of being, this human sphere is coming?

First, 2012 is not meant to be a completion, nor was it ever meant to say that it was a time when the resonance was in brilliance or that the resonance was in an awakening. ***2012 is the time that is seen as the beginning of the inevitable dawning, the inevitable return of the awakening of consciousness***. There is no question; it is not to be questioned.

2012 is not an exact moment. There is an epitome of change within the whole physical and energetic universe that is held at that time. The aura of that time has been great before and after, the meaning of that time is the early dawn, the very beginning of the inevitable dawning, the inevitable expansion that will overtake all beings with no question. It is a time of celebration and a time of no doubt. There is no place for doubt. **A time when Grace becomes the most thunderous drum that everyone hears.**

Describing the conscious change ahead: if someone is dying in their contractions, into their choices, they're dying into a sphere of such tremendous potency they will know every micro reason why they're dying. They will know everything about how they have poisoned their soul. Every being in any stage they are in, becomes absolutely aware of their state of being and how it has come to be.

It is as though choice has come in and consciousness has been delivered. Those beings that would deny, and would keep reaching for unconsciousness will find it impossible and intolerable. They will find there is no place and no way, and they become like infants. Innocent infants that will appear to you like children, children that are just slowly starting to be curious, slowly starting to wonder. They may go through many embodiments just as children, not even living far past being children. And for those like yourself, the dawning moves into your very heart. It moves into the core of your being.

Your question of how to prepare is to hold no doubt, to host no doubt. To erase forever the sense of: "Will we make it, did we measure up, do we pass the test?" It is much bigger than that; this human being has been in evolution for so long. It is not a little moment that is a failure or success. The tide is much bigger, no one can hold out against the tide, nobody. It is a tide of grace, a tide not to be feared nor doubted, nor questioned. Include everything into the tide that you see and hear of, and if there is dying in greater and greater numbers, know they are dying either into childhood or into freedom. Look then, for the generations to follow that manifest freedom and childhood.

In the generations to come there will be stories of the great darkness, of the wars and of the tremendous contractions. There will be the questions: "Where did the darkness go, what changed that?" and there will be an impassive, peaceful answer: "I don't know, what changed it." It was as though a race died out, or darkness died out and all the efforts that can be remembered: "Well, these people tried to do this and this government tried to make this change." What was it, in all of this, which caused the change? None of it was big enough to create the change that is there. It is simply as though a race died out.

There will then be the calling inside, because these are the same beings. "What did we do so that we won't do that again, and what were the factors in all that so that we won't create that again?" Even the question seems to carry no content, because everyone knows that it won't be like that again. The only punishment for a soul that wants to contract is that they retain childhood and stay in the innocence and the reduction of childhood.

There is a purity arising within the human being and the yearning from that purity arising within the human being as though the hardened sheaths of the heart are shattered and broken off. The purity of love and open heartedness dictates the formation of culture and of life. And as those that would try to repeat the pattern of contraction and dominance and power through fear, as they try to establish and reach back, it is as though they can't. If they keep trying, they die because there is a new message now in the genetic substance that the body cannot live in contraction. As though there is built in a karmic ending, as though (and truly it is so), that the frequency of the entire universe and planetary body is too high to sustain contraction and contraction falls out. Where does it fall to? You don't need to know. A sphere of lower frequency, like a holding place.

*What is our relationship and link to **the Mayan Civilization**? What* *are our similarities and what more can we learn about their culture?*

Cultures are like waves over history, waves of consciousness. Some are small waves and some are very significant. The Mayan wave is a significant one. However, the cultural name 'Mayan' isn't a true representation of this wave, there were many peoples that were a part of the wisdom and development of its consciousness. 'Mayan' is used because it is most recent, but the true roots are not Mayan at all. However, for these purposes we will continue to use this term with the knowledge that this wave was a consecutive progression of peoples developing the wisdom we speak of.

The Mayan culture was actually the demise in that wisdom when the wave had already broken and was receding. Because of the demise, there was great purpose in that time. All manifesting purposes are a part of the network of consciousness within the whole and they all have their own wave, complete with a peak and a recession.

There existed a unique purpose in the Mayan culture. They were a people of remembering and of bringing forth of original beings and their consciousness, bringing forth the most original flowering of consciousness within the human form. They knew that the cultural structures were aligned with the original. Their culture was a resonant bell, a similar note to the first ringing.

There is a thread of truth that carries on through all of time, cloaked in many different ways. The purpose of the Mayan people was to be the messengers and to carry the thread. **With the knowledge of all that came before and will come ahead, their mission was to carry the true identity and capacity of the human being right through until now.** Whether they were embodied and their temples existed did not matter. They needed to formulate and set down the continuing thread of all the knowledge that is held in the purposes of human evolving. The knowledge of the waves, the cycles, and the progression of consciousness that human beings are a part of. The progression is not just of the human realm; it is of this sphere, of the animals and the Earth.

The Mayan people knew that this knowledge must be brought forward, through living it, making ceremony of it, and creating a culture out of it, to embed it into the collective consciousness. Their wisdom leaders, the ones creating the epicenter of their culture, strove to intimate the knowledge and detail to this point. This is the relationship to now; it is like a relay race.

The information we speak of peaked in the epitome of its perfection far before the Mayan time, as we know it. Following the peaking came the implanting of the information into image, language, philosophy, astronomy and mathematic understanding. So deeply embedded was it that it became a holistic knowing, as though the entire scope of the wisdom was manifesting in daily life. Following the implanting was the beginning of another period of unconsciousness.

There was an inability to culturally sustain the ongoing development. Unconsciousness began to enter because beings, not of that wave, began to be born. This was the beginning of the next phase of beings that did not hold in their consciousness the personal mission to carry the thread. So they lived within the structures that had been built, animated the philosophy and cultures, but with less and less belief and true awareness. It was the recession of the wave and the wisdom elders knew that. Their purpose was *to know;* they understood that the next phase consisted of beings born from a whole different part of evolution and that their ideals would become invisible for a time. The new wave of people were like broken children who needed to evolve themselves, children that needed to be given a new land, a clean slate. Who knew how much of the old structures would be carried with them? The Mayan wisdom elders understood that in order for the information to be held until now, it could not be stored only on physical structures on the Earth, but held in invisibility by the Guardians in ways that don't age.

Today, at this point in our present wave, the information is emerging and one must only look around to see why: the re-birth of the wisdom elders; they knew their timing. The re-birthing is all around and within you. Beings that know the culture already, or that have the interest in it, reach for it, bring it forth, write books about it, study it, seek it: it is emerging from within. They are simply human beings, committed to truth and the meaning of the whole picture of universal creation. We have a direct, intimate relationship to what the Mayan culture was because it is *them* that are here now; the re-embodying of those that have been waiting for the time to continue their mission (many have not re-embodied until now).

The concerns around the barbaric nature of Mayan ceremonies can be put to rest with the knowledge that the people responsible for the structures of barbarism were born in the new wave of evolution and did not carry the thread. The question is raised, how did it change so drastically and so quickly? The answer is, that the wisdom elders, with their active bodhisattva mission to ripen the information into a high degree of physical manifestation, knew when the peak had come and when it was time to step away. They left the space open consciously and didn't re-enter until it was time.

The period of time following the recession of the wave we speak of, is also known as a time of very little birth at all. Many infants were stillborn, and there was a lack of ability to conceive. It was like a physical numbness and emptying of those of the previous era. At the same time, an emptying of the sacred sites took place and villages and rudimentary beginnings of new culture spread out all over. The sacred sites literally repelled inhabitation. Those that re-entered became fearful of the structures, and feeling the repelling energy chose not to live there, leaving them intact.

Now we can celebrate the re-entry of the thread carriers, the continuation of the information. They are amongst us and are entering more and more places within the world to direct us. Yet it must be remembered that what they do or say may not sound the same; the information is a pure stream of truth, cloaked in different symbols and ceremonies each time it comes forth.

*What does the **New Earth** look like? How is it manifesting at present? How can we recognize and help it?*

This question is large. This question is sweeping, and yet we go to its most fundamental happening, its most fundamental manifestation at this time. We show her the genetic strands within and throughout the entire Earth. This descriptive has many versions. We begin with the human being where this genetic strand, in its readiness now, has a new development. We show her the portion of the genetic strand that is now actively creating its new incarnations, its new potentials and possibilities in the children being born and the children to be born. By the third generation from now these children will have this genetic activation fully in place.

The meaning of this genetic portion of development is that every nerve ending throughout the whole body, throughout the brain and nervous system, has the ability to receive and incorporate information, sensing, and nutrition - beyond itself. There is the ability in the nervous system, in the sensory brain that exists flowing through every nerve, to sense, to interact, to be informed, and to engage beyond itself. Therefore, the isolation and separation is disappearing. There is the ability to integrate more subtle energy within the nutritional field. There is the ability to integrate and interact with other beings more subtly, to identify with other beings, to know other beings more deeply and intricately. There is the ability to understand, in much larger spheres, one's being and identity and to move out of the prison of self-nature. There becomes far more subtlety in the whole physical organism, less imprisonment within the physical organism.

This will be seen directly as far more empathy, far more sensitivity and far more intelligence in the children and the animals, far more fusion, far more lightening quick understandings of what is happening in the other, happening around. The word empathy comes close to this, though there will be new words created for this engagement, this direct knowing from one to the other. Problems that arise from isolation and separation, from self-serving natures, begin to disappear as though by magic. Beings will identify with the ones around as much as with themselves. There will be an unforeseen collaboration of consciousness in every group, as though the consensus is easily found. The group consciousness is there from the beginning. You will see it in this generation.

You will see this in the animal world in other ways. You will see the animal world less barred, less blocked from the human being. Remarkable abilities and changes the animal world. You will see the animal, physically, looking up more often. This is a sign.

You will notice the human being, physically, more directly looking into the eyes of others, as if needing to feel their own being-ness. You will see faster and faster resolutions in the problems, in the conflicts in any group, anywhere and the sense of ease and wonder at how such a remembered lock and struggle of conflict seemed to dissipate so quickly. You will see the swifter and swifter finding of resolution due to being part of all others present. This is the most succinct, direct change in the new time that is facilitated now. The fixed nature of the patterns of the past, consciously, and we will say genetically, is leaving and dropping away. That portion of the genetic strand that we began with, that holds fixed the patterns of the past, is dissolving as the new potion of the genetic strand becomes active.

The New Fruit, *"A fruit never before known in the creation"*. What does this mean?

Orientation and Context:

We are at a time of two significant calendar endings, one is for the Great Cycle of the Mayan Astronomical Calendar, or Sacred Calendar, also called the Eagle Bowl. It defines the great cycle from 3113 B.C. to 2012 AD and is composed of 13 Baktuns /5200-tuns in the reckoning of the calendar. This ending is called AHAU, Complete Transformation.

The other calendar and end-point was given by the first Quetzacoatl. It was carved on the Palenque stone in glyphs an unknown time ago. Quetzacoatl was an original teacher and creator of the ancient culture. The prophecy of Quetzacoatl's return in 947 AD is a very old one. This prophecy, and all that it meant, was held and passed on through the centuries by priests who were the guardians of Quetzacoatl's sacred tablets. They knew that he would be re-born at Xochicalco, south of Mexico City. This 2nd Quetzalcoatl became a perfect manifestation or Avatar and brought spiritual awareness to the people of America. His name means 'the plumed serpent', a combination of sky (bird) and earth (serpent). He returned to remind and enlighten them. The time span, from the original prophecy has been described in this way: Thirteen heavens of decreasing choice and nine hells of increasing doom (or thirteen fifty-two year cycles of choice and nine fifty-two year cycles of doom).

"The sacred tablets told of his birthday and laid out a tentative description of his life. Those tablets went further to describe this entire epic, which was now taking place, as but a fragment of what was to come. The sacred tablets predicted the future of the entire continent, not a vague prophecy, but one of magnitude. Using the fifty-two year cycle of the sacred astronomical calendar of ancient Mexico, and defining a number of checkpoints in its 1144-year periods. They prophesize coming events of the continent, both land and people by a series of symbolic heavens, thirteen all tolled, and nine hells. All in all, twenty-two cycles of the fifty-two year calendar. The first heaven had been entered one-hundred-and-four years before the birth of Quetzalcoatl. In other words, two heavens had gone by. He was the long awaited Lord of the Dawn."

Quetzalcoatl initiated a renaissance of culture in the city of wonder known as Tollan. Tollan was an empire of beauty and peace, an apex of grandeur and accomplishment.

"They say the people of Tollan were the most beautiful in all the world because of what they had done. They had learned that the secret of peace was the unity of all things"

Following the glory of Tollan under the rule of The Lord of the Dawn, there was a long decline towards the decreasing consciousness of the thirteen heavens. The thirteenth heaven began in the dark ages of 1467. The nine hells began in the year 1519, which was the year Cortez came to Central America. The ninth hell began August 3 1935, the year of Adolph Hitler's rise. The end of this prophetic time period was August 16, 1987. The prophecy goes on to say:

"And after the ninth hell, the tree of life shall blossom with a fruit never before known in the creation, and that fruit shall be the new spirit of man."

The Quetzalcoatl prophecy takes us to 25 years from the end of the last Baktun of the Great Cycle charted by the Sacred Calendar (Mayan or Aztec). After the calendar ends, it is suggested that mankind and Earth shall undergo a transformation to become part of the galactic or universal community. The end of the Quetzacoatl prophecy also says that there shall be a new development in creation. It has been said that the 25-year gap was a period of integrating the alignment that had occurred on August 16, 1987, the Harmonic Convergence, leading us to an end point in the purposes of the calendar recordings, in December of 2012.

Question:

I would like to go into Guidance now and open up as a receiver of more knowledge for us all, of what this means:" A fruit never before known in the creation".

The truth of this calendar and the prophecies is absolutely not questioned by my being. The truth of Quetzalcoatl, of the being who manifested to guide and teach is absolutely not questioned by my being. My heart knows its truth, and my being remembers this.

I see that there is a stirring, a very deep stirring in the entire entity of Earth, its being and its inhabitants. It is like a stirring in the womb of the Earth, with this reaching in, this questioning. The power of the stirring of this entity of Earth is truly felt and I hear the words:

Do you know what you are asking?

Do you know who you are yet?

Do you know who the human being is yet?

Do you know where you stand?

Do you know who this Earth is yet?

Do you know your place in the Universe yet?

How ready have you become, to know forward?

How ready have you become, to host the new creation in your being?

The Earth holds weariness now, and sickness. You host weariness and sickness. We find the Earth beleaguered and tired. We find you tired. We find the life spark is dim. We find the sacred moment cluttered with debris. *And yet, you have made it.* You are here to ask the question. You are here to notice this day. Look around at the thousands who are here to notice this day. There is a stirring and there is a celebration, that you have made it through the darkness that threatened to shear away all of the light within your spirit. We are speaking to all: you made it through the crushing weight of unconsciousness. Even if there is only a glimmer now, you made it. A glimmer is enough; it is the glimmer of fortitude, of courage, of the indestructible truth, the indestructible spirit of thy being, of All Being. We knew it would be this way, we knew that the cycles of darkness would be so crushing, and we knew that it was the labour pains of the new creation. We knew it was the process necessary, and yet we didn't know that there would be anyone here to ask this question: "What now?" or anyone that would notice after all this time. The Guardians have done their work well. They have walked steadily drumming around the earth, tapping it continually, birthing within the most clear, stirring the knowledge continually, and not letting it sleep.

What is the forward movement of the spiral? What is 'the years of increasing choice'? What is the new creation that can now be born?

We will show you. We show you the eyes of the new creation, of the human spirit and the human being:

The Eyes

We show the illumination of the eyes and of the mind behind the eyes, of the upper brain, the luminous extension that is the dominant feature of the new creation. The eyes are actually emitting light. The eyes have the capacity to see life force flowing in every form of creation. To not only see life force, but the life principle, which is the stream of Grace, of God, the stream of creation that is animating and flowing through all life forms. To not only see this directly, but in seeing, to be part of. So, by looking at a tree, for example, one sees the density of its molecular skeleton, and also sees the life force flowing in the tree. By seeing the life force flowing in the tree, one has entered it; there is no outside, there is no separation. To see the life force is to give to the life force, and to receive from it.

End of Separation

Whereas the human being, in the darkness of human sight, is separated and sees the tree as an outside entity of fixed nature. The new creation enters the tree, is part of the tree, and shares life force. The superior of the two assists the other, so the evolution of all life forms enhances light speed. If the tree in the example is wounded, has injured life force streams, the being observing the tree, entering the tree, instantly corrects that. If the human being was to gaze upon an animal, they would see the physical, skeletal, molecular structure, and they would see the stream of life, and the stream of consciousness within that creature at the same time. If that creature was cramped and injured and held in fear or injury, the entry would heal. Every glance, every mergence introduces the refined and superior into the less refined. Therefore, there is a speeding of light speed to all evolution of all life forms. Separation is a story of the past, between human beings as well. There is the entry into each other's beings, the enhancements of each other's life force, of consciousness, of spiritual linkage.

Resistance is the journey for the first series of cycles. There is a relearning of your identity. Your identity is not of separation, your name does not mean you are separate from the one next to you. Your individuality is redefined, but you still maintain your individuality. You still become a very individualizing beauty of being-ness. Yet the very nature of the beauty of your being-ness is that you know that you are no longer separate from the beauty of the entire creation.

End of Illness

The new creation hosts no illness. Once the state of unity has been learned, and accepted, and the new identity is known, there is no illness. Illness is entirely a result of separation and unconsciousness. In the first series of cycles, there is still illness, if not great illness. The illness of resistance and a fear of letting go of separation, for separation has become the stronghold and the protection in all life forms. Yet the deeper, truer message of unity floods every birth, every sleep, every moment like a great tidal wave of truth that overtakes all beings, more and more. The reward of one who yields even for a moment to the identity of unity is that they are filled with peace, with a sense of belonging, of joy and of contentment. When the reward of that little moment speaks so loudly, the separation becomes easier to let go of. As each being learns to identify with their true nature, the true nature of Universal Identity, and as they relate one to the other, there is the healing of all injuries and traumas of the past, all of the agonies. We acknowledge the agonies, for the heart has been broken millions of times. The healing lifts that heart out of its rubble, out of its patterns of grief, forever.

We say again, there is no more illness in the new creation, there is no more cancer, no more epidemics. Healing occurs instantaneously as one life being merges with another, and has the identity that you are mine. Every being is in service to every other. This is the new creation, which has never yet before walked embodied. This is the manifestation of the embodiments of Love. Love incarnate within all eyes. The Earth awakens and brings forth the sweetest life forms yet. The flowers learn to sing, and the plants emit sound, and the animals drop their fear, and all metabolisms learn to exchange directly with light, and need not hunt and kill each other. And the animal forms become a people of their own shape, of their own language, and of a very refined nature. The human being becomes less bound to the physical, molecular embodiment. They become truly free. Death is more a choice of transition, a changing of forms by choice, by a deep understanding. The sphere of embodiment, of incarnation, becomes less limited to this one.

The New Fruit

In the new creation, in the freed identity, the Universe is looked at with new eyes, not as millions of distant lights measured in light years or literal years away. Time changes, distance changes as the rest of your brain lights up and knows the truth about time, about distance and about molecular formation. Evolution moves into other spheres of hosting this tremendous creation. But not before this Earth has flowered with its plants of singing nature, not before every being has been healed. Not before the broken heart is just a chronicle, an honoured chronicle of this journey, a lesson never forgotten throughout the whole universe: the fruits of unconsciousness, the results of separation.

And listen to this: The lesson of separation resounds through the entire universe, and you have walked in the middle of it. You are the courageous ones that made it. You are the ones who demonstrated and who walked through the narrow tunnel of separation setting forth the foundational knowledge, throughout the Universe, that creating separation creates amnesia within consciousness. Never before, and never again shall the identity of separation be hosted. This is the new fruit blossoming, the never before seen. This is the all-encompassing freedom. All shall be gathered into this and none shall be left out.

You ask of the time periods, you ask of the calendar cycles, and we speak of the vast summation of this: The process of these cycles cannot be pinned into a definition of what happens when. The cycle of the fifty-two years is still printed into your genealogy. The cycles of alignment and misalignment are still printed into the universal genealogy, and yet what is being born will not relate to the cycles of decrease in the same way, ever again. The cycles of decrease shall be cycles of purification, a resistance arising in order to be purified, but a lesson will have been learned. The cycles of increase and decrease shall continue on into time ahead, and as to how many of these cycles before this new creation is fully unfurled: it is not set at just the one ahead, but three times ahead. Yet, you shall see the fruits beginning within you now, and tomorrow. If you develop your being, and you open the map of your brain, you can hear the flowers singing even now, because they are, and they always have. It is when they are heard that you have merged with them. You have increased their evolution. You have said to them, from your highly developed being-ness: "I hear you, I see you, you exist in a whole new way to me." And that flower will then exist in a whole new way as it forms its seeds. You've awakened its genealogy with your own. So it begins now, and yet the summation is far steps ahead.

Postlude

The Singing Flowers ~ a parting thought

I stand before roadside flowers, moved so deeply by all these words of possibility and potential, all these teachings of wonder.

This creation is infinitely more than my humanness and my senses gather. So much more than we ever hoped or thought could be: that we, ourselves, are actually created to become such beautiful beings!

I walk through a logging slash, the apparently destroyed landscape with the news story of the nearby water contamination from a mine, clashing in my heart and mind.

What are we doing? Where are we going? Stumbling through the debris, I go back to the words of Guidance. We *are* going somewhere, by all of this thought, we *are* going into a magnificence of being and becoming that is all we've ever dreamed and yearned for. Beyond Disney, beyond happily ever after, beyond limitations that were all our own process and making, all along.

Flowers evolving into songs of beauty and colour, and giving even more to our hearts. Flowers singing!

Now I visit the flowers as a wondering child, listening, waiting, wanting to believe in magic. Magic that was real all along and is our process after all.

A flower showed its joy to me once
Stunned, yet I was so exhilarated
By life at the moment that I took
It in as one seamless event
It was a wild rose and its deep pink
Matched its voice of glory

I visit the roses often since, feeling their

Vibrancy, drinking in their sweet smell

Never have I forgotten that wild exchange

That instance where in my heart I matched

The glory of a rose

Made in the USA
Charleston, SC
16 March 2015